Female Heroes in Young Adult
Fantasy Fiction

Library of Gender and Popular Culture

From *Mad Men* to gaming culture, performance art to steampunk fashion, the presentation and representation of gender continues to saturate popular media. This series seeks to explore the intersection of gender and popular culture, engaging with a variety of texts – drawn primarily from Art, Fashion, TV, Cinema, Cultural Studies and Media Studies – as a way of considering various models for understanding the complementary relationship between 'gender identities' and 'popular culture'. By considering race, ethnicity, class and sexual identities across a range of cultural forms, each book in the series adopts a critical stance towards issues surrounding the development of gender identities and popular and mass cultural 'products'.

For further information or enquiries, please contact the library series editors:

Claire Nally: claire.nally@northumbria.ac.uk
Angela Smith: angela.smith@sunderland.ac.uk

Advisory Board:
Dr Kate Ames, Central Queensland University, Australia
Dr Michael Higgins, University of Strathclyde, UK
Prof Åsa Kroon, Örebro University, Sweden
Dr Andrea McDonnell, Emmanuel College, USA
Dr Niall Richardson, University of Sussex, UK
Dr Jacki Willson, University of Leeds, UK

Previously published titles:

The Aesthetics of Camp: Post-Queer Gender and Popular Culture
By Anna Malinowska

Ageing Femininity on Screen: The Older Woman in Contemporary Cinema By Niall Richardson

All-American TV Crime Drama: Feminism and Identity Politics in Law and Order: Special Victims Unit
By Sujata Moorti and Lisa Cuklanz

Are You Not Entertained?: Mapping the Gladiator across Visual Media
By Lindsay Steenberg

Bad Girls, Dirty Bodies: Sex, Performance and Safe Femininity
By Gemma Commane

Conflicting Masculinities: Men in Television Period Drama
By Katherine Byrne, Julie Anne Taddeo and James Leggott (Eds)

Fat on Film: Gender, Race and Body Size in Contemporary Hollywood Cinema By Barbara Plotz

Fathers on Film: Paternity and Masculinity in 1990s Hollywood
By Katie Barnett

Film Bodies: Queer Feminist Encounters with Gender and Sexuality in Cinema
By Katharina Lindner

From the Margins to the Mainstream: Women On and Off Screen in Television and Film
By Marianne Kac-Vergne and Julie Assouly (Eds)

Gay Pornography: Representations of Sexuality and Masculinity
By John Mercer

Gender and Austerity in Popular Culture: Femininity, Masculinity and Recession in Film and Television
By Helen Davies and Claire O'Callaghan (Eds)

Gender and Early Television: Mapping Women's Role in Emerging US and British Media, 1850–1950
By Sarah Arnold

The Gendered Motorcycle: Representations in Society, Media and Popular Culture
By Esperanza Miyake

Gendering History on Screen: Women Filmmakers and Historical Films By Julia Erhart

Girls Like This, Boys Like That: The Reproduction of Gender in Contemporary Youth Cultures
By Victoria Cann

'Guilty Pleasures': European Audiences and Contemporary Hollywood Romantic Comedy
By Alice Guilluy

The Gypsy Woman: Representations in Literature and Visual Culture By Jodie Matthews

Male and Female Violence in Popular Media By Elisa Giomi and Sveva Magaraggia

Masculinity in Contemporary Science Fiction Cinema: Cyborgs, Troopers and Other Men of the Future By Marianne Kac-Vergne

Positive Images: Gay Men and HIV/AIDS in the Culture of 'Post-Crisis' By Dion Kagan

Postfeminism and Contemporary Vampire Romance By Lea Gerhards

Queer Horror Film and Television: Sexuality and Masculinity at the Margins By Darren Elliott-Smith

Queer Sexualities in Early Film: Cinema and Male-Male Intimacy By Shane Brown

Screening Queer Memory: LGBTQ Pasts in Contemporary Film and Television By Anamarija Horvat

Steampunk: Gender and the Neo-Victorian By Claire Nally

Television Comedy and Femininity: Queering Gender By Rosie White

Tweenhood: Femininity and Celebrity in Tween Popular Culture By Melanie Kennedy

Women Who Kill: Gender and Sexuality in Film and Series of the Post-Feminist Era By David Roche and Cristelle Maury (Eds)

Wonder Woman: Feminism, Culture and the Body By Joan Ormrod

Young Women, Girls and Postfeminism in Contemporary British Film By Sarah Hill

Female Heroes in Young Adult Fantasy Fiction

Reframing Myths of Adolescent Girlhood

Leah Phillips

BLOOMSBURY ACADEMIC
LONDON • NEW YORK • OXFORD • NEW DELHI • SYDNEY

BLOOMSBURY ACADEMIC
Bloomsbury Publishing Plc
50 Bedford Square, London, WC1B 3DP, UK
1385 Broadway, New York, NY 10018, USA
29 Earlsfort Terrace, Dublin 2, Ireland

BLOOMSBURY, BLOOMSBURY ACADEMIC and the Diana logo
are trademarks of Bloomsbury Publishing Plc

First published in Great Britain 2023
This paperback edition published 2024

Copyright © Leah Phillips 2023

Leah Phillips has asserted her right under the Copyright,
Designs and Patents Act, 1988, to be identified as Author of this work.

For legal purposes the Acknowledgements on p. xxii constitute
an extension of this copyright page.

Cover design: Charlotte Daniels
Cover image: Installation detail of Reciprocal Pain (2009) by Kako Ueda in Slash:
Paper Under the Knife at the Museum of Arts and Design, New York.
(Photo by Ed Watkins, Courtesy the Museum of Arts and Design)

All rights reserved. No part of this publication may be reproduced or
transmitted in any form or by any means, electronic or mechanical, including photocopying, recording, or any information storage or retrieval system,
without prior permission in writing from the publishers.

Bloomsbury Publishing Plc does not have any control over, or responsibility
for, any third-party websites referred to or in this book. All internet addresses
given in this book were correct at the time of going to press. The author and
publisher regret any inconvenience caused if addresses have changed or sites
have ceased to exist, but can accept no responsibility for any such changes.

A catalogue record for this book is available from the British Library.

A catalogue record for this book is available from the Library of Congress.

ISBN: HB: 978-1-3501-1933-8
PB: 978-1-3501-9423-6
ePDF: 978-1-3501-1931-4
eBook: 978-1-3501-1932-1

Series: Library of Gender and Popular Culture

Typeset by Integra Software Services Pvt. Ltd.

To find out more about our authors and books visit www.bloomsbury.com
and sign up for our newsletters.

Contents

Series editors' introduction		viii
Preface		x
Acknowledgements		xxii
1	The hero's prize: The myth of 'successful' adolescent girlhood	1
2	Mythopoeic YA: Bringing new worlds into being to conceive new ways of being	23
3	Disrupting the myth: Alanna becomes a warrior-maiden	55
4	Breaking the mirror: Cinder(ella) is a cyborg	79
5	Engendering a new myth: Daine is 'of the people'	111
6	Being-Hero: Relational, embodied, procreative selfhood	139
Appendices		150
Notes		151
Bibliography		160
Index		178

Series editors' introduction

The Library of Gender in Popular Culture features many books that explore the role of the heroic character, whether how one character has changed with the times, such as in Joan Ormrod's analysis of *Wonder Woman* (2020) to the rise of 'action babes' in Maury and Roche's *Women Who Kill* collection (2020). As part of this agenda, *Female Heroes in Young Adult Fantasy Fiction* by Leah Phillips explores that role as found in female characters aimed at the young adult market. This particular audience has grown as a specific target for media producers and authors in the last few years, and the range of texts Phillips explores allows for a more nuanced picture than the focus on one character would otherwise permit in this context.

In relation to gender stereotyping pitched to a young adult audience, Victoria Cann's *Girls Like This, Boys Like That* (2018) sheds light on this key issue. In *Tweenhood: Femininity and Celebrity in Tween Popular Culture* (2019), Melanie Kennedy has explored how pre-adolescent girls are bombarded with often contradictory messages from a wide range of sources, all of which construct a feminine identity. These texts often seek to instil a strong sense of identity formation, and with it, an achievement of a secure, stable, heterosexual identity.

Therefore Phillips considers how Western patriarchal ideology depicts successful adolescent girlhood as peripheral to 'normal' adolescence, the default of which is male. This theme is central to the book, where the concept of heroism is almost always associated with masculinity. In *Are You Not Entertained?* (2021), Lindsay Steenberg has explored the role of the gladiator character across visual media, allowing us to see just how stereotypically male this is. Phillips shows how the heroic lead can be reclaimed by female characters who do not conform to the stereotype of self-sacrificing heroine figures (those who are there to be rescued or won), but who exist in a gap in language that represents them as 'female heroes'. The dominant liberal humanist ethic is one that privileges concepts such as the uniqueness of the individual and the essentiality of self, as opposed to concepts of the self as fragmented or plural. As Phillips argues, this twenty-first-century ethic has heightened and intensified through neoliberal narratives of self, proposing that both discourses refuse conceptualizations of the self as related to and interdependent with other selves. A discussion of the body and what it means to be a self is particularly imperative for adolescent girls, who are, within the hegemonic discursive fantasy, both constructed as more corporeal than their boy counterparts and yet, simultaneously, told to disavow that corporeality through the silencing of the body and its processes.

Phillips explores the mythopoeic young adult sub-genre, which is the space occupied by nontraditional heroes (i.e. not the archetypal white, able-bodied, handsome male). As such, the female hero is central to reframing dominant, patriarchal myths, place, space and time. As several books in this Library show, cyborg characters are also found to be a useful way to explore issues relating to identity. As Phillips shows here, they can be employed to embody female characters in both body and mind. In looking at specific examples, Phillips shows how the female-hero expands what it means to be a hero, girl and, even, human, and offers a model that might make such a being possible.

Claire Nally & Angela Smith

Preface

Female Heroes considers how the female-heroes of mythopoeic YA are reframing what it means to be an adolescent girl. To name a few of these heroes (and the ones I focus on), I offer Alanna the Lioness, a cross-dressing female-hero emerging from Tamora Pierce's Tortall Universe. This universe, or imaginary world, has been a part of our consensus reality since the early 1980s, when it kick-started mythopoeic YA, as I discuss in Chapter 2. I also submit Cinder, a cybernetic Cinderella, and Iko, her android friend. These female-heroes emerge from Marissa Meyer's Lunar Chronicles (2012–2015). This futuristic imaginary world and its female-heroes illustrate mythopoeic YA's generic flexibility and inclusivity – which are also integral to how female-heroes reframe adolescent girlhood. Finally, I name Daine the Wildmage, a shape-shifting demigoddess who, like Alanna, is from Pierce's Tortall. Daine's story takes place after Alanna's, according to their world's timeline and ours, although book order does not dictate reading or listening order, a significant intervention in linear, teleological storylines. In distinct yet not unrelated ways, these female-heroes are pushing the boundaries of what it means to be a hero, girl and *even* human. They do so by including the body – fleshy, material, prone to change and capable of producing new bodies – within what it means to be a hero. This inclusion makes it possible for them to disrupt and dismantle one of Western Culture's most dominant and enduring narratives: the heroic romance, a form of quest myth permeating every layer of Western belief and culture.

The heroic romance is one of the West's most enduring narratives; its seemingly simple premise (good guy wins, the bad guy doesn't, order prevails) shapes how we, those who see and hear it, understand the world around us. Importantly, this shaping is not passive. In patterning the acceptable appearance and behaviour of heroes – while demonstrating how all others should serve (or love), honour and obey them – this story creates, structures and organizes dominant consensus reality (the generally agreed upon, by the dominant group, way of seeing and understanding the world). It tells us how to live and be in this world, and the story undertakes its social and cultural work through the archetypal hero: a white, often 'god'-touched, middle-class, cisgendered and heterosexual, 'fit' young man who exists in opposition and superiority to that which he is not. He is recognizable as Beowulf, Odysseus, Aragorn son of Arathorn, Luke Skywalker, Percy Jackson and the 'normal' adolescent. These young men battle some evil foe (even if, as is the case with the latter, that 'monster' is only puberty) to restore the world to its 'proper' order. As the personification of reason, order and that which is 'good', the archetypal hero models what it means to be human within the West – at the expense of those who do not look (male, white, young, 'fit') and act (with superiority) as he does. For his efforts, the hero usually wins a prize, frequently a princess's hand in marriage.

The hero's bride, in turn, models 'successful' adolescent girlhood, establishing prize as the goal of what it means to be a girl. In doing so, this narrative excludes girls from the role of hero because they are his bride, while also barring them from that position if they do not look, and to a lesser degree act, the part. In contemporary Western culture, Walt Disney's Cinderella – typified by the 1950 feature-length animation and found in many books, films, television programmes and products – is the most iconic bride. Her passage from pauper to princess patterns the same ritual movement from child to adult as does the hero's, with a few crucial modifications: rather than slaying the monster, Cinderella is tasked with achieving a suitable appearance while joyfully attending to household duties and chores. For her efforts, she wins a makeover. This makeover transforms Cinderella into the 'maid predestined to be his bride' (Geronimi, Jackson, and Luske 1950). Crucially, although the girl's exclusion from heroic selfhood affects all girls, it does not do so evenly. If a girl is also Black or Brown, disabled or otherwise not performing Cinderella's version of femininity, alterity increases, and it does so, even more, when markers overlap; for these girls, even the relative privilege of existing within the system as the hero's prize is impossible.

Despite the prize's appeal and Cinderella's fame, popularity and astronomical worth, she is merely a prop – albeit a pretty, sparkly and appealing one – in the hero's story. Indeed, while ensuring cultural visibility and contributing to her iconic status, the films, franchise, boutiques and Cinderella's sparkly femininity merely ensure her position as the hero's bride. While it might appear otherwise, the hero's bride is not equal to the hero. Structurally, she is synonymous with the elixirs, trophies and other treasures a hero receives to mark his glory. She is undoubtedly just as sparkly, often golden (at least her hair), and usually just as hard to win as any other prize. Prizes, or the objects of the hero's quest, are part of the closure the story offers him. In this view, the hero's bride is a mirror by which the hero secures his identity as a person who is whole, rational, autonomous and unaffected by embodiment. As the mirror, Cinderella is an object, trapped in her image and unable to secure one of her own (let alone one that could apply to them both without alienating one or the other), and YA's 'exceptional' heroines – Katniss Everdeen, Tris Prior, Hermione Granger – have done little to change the girl's ancillary role, despite how empowered they may seem (Wilkins 2019, 19).

Heroes and prizes look, act and relate to one another as they do because of the structure of opposition underpinning the patriarchal ideology structuring and supporting mainstream Western culture. As Margery Hourihan argues in *Deconstructing the Hero: Literary Theory and Children's Literature*, the heroic romance, a tool of patriarchy, 'inscribes male dominance and the primacy of male enterprises' (1997, 68). She further argues that the myth's 'conceptual centre', its way of seeing, understanding and engaging the world, is characterized by 'a set of binary oppositions: the qualities ascribed to the hero on the one hand and [...] his "wild" opponents on the other' (15). Hourihan argues that this centre gives rise to seven markers of the archetypal hero. Briefly, these are his 'race' (58), 'class and mastery' (62), 'gender' (68), 'age' (72), 'relationships' (76), 'rationality' (88), and 'action and violence' (96). This centre, because binary oppositions are not neutral, also imposes radical alterity on that which is 'not-hero' (monster, darkness, woman, other) to violently ensure the hero's heroicness while setting him above and apart from those 'others'. For this binary logic to function, a clearly defined void, a schism, must exist between oppositional sides lest they risk bleeding into one another. If there is no indisputably blank space between hero and 'monster', they might not be so different; they might be the same.

While the hero story insists that 'monsters' are external to the hero (they are that which he is not), the body is the first and most intimate monster. Yes, it serves to mark the boundary between self and other, but the body is also the other within the self, ever-threatening order, stability and control. Archetypal hero stories erase the body and its fleshy materiality to mitigate the threat the body poses to heroic logic and rationale by erasing signs difference, enforcing linear, teleological development and insisting on isolating individuality, superiority and success. As such, while heroes obviously have bodies (usually quite 'fit' ones), the body is a tool he wields. It is not an integral part of himself, and the repetition of the same body (white, fit, able) across hero stories allows the body, and the threat it poses, to fade from focus. Owing to their intense association with the body – their identification as body – and ties to the cyclical patterns of menstruation, adolescent girls are relegated to the status of prize, if they can look and, to a lesser degree, act the part.

Female-heroes intervene in this narrative by occupying the spaces between oppositions, foregrounding the body's fleshy materiality, including its procreative potential, and demonstrating relationality, that is how seemingly opposing sides might exist in relation to one another without losing their uniqueness. Relation, instead of inversion, is crucial because it frustrates the system while also offering an alternative. Inversion offers nothing new as it leaves in place the structure of opposition inflicting radical alterity on anyone not meeting the norm or standard. For example, YA's 'exceptional female hero' offers the appearance of heroic equality (Wilkins 2019, 19). These girls, such as Hermione Granger, Bella Swan, Tris Prior, and Katniss Everdeen, are not prizes to be won. They are smart. They can fight, hunt, be the face of rebellions and save their respective worlds. Their books, films and related franchises command huge consumer capital. However, rather than offering any real alternative to the heroic ideal, these 'exceptional YA heroines' – who are white, able-bodied, attractive, young women – perpetuate the system of binary opposition at the very centre of Western thought in their reifying of heroic norms, recapitulation of bodily erasure, and continuation of heightened fantasy femininity.

Female-heroes incorporate the body and its fleshy materiality, including the body's capacity to produce new bodies, within what it means to be a hero, making spaces for bodies that grow, break, bleed and change. The figuration 'being-X', for example, being-hero or female-hero, is fundamental to how mythopoeic YA intervenes in dominant mythic paradigms and, by extension, hegemonic discourse in its relation to those paradigms. The liminal disrupts and denies the power of binary opposition by occupying the spaces between oppositions. Throughout, I use the figuration 'being-X' to demonstrate this liminality. This figuration couples the dynamic 'being' (the action of existing and actively occupying a place or position) with, in this case, hero. Concomitantly, I see the 'female' of female-hero performing a similar function: dynamically occupying a gendered identity, which is then, of course, coupled with hero. Importantly, this female is not one tied to biology in an essentialist way, even as biology (menstruation) is, for many, a part of that being, an issue Chapter 4 considers in depth. The hyphen insists upon the correlation of 'being' and 'X' while also physically occupying the space between the two terms, thus visually emphasizing their combined meaning.

In another sense, the body – the very thing by which adolescent girls and others are excluded from the hero story – is a kind of hyphen. It is the boundary between self and other. Archetypal hero stories erase the body and its fleshy materiality by associating the hero with the mind, reason, truth and rationality. That is, while heroes have bodies (usually quite 'fit' ones), the body is a tool he wields, and the repetition of the same body across his stories allows it, and the threat it poses, to fade from focus. Owing to the 'real' presence of adolescents (even as the category is discursive), the paradigm of 'normal' adolescent, which is a displacement of the archetypal hero (Frye 1961), cannot erase the body in quite the same way. Rather, this iteration of heroic discourse 'doubles down' on the body using the biological changes of puberty to kick-start the period and to pattern its success. The adolescent girl's intense association with the body and the cyclical patterns of menstruation means she can never fully achieve heroic or 'normal' adolescent markers. The female-hero includes bodily instability in what it means to be a hero. In so doing, they work to reframe the myths not just of adolescent girlhood but of what it means to live and be within this world.

Across mythopoeic YA, there are many female-heroes undertaking the social and cultural work of reframing myths of adolescent girlhood, and I mention several of them throughout, but in the following chapters, I focus on Alanna, Cinder and Iko, and Daine. Through cross-dressing, being-cyborg and shape-shifting, these three examples not only question key binary oppositions (male/female, human/machine, animal/machine) but they also collectively offer a revision to, a disruption of, the heroic romance's pattern of separation, initiation and return. However, before turning to the inclusive model of selfhood female-heroes offer, I want to do two things. First, I want to take a closer look, a deconstructing look, at the archetypal hero. I do so to show how the hero's fleshy, material body is his first and most intimate monster – and the key to reframing what it means to be a girl.

The Archetypal Hero: Or, On Monsters

There are a number of 'hero patterns', and the field of hero pattern studies is lengthy. As the folklorist Alan Dundes argues, Johann Georg von Hahn's 'Arische Aussetzungs-und-Rückkehr-Formel' (The Aryan Expulsion and Return Formula) initiated the field while also encoding the pernicious standard around race that lingers in conceptions of the hero today. While other notable players include E. B. Tylor (1958), Vladimir Propp (1968), Lord Raglan (1934; 1936) and Joseph Campbell (1949), Otto Rank's *The Myth of the Birth of the Hero* plays a central role: not only is his pattern a typification of hero pattern research but it is also a project forging new ground (1914).[1] Rank was not only the first to analyse his pattern, a trend Raglan and Campbell continued, but his was also one of the earliest, and still most well-known, studies exploring the convergence of comparative mythology and (Freudian) psychoanalysis (Segal 1990, vii). For my purposes, Hourihan's deconstruction of the hero is particularly useful, not only because it links the hero to children's literature (which for Hourihan included YA) but it condenses the above patterns into those seven markers I mentioned above. For Hourihan, they are the most basic or essential markers of the archetypal hero, and while I agree, I would add one more – or, more specifically, I would explicitly discuss the marker underpinning each of Hourihan's categories despite remaining undiscussed: bodily stability.

Bodily stability, or the fleshy material body's ability to disappear from concern, underpins each of Hourihan's markers, including those more focused on his journey or actions. Yet, while present, the body is also suspiciously absent. It hovers in the background, never specifically addressed, never discussed. The absence of discussion – the refusal to acknowledge, theorize and address the body – is not limited to Hourihan's deconstruction of the hero. The body – fleshy, material and biological – is a 'volatile site', even for feminist theory, a discourse that should be deeply concerned with bodies, if only because the body is at the centre of the gender inequality it seeks to understand (Alaimo and Hekman 2008, 1). The discursive turn within feminism, 'taking refuge within culture, discourse, and language', came as a solution to the biological determinism, essentialism and reductionism that too often comes with focusing on the body. However, not speaking about the body, about its materiality, corporeality, biology perpetuates both the conceptual centre of binary oppositions (that refuse the adolescent girl) and the limiting dependence on bodily wholeness and stability, as a symptom of that conceptual centre. Thus, in this section, I aim to talk about the body, to consider how the fleshy, material body gives rise to heroic markers and how each marker is a response to the threat of the body.

Hourihan begins her deconstruction of the hero by discussing his race. Of this marker, she writes, the 'hero is white' (1997, 58). This is not the hero 'is always' or 'is traditionally' white, but he *is* white. Whiteness is fundamental to the hero, and due to the story's binary logic, his whiteness, as manifested by his skin colour, is associated with his success at 'oppos[ing] darkness' (88). Race and ethnicity are far more complex than skin colour. Still, in the hero story, there is a one-to-one relationship between the hero's white appearance and his status as a hero, as Ebony Elizabeth Thomas demonstrates in *The Dark Fantastic*. Specifically, Thomas shows how darkness – not just a metaphor but a 'personified, embodied, and most assuredly racialized force' (2019, 20) – drives hero stories while also drawing our attention to the real-world implications of this positioning. Darkness and monsters are synonymous, so people with dark skin tones are monstrous owing to how this story links and layers alterities. Thus, 'is white' establishes, in racial and racist terms, not only the hero's 'normal' body colour but it also, by refusing difference, models a kind of bodily stability: the hero's skin colour does not change; it is white.

The hero's skin colour is most obviously implicated in racial and ethnic hierarchies, but it also relates to blood, mainly, menstrual blood. The archetype does make space for 'bloodshed on the battlefield' because this blood contributes to the hero's heroicness, as Peggy McCracken notes

(2003, x). However, as Catherine Batt describes, heroic injury is also 'part of a general strategy' in medieval literature 'that uses the body as the focus for issues of integrity' (1994, 270). (Medieval literature is a rich source of hero stories.) To make her argument, Batt cites how, in Malory's 'Tale of Sir Gareth of Orkney', an injury to Sir Gareth's thigh represents 'sexual activity constitut[ing] a moral transgression' (270). This injury signals that Sir Gareth is not acting heroically; he's not living up to the archetype. Its location, on his thigh, also alludes to menstrual blood, which this story sees as unclean, polluting and abject (Kristeva 1982). In Chapter 3, Alanna learns that she has begun menstruating when she wakes to discover her 'thighs and sheets smeared with blood' (Pierce 1983, 132). The bleeding, the conversation following it and the change it brings to Alanna's hero's journey – she is crossed-dressed and living as a boy, Alan, when this bleeding happens – disrupt the linear teleological impetus of the hero story while also including that which it would reject (menstrual blood) within the story's frame. Thus, for Sir Gareth, the location of this injury adds symbolic weight to what is, effectively, a body problem, specifically the body's capacity to break, bleed, change and produce new bodies from within the embodied self.

Briefly, it is worth explicitly stating my use of archetypes does not see them as universal, timeless, pure or inborn concepts or forms. Indeed, one of this book's tasks is to disrupt that conception inasmuch, at least, as it impacts adolescent girls. As such, I prefer to think of archetypes as the 'model from which copies are made' and to acknowledge the cultural and historical implications of the model and any copies (Cuddon 1999, 53). For example, the archetypal hero is the paragon of his people, and the markers describe what it takes to be that paragon. Not all heroes will meet all markers, but there is a tipping point; there is a point at which not-hero occurs. Thus, when an archetypal hero diverges from the model but remains a hero, it is worth paying attention to which markers he fails to meet (or might eschew) and what the divergence might entail or mean. For example, the 'change' might be nothing more than a displacement or permutation that leaves the structure of opposition intact as is the case with YA's 'exceptional heroines' who I discuss in Chapter 1 (Wilkins 2019, 19). Changes will also reflect the shape of cultural norms and expectations when they occur: what does it say about twenty-first-century Western culture when the form can stretch to include girl power, but it cannot expand to include darkness, as Thomas describes (2019)?

'Class and mastery', Hourihan's second marker, is a residual effect of the 'god'-touched aspect of mythic patterns, and it speaks to contemporary hierarchies and inequalities. The hero's existence as a 'symbol of an elite' bestows authority and power upon that group while also setting narrow parameters around who – the white, young, able-bodied male – might be included within it (1997, 62). Like the raced, injured, or menstruating body, the 'poor' or working-class body would bear traces of its existence on the body. It would be impossible, according to the logic, for this body to disappear. 'Class and mastery' also intersect with the hero's race, establishing and engendering superiority along both lines. Indeed, while unique, each of the heroic markers intersect, and they do so on and through the body, again illustrating why the body must be considered within what it means to be a hero. Class and mastery, for example, directly engage the hero's whiteness by insisting that because of his skin colour the hero exists in an elevated position, a position rendered evident and knowable by his body.

The hero's body is also a tool for signalling his age, as Beowulf, the heroic deliverer of King Hrothgar's halls from the terror of the monstrous Grendel, demonstrates. In all his battles with Grendel, Beowulf is never injured. He is never injured until when, in old age, he meets the dragon.

> Beowulf was foiled
> of a glorious victory. The glittering sword,
> infallible before that day,
> failed when he unsheathed it, as it never should have.
> For the Son of Ecgtheow, it was no easy thing
> to have to give ground like that and go
> unwillingly to inhabit another home
> in a place beyond; so every man must yield
> the leasehold of his days.
> (Donaghue 2002, vv. 65, lines 2583–91)

Dragons are potent symbols in myth and legend. In one sense, they represent the cosmic abyss, hidden knowledge and the unknown. In this view, they are linked to the serpent who tempted Eve in the Garden of Eden (and the origin story linking menstruation to a curse (Delaney, Lupton, and Toth 1976; Lerner 1986; McCracken 2003). Here, the dragon serves as the border between life and death; Beowulf will pass on into the unknown.

Representing Beowulf's failure as the failure of his unsheathed sword suggests his strength, youth, virility – his manhood – has failed. Northrop Frye describes a 'thigh-wound' as one 'being as close to castration symbolically as it is anatomically' (Frye 1957, 189). In this case, Beowulf is old, and the hero archetype requires youth. Hourihan even suggests, 'the archetypal hero is not merely young, he is essentially adolescent' (1997, 74).[2] In one very important sense, Hourihan's 'essentially adolescent' has nothing to do with age. It describes an outlook and engagement with the world, one marked by liminality, the push and pull of being in-between, and – because I'm talking about the hero story – an impetus to 'move on'. In another, it overtly links hero stories to YA; as YA is the field of literature ostensibly 'for' adolescents, I believe we can take the axiom further: in contemporary Western culture, the 'normal' adolescent is the archetypal hero, and he has been since G Stanley Hall gave birth to the myth of 'normal' adolescence in 1904 as I discuss elsewhere. Beowulf's death also suggests that the failure is integrally tied up with masculinity, at least because the story assumes masculinity to be rugged and virile.

Of the hero's gender, Hourihan writes 'the essence of the hero's masculinity', that is the essence of the archetypal hero, 'is his assertion of control over himself, his environment, and his world' (1997, 68–9). Control is the hero's *raison d'etre*, the sole purpose of his existence, and he directs that control outwards, projecting his will onto the world to make it more like himself. In contemporary Western culture, adolescent girls must 'get [and keep] their bodies under control' (Brumberg 1998, 49). The difference between the hero's assertion and the adolescent girl's task is crucial: the hero has always already asserted bodily control, freeing him to exercise control over others, while girls (and women) are tasked with pursuing bodily control, coded as beauty if they want to succeed within the system. It also does not allow identities beyond or outside the man/woman binary because the bodies associated with these identities could never be contained as the story requires. Where the hero story delineates control, the body – or that which must be controlled before all else – never appears because it is already controlled. There are no hero stories about conquering the body, though popular culture offers plenty of narratives in which girls must, through makeover practices, conquer theirs, so the hero may have his prize.

The questions I ask throughout this book are as follows:

- What would it take to change the girl's ancillary role, to free her and others from the patriarchal ideology that pits heroes against monsters, men against women and people against their bodies in a relentless competition for superior, rational and autonomous selfhood?
- What would it take to create an initiation pattern that is responsive, reflexive and dynamic enough to include rather than exclude nonlinear, relational and embodied patterns of development and selves?
- What would it take to conceive identity and selfhood through an embodied subjectivity that does not repudiate or abject that which it is not, but, instead, finds ways and means to include it within what it means to be a 'hero' and without overriding or engulfing the self?

The book's journey

Chapter 1, 'The Hero's Prize', argues that Western patriarchal ideology depicts the goal of successful adolescent girlhood as a journey towards becoming the hero's prize, or 'the maid predestined to be his bride' (Geronimi, Jackson, and Luske 1950). It not only excludes girls from the role of hero because they are his bride but also relegates their story to what it considers the margins: folk and fairy tale, romance, and YA. Moreover, it bars girls, and by this, I mean anyone identifying as a girl, from the role of hero's prize if they do not look and, to a lesser degree, act like Walt Disney's Cinderella (1950), currently the most iconic prize. Cinderella's sparkly, heightened, fantasy femininity as well as her cheery disposition in the face of hardship delimits what it means to be a girl, setting the standard for later versions. The chapter concludes by showing, first, how Cinderella's model of selfhood works outside the films and in contemporary Western culture before, finally, arguing that mainstream YA's 'exceptional heroines' have done little to change the girl's ancillary role, despite how often they save the day or how much they kickass. Twilight's Bella achieves the status of the prize by embodying, not just displaying, the sparkle. The Hunger Games' Katniss becomes an exceptional heroine (an intensification of a straight gender swap) by displaying many traits of heroic masculinity and offering a postfeminist rearticulation of the sparkle: fire. Neither girl, however, offers an alternative to the prize's narrow and limiting expectations. In fact, they heighten, intensify and internalize them.

In Chapter 2, I turn to Mythopoeic YA – the genre of YA speculative fiction giving space to female-heroes. It is worth remembering that I use this figuration to signify the, usually, girl heroes pushing the boundaries of what it means to be hero, girl and maybe even human. The hyphen signifies their liminal status between hero/prize. While female-heroes are central to this book – and the focus of chapters Three to Five – they could not exist without mythopoeic YA and the imaginary worlds from which they emerge. Beginning in the early 1980s with the work of Tamora Pierce and still being published and consumed to this day, mythopoeic YA is an imaginary world, speculative fiction drawing on the creative world-shaping power of myth and YA's liminal potential to build a new myth, a new story of what it means to be a girl. This myth is founded in relation, ambiguity and hybridity, not opposition. It not only makes space for difference and change but includes those things – or that which the archetypal hero excludes – within what it means to be a hero. At its core, mythopoeic YA brings new worlds into being to actualize new modes of being. It does so by displaying what I call a 'mapping sensibility', a creative impulse and proclivity to change, and through forming networks of relation that may cross genre boundaries. Indeed, mythopoeic YA denotes an outlook, or an ethos, more than it delimits a specific generic label or an age range.

Chapters 3 to 5 stand independently but also work together to disrupt the heroic romance and its linear teleological imperative, isolating individuality, and radical alterity, especially the erasure of fleshy materiality and procreative potential. I considered structuring these three chapters thematically, rather than, as I have, focusing on a single female-hero and her intervention – cross-dressing, being-cyborg and shape-shifting – in what it means to be a self. In fact, there is overlap between chapters that seemed to push for such a structure. For example, the third section of each chapter (Alan, android and animals) all engage what it means to be outside of discourse, the symbolic, but they each work from a slightly different perspective:

- Alanna must silence her female body to become **Alan**, but her female body breaks through that disguise to disrupt the hero romance.
- Iko can only approximate femininity as an **android** because she lacks the biology the story associates with femininity, but her movements across bodies show there is no such thing as a 'right' body.
- Daine's gift with **animals** appears to be nothing more than a knack but is really a powerful bond that gives her the ability to communicate with, heal and shape-shift into animals.

In each section, issues of the real, what it means to be a girl and epistemology (how we know what we know) come into play – with profound ontological implications for what it means to be human. These threads could form a chapter, and just as the second sections of each chapter might be read in order: 'on the road' 'appearances may be deceiving', requiring a female-hero 'look inside herself'. However, structured as they are, the chapters – together – offer a revised pattern of initiation.

The female-hero's journey offers a pattern of development or growth that brings cyclicality, repetition and kinship into the linear teleological hero's journey. Alanna's journey, as Chapter 3, considers, offers a model of selfhood that spirals, providing her a developmental path that accounts for her male/female, masculine/feminine, warrior/maiden selves and one that proliferates her 'self' beyond the boundaries of her body: Alanna's three children – Thom, Alan and Aly – complicate an easy resolution of Alanna's self as individual or singular. The model put forward by female-heroes also refuses flatness and makes space for history, depth and ambiguity. In Chapter 4, Cinder, as a Cinderella figure, should be the hero's prize, but owing to her status as a cyborg, her body is unfit to be the hero's prize. Specifically, it is unfit to be the mirror by which the hero secures rational, autonomous and unembodied selfhood. Instead, Cinder breaks the mirror to offer a 'girl full of wires' (Meyer 2012, 82). Building on the work of Chapters 3 and 4, Daine's chapter renegotiates the human/animal, self/other, mind/body oppositions central to the heroic romance to offer a model of self 'impregnated by otherness', 'scored by relationality into uniqueness' and 'with the potential to generat[e]' new selves 'from within the embodied self' (Battersby 1998, 7 and 18).

The book's conclusion, Towards a New Myth, draws together the central arguments of Chapters 3–5 – of the model of selfhood offered by female-heroes and the initiation narrative they build. In three sections, focusing on repetition, touch and kinship, the conclusion illustrates what being-hero means; that is, what a relational model of selfhood combining antithetical states to offer an embodied subjectivity recognizing plurality and change, forming through connection and kinship and underpinned by a sense of ethical responsibility looks like and how it works. My model building is particularly interested in children and in making space for relationships between mothers and children (specifically by showing how the mother lives on in and through her children) to radically disrupt the autonomy, coherence and isolating individuality of dominant models.

Acknowledgements

Finally, *Female Heroes* would not have been possible without several midwives, women who read drafts of chapters, paragraphs, and sometimes, even sentences. Emily Corbett, Catherine Charlwood, Alison Waller, Rebekah Fitzsimmons, Aishwarya Subramanian, Catherine Lester, Jennie Gouck, Abigail Fine, Melanie Ramdarshan Bold, Jamie Bienhoff, Ikram Belaid and Catherine Garner – thank you all. Karen Coats, you also fit here for one very, very helpful Zoom to help me work through a bit of Lacan (I think I did, maybe; if I didn't, it's on me). Along the road, Lucy Pearson, Kelly Gardiner, Chloé Germaine, Dimitra Fimi, Alison Waller and the Children's Literature Studies Association gave me wonderful opportunities to present bits of the project, and all were as much fun as they were helpful – thank you. Rebekah Fitzsimmons and Casey Wilson deserve a special thanks for Beyond the Blockbusters; Chapter 2 got its start there, and I owe them a great deal for what it became. There are also some peer reviewers along the way who also deserve thanks. In the scheme of things, I'm not meant to know who you are, so please take these anonymous thanks.

I also want to thank fellow Tamora Pierce fan and scholar Corinne Matthews for endless Twitter messaging about Pierce; Corrine also deserves thanks alongside Ayanni Cooper, as the co-hosts of Sex Love Literature, for one delightful podcast episode on Pierce. On that note, Aisha, be on the lookout for the 'Quite Large Inlet', and the ladies of the Twitter thread about knacks – I owe you! The YA Studies Associations' Critical Theory Reading Group also deserves a huge thank you, not least for putting up with me mentioning Tamora Pierce in (I'm guessing) every single reading group from the last couple of years.

This book began as my PhD project, and I could not have finished that without Rachel Moseley. I also need to thank a number of friends: Savita Kalhan, Alice Broadway, The Pub Gang, Amy Montz, Miranda Green-Barteet, Emily Murphy, Stephanie Toliver and the ones I know I'm forgetting in the fog of (finally) finishing. In more ways than you know, you impacted this project, and me. Thank you. Jessica Reid, as a sister you are more than a friend and you also probably know more than anyone just what this book represents. Love you.

Finally, two cats, several house plants and one incredibly long-suffering human deserve the most thanks of all.

1

The hero's prize: The myth of 'successful' adolescent girlhood

Against a backdrop of girl power, neoliberal narratives of self and a sort of common-sense feminism, the adolescent girl appears to have won the day. Popular culture is awash with 'heroic' girl heroes: Hermione Granger, Bella Swann, Clary Fray, Tris Prior and Katniss Everdeen, to name just a few. These girls are smart. They can fight, hunt, be the face of rebellions and save their respective worlds. Moreover, their books, films and related franchises command huge consumer capital. However, rather than offering any real intervention in heroic norms and standards, mainstream YA heroines – who overwhelmingly look and act like Cinderella, even as they kick ass and save the day – perpetuate the system of binary opposition at the very centre of Western thought. Mainstream or 'blockbuster' heroines offer an exceptional and expectational model of adolescent girlhood, offering the illusion of empowerment and equality *because* they look and act like Cinderella while kicking ass and saving the day. In other words, while prizes may have started to look and act like heroes, 'brass tits on the armour' leaves the wearer just as trapped, possibly even more uncomfortably so, than his prize is in her fragile glass slippers (Altmann 1992).

The hero emerges from quest-myth, a form of myth deeply concerned with renewing the world and its 'proper' order; the hero is the 'reviving power of spring' (Frye 1983, 188). In this sense, the hero story, or heroic romance, is also an initiation narrative. It maps the movement, or rite of passage, from one clearly defined and 'relatively fixed or stable state' within the social order to a new one (Turner 1967, 93; see, also, Gennep 1910). Such narratives accompany many transitory periods of life: birth, adolescence, marriage, pregnancy and death. Incidentally, this makes YA, as one of the cultural products addressing adolescents, a passage narrative participating in the adolescent's ritual transference from childhood to adulthood. It is also one of the reasons why identifying YA as an 'age category' does not work: numerical age is concrete, even as it, at least historically, has not been without ambiguities (Kett 1977; Chinn 2009; Stockton 2009; Owen 2020). Passage does not depend on age, as I discuss in Chapter 2 when considering the shifting and expanding age range of the YA protagonist and, consequently, the reader YA hails. Here, initiation narratives are not passive; they imply action and script behaviours. The heroic romance maps a linear, teleological and violent passage from potentially-but-not-yet-hero to hero and potentially-but-not-yet-bride to bride. However, the bride's journey is radically different from his.

Rather than setting off on some grand adventure to defeat a monster, the bride prize must perform normative white femininity, joyfully attend to house duties and chores and be made to sparkle so that she might secure a husband (the hero). As such, the makeover, or sparklemation as I name it below, sits at the centre of the girls' rite of passage. It is the turning point, or, in heroic terms, her 'symbolic rebirth' as an eligible maiden (Eliade 1956, 187–200; Turner 1967). Rebirth is the most central and crucial part of any initiation narrative, and conventionally (i.e. in the hero story) rebirth is difficult, dirty and, often, disgusting. The shift to the sparkle as the primary symbol of the girl's ritual rebirth marks the changed nature and goal of the bride's journey: she is not to be the hero but his prize. The sparkle produces femininity, and it is heightened, fantastical, superficial and exclusionary, and it does not affect all girls evenly, if a girl is not or cannot perform Cinderella's sparkly femininity, alterity increases and it does so even more when alterities overlap.

Finally, to be clear, Cinderella's journey from pauper to princess is not an alternative or parallel journey to the hero's; rather, it is part of his story. Indeed, it is possible to think of Cinderella's story – as it exists in the contemporary Western zeitgeist – as how the girl finds her 'place in man's life cycle' (Gilligan 1979). This is one of the reason's Cinderella's story is located in folktale, not myth and why it maps onto the 'marriage plot' or 'family romance', as described by Freud and interrogated by Marianne Hirsh in *The Mother/Daughter Plot: Narrative, Psychoanalysis, Feminism* (1989). In short, this story domesticates women, contains them, by placing them within an acceptable, to patriarchy, family structure, a structure of which the hero is head – and it makes the domestication look terribly appealing, as Walt Disney's Cinderella, the most iconic bride prize, makes clear.

In complex and complicated ways, heroic norms and standards have come to appear natural and immutable. Consequently, the model of selfhood mainstream Western culture offers and expects of men (heroes) and women (prizes) is difficult to dislodge, and I am not the first to undertake the work of doing so, as I discuss below when considering the female-hero's model of selfhood more fully. However, before turning to their inclusive model, I want to explore the West's dominant model of 'successful' adolescent girlhood and to show how Cinderella's legacy lives on in the apparently competing but, in reality, overlapping model of adolescent girlhood offered by Twilight's Bella

Swann and The Hunger Games' Katniss Everdeen. Encapsulated by Kim Wilkin's 'exceptional' YA heroines framework, Bella and Katniss illustrate in different ways the expectational nature of adolescent girlhood in the twenty-first century, a feat Bella achieves by embodying, not just displaying, the sparkle, while Katniss offers its postfeminist iteration, fire. In short, despite a recent YA novel declaring *Cinderella Is Dead*, she isn't – yet (Bayron 2020). The patriarchal ideology she represents and the model of selfhood she offers – to *some* girls – still dominate, and they will do so until the structure of opposition residing at the heart of the heroic romance is disrupted and dismantled.

Disney's Cinderella: The most iconic prize

In the twenty-first century, Walt Disney's Cinderella is the most iconic prize. She is two feature-length films (1950 and 2015). Cinderella also spearheads the Disney Princess court, a media franchise and toy line featuring twelve Disney princesses.[1] Her magical transformation at the hands of Fairy Godmother not only plays a key role in the makeover paradigm at the centre of the girl's developmental trajectory but also provides the premise and framework for Disney's Bibbidi Bobbidi Boutiques. These are 'magical' places where girls between the ages of three and twelve can – for a considerable price – experience Cinderella-esque makeovers from Fairy Godmothers-in-training. Disney's Cinderella is also at the forefront of the wedding industry, where the ubiquitous 'princess-style' wedding gown invariably means her ball gown. However, despite the saturation of Disney's Cinderella, her history is rich and deep.

In the language of folktales, Cinderella is a 'persecuted heroine', a being that profoundly impacts the femininity she offers. According to the Aarne-Thompson-Uther (ATU) tale type index, a catalogue of folk tales grouped by recurring sets of motifs, the Cinderella story is tale type 510a.[2] Disney's version notwithstanding, the core of the story is simple: a young girl exists in a state of persecution, frequently at the hands of a stepmother. Throughout her ordeal, Cinderella (or girl, as she is often known) remains both cheerful and pretty. However, her beauty, and thus inner worth, remains unrecognized until some form of supernatural intervention. This intervention allows her to escape her mundane existence and conflates inner goodness with outward appearance. It equates inner with outer and goodness with beauty (Stephens 1999). Cinderella's subsequent rebirth as a beautiful and appropriately dressed woman makes her eligible to attend the ball (or church) where she meets a (young) man, usually a prince, who falls instantly in love with her.

There are countless versions (and revisions) of the Cinderella tale, but there are two particularly well-known traditional versions in the West: Charles Perrault's *Cendrillon, ou la Petite Pantoufle de Verre* ('Cinderella, or The Little Glass Slipper') (n.d.) and the Grimms' *Aschenputtel* ('Cinderella') (1812). As Cinderella stories, both share a few key tropes – 'once upon a time', a wicked stepmother, unpleasant step-sisters (the Grimms allow them physical if not inner beauty), Cinderella herself, magical helpers, a glass slipper, the prince. However, two more different stories are difficult to imagine. Perrault's is a literary version of the tale ending with two morals: one extolling girls to beauty within and without and the second noting that with 'a godfather or a godmother' even that beauty might not be enough 'to bring you success' (n.d.). The Grimms', on the other hand, ends with, well, the wicked step-sisters getting their eyes pecked out: 'And thus, for their wickedness and falsehood, they were punished with blindness all their days' (1812). However, while the shape of their endings differ, there is a similar core message: the feminine identity rewarded within both versions is Cinderella's 'beauty within and without', not the step-sister's 'wickedness and falsehood' – these things bring 'punishment'.

This grounding in fairy tale is important, for it is upon the fairy tale that Walt Disney constructed his Cinderella. In fact, the film's opening credits claim that its Cinderella is 'From the Original Classic by Charles Perrault'. Crediting Perrault in this way not only establishes a direct lineage between the film and the fairy tale but also (re)establishes Perrault's story as a classic, perhaps aiming, even before it begins, to bestow the same 'classic' status on this new incarnation. As Linda Parsons argues, it is also quite telling that the Disney film links itself to Perrault's version of the tale rather than the Grimms'. For Parsons, 'the Grimm version is based on female empowerment enabling its reclamation by women, while the Perrault version embodies a patriarchal point of view' (2004, 143). While this makes the Perrault version unsuitable for the feminist revisions with which she is concerned, the connection illustrates precisely the kind of feminine identity offered by Disney's Cinderella. Thus, it is this positioning – emanating from a patriarchal point of view, or the 'powdered sugar' nature of the heroine, as Erika Jarvis describes Disney's live-action remake (2015) – that describes the feminine identity available through Cinderella: if you work hard and believe in your dreams, you too might be saved from domestic drudgery by some 'rich and handsome Mr. Right' (Wood 1996, 34).

First, Cinderella's appearance as a comely young woman dressed for housework is just as integral to the feminine identity she depicts as is her heightened fantasy femininity, without this foundational level of normative white femininity she could not achieve the other. In traditional versions of folktales, characters are 'ordinary' representatives of the people, so the people can see themselves in the tale and place themselves in the role of the protagonist (Bettelheim 1976, 8).[3] This is one of the ways folktales undertake the social and cultural work of shaping the lives of those who encounter them. Discussing *Cinderella*, Linda Parsons argues that 'fairy tales', and their vestiges, 'are sites for the construction of appropriate gendered behaviour', and that in so being, these stories offer those who encounter them 'positions to occupy' (2004, 135–6).[4] The lack of difference (white, ordinary characters) and the framing of otherness when it does appear ensures 'the people' take up the 'right' position. In short, therefore Cinderella must be a pauper *before* she is a princess.

In the case of Disney's Cinderella, Cinderella is also a particularly domestic pauper. As Naomi Wood argues, Cinderella is '[t]he ideal housewife' (1996, 35). She is 'beautiful (in a softly curved, Miss America, girl-next-door kind of way ...); innocently sexy (one of our first views of her is her rear end charmingly presented under the bedcovers); a loving caregiver (she tends animals in lieu of children)' (1996). Significantly, the predominant aspects of Cinderella's 'ideal' nature have to do with her appearance: 'beautiful' and 'innocently sexy'. Yes, she is an 'ideal housewife', but she is thus, at least partly, because she is beautiful and innocently sexy. Caregiving is important, but appearance is more so. Cinderella's 'innocently sexy' – sexy without the sex and certainly not desire – establishes a benchmark for feminine appearance still present in the twenty-first century.

Cinderella's appearance as innocently sexy is also paramount because, while necessary, the caregiving is problematic: the hero's prize cannot have children, even as she represents their promise. The hero's prize is a symbol; she plays a function in the hero's story. As the representation of his success and the mirror by which the hero secures his wholeness, Cinderella must remain flat. She cannot have depth or history, or exist in relation to anyone else. Moreover, symbols cannot overlap, thus while the bride is deeply related to the mother, these two symbols must remain distinct. It gets messy otherwise, and the heroic romance cannot tolerate mess; it actively works to resolve mess, disorder and chaos (all of which are 'other' to the hero). The film gets around this problem by having her care for animals, especially the mice. As pseudo-children, the animals mitigate the threat pregnancy poses to the hero story, or more accurately, the 'monstrosity' associated with the capacity to 'birth new selves from within the embodied self' (Battersby 1998, 19). There is no way Cinderella gave birth to these 'children', but she can 'mother' them in all the ways valuable to the femininity she depicts.

Given the role as pseudo-children, the animals also play a central role in Cinderella's feminine identity (not least owing to how women are associated with animals within the heroic romance's binary logic).[5] In the film, they often serve as foils or avenues to discuss norms and expectations, particularly in terms of clothing. Gus, for example, does not get a dress because he is a he – and 'that does make a difference', as Cinderella intones. In this space, dresses contribute to one's feminine identity, an identity that presupposes femaleness: Gus, as a boy mouse, cannot wear a dress. In Chapter Three, Alanna disrupts this assumption when trading places with her twin brother Thom, an act that requires her to wear 'boy's clothes'. Here, Gus is also fat. Within heroic discourse, the fat body is monstrous. It signifies disorder and a lack of (self)control, including the (re)productive, relational potential of pregnancy. In the first sense, fat is 'opposed to the self, not part of the self' (Kent 2001, 135–6). Fat makes the fleshy materiality of the body too visible, which threatens the system. As Lauren Berlant writes, fat bodies indicate 'more' – 'more surface, more depth, more dimensionality: the fat subject has explicitly and paradoxically given up control and become a stereotype of compulsive, helpless choosing, of selflessness and an excess of self' (1994, 163). Fat represents chaos and excess, and while the threat of this 'more' touches both heroes and prizes, the risk is more significant for women because they are already one step closer to excess.

Gus, as a wild, fat boy mouse, cannot be the hero's prize and so he cannot wear dresses, but as a (slim, white, 'fit') girl, Cinderella can wear all kinds of dresses, although even she must work to wear some of them – if she were fat (or disabled or otherwise not performing her normative white femininity) this would not be the case. Cinderella's 'rags', a simple dress, apron and headscarf, mark a basic level of femaleness and femininity. Her ball gown, on the other hand, represents the epitome of sparkly, heightened, fantasy femininity, and Cinderella's thinness certainly contributes to her ability to wear this dress. For example, Lindsey Averill describes in an article questioning whether or not fat-positive representations exist in YA (at her time of writing they did not), that positive understanding of thinness is 'rooted to the dualistic construction of the physical body as the marker of humanity's uncivilized animal instincts, which need to be controlled by the civilized and sanctimonious mind' (2016, 16). In the binary logic of hero stories, the hero is the mind (civilized and sanctimonious) and women the body (uncivilized and animal).

Finally, Cinderella's status as the most iconic prize is down, at least in part, to the cultural work Walt Disney undertook in the middle of the twentieth century: the animated feature-length *Cinderella* was part of a deliberate attempt to build an American märchen, a sort of body of American folklore (Wood 1996). While *Snow White* began this work (Hand et al. 1937), and *Sleeping Beauty* also played a key role (Geronimi 1959), *Cinderella* was vital (Geronimi et al. 1950), not least because Disney most clearly begins articulating his version of the 'American dream' in the film, as Naomi Wood argues in 'Domesticating Dreams in Walt Disney's Cinderella' (1996, 34). As the iconic song declares, this dream promises 'No matter how your heart is grieving/ If you keep on believing/ The dream that you wish will come true') – if you also meet the basic parameters and are fortunate enough to have a Fairy Godmother. Of course, Cinderella's dream is not shared explicitly with the audience (as she tells the mice, it won't come true if she says it aloud). However, her dream – to find true love through a traditional, heteronormative marriage and escape her present situation – is very much implied by how she gazes at the castle in the distance.

Cinderella's dream is 'appropriately' feminine to traditional ideas/ideals of femininity on two levels. First, as Wood suggests, Cinderella's dreaming is contrasted with and underscored by the household jobs she dutifully completes. It is 'shaped by the values of self-control and devotion to duty, as defined by a patriarchal order' (1996, 26). The work is for the present; the dreams are for the future. Furthermore, and as the happily-ever-after ending indicates, her dream is allowed because it is the dream of the heroic romance. In this sense, Cinderella is a narrative that reinforces the binary opposition between men and women that resides at the heart of the heroic romance, and in the case of *Cinderella*, it is an opposition that sees women as a Bride-to-Be-Had (if they look the part).

'Arranging the conditions' for a boy to meet a girl

My reading of Cinderella as the hero's prize and thus an image of successful adolescent girlhood depends, at least in part, on the purpose of the ball, which is also the plot of the film: 'arranging', as the King describes, 'the right conditions for a *boy* to meet a girl' (Geronimi et al. 1950, emphasis added). At least from the King's point of view, the film is about finding a bride for Prince Charming who is presumably on some sort of heroic adventure. Indeed, it is the King's decision to host a ball, ostensibly to honour the Prince's return home, that kick-starts the action of her story; without the letter instructing, 'by Royal command, every eligible maiden [...] to attend' the ball, there would be no film; Cinderella would be no bride. In other words, while the film may be called *Cinderella*, its plot is about the men, particularly about finding the hero a bride. As the King makes clear by throwing a temper tantrum about his son 'avoiding his responsibilities [giving the King grandchildren] for long enough'.

After establishing why he wants to throw the ball, the King further describes the film's purpose while manipulating a pair of bookends. These bookends depict, in porcelain, a pretty young couple separated by a trio of books. The handsome young man holds a small bouquet in one hand and his hat in the other. Staring entreatingly at the girl, he appears to be coming out of or at least peaking around a book by Homer. While these books lack titles, they do indicate authors: Homer, Plato and, authoring a shorter and fatter book, Rabelais. While these books lack titles, Homer is most well known for *The Odyssey*, the epic poem featuring the archetypal hero Odysseus (to which the traditional Greek helmet on the book's cover might nod). Rabelais, on the other hand, is known for satirizing such traditions. Indeed, his work might represent the inversion or opposite of Homer's lofty epic poetry. Clutching a basket, the pretty young girl coquettishly peaks over her shoulder next to this book, visually aligning the boy with epic poetry (and hero stories) and the girl with, well, not hero stories. These two books (and thus the boy and girl) are separated – and yet also bound – by a book by Plato, which might very well include discussions of Platonic ideals such as Love and Beauty. The ornate 'S' suggests it might be Plato's *The Symposium* (385–370 BC), a text containing speeches praising Eros, the god of love. In many ways, the King's speech is another speech on love, marriage, duty and responsibility.

As the King continues describing the purpose of the ball (arranging the conditions for a boy to meet a girl), he violently pushes the books away to bring the boy and girl statues together. This scene does (at least) two things. First, it redeploys the violence at the heart of the heroic romance, insinuating that the bride is simply there to be conquered – just as much as that unknown continent or monster. Second, in pushing these sign systems away, the King-in-the-film, and by proxy 'Disney', signifies something new is at work, a new myth is emerging. However, this 'new' does little more than inscribe a sort of 'American-style' into the old system (the heroic romance and/or Western, European mythology) (Wood 1996, 34).

The 'true love', as the film continually describes it, is not as 'real' or natural as the King's violent disregard of those books would suggest. Yes, the bookends fit perfectly together once the books go, but the King and his advisor undermine any naturalness by throwing a ball, by 'arranging the conditions for a boy to meet a girl'. In other words, true love and this myth of girlhood might be possible, but only if you are a porcelain white girl, meeting a porcelain white boy; then, and with the help of a Fairy Godmother, might you be an 'eligible maiden'. While as the daughter of a nobleman, Cinderella is intrinsically an 'eligible maiden', her social positioning and consequent ash-covered appearance make her ineligible. In other words, while the King's missive may insist that 'every eligible maiden' attend, it takes Lady Tremaine to clarify: Cinderella's chores must be completed (appropriate feminine work) and she (like all other girls) must find something 'suitable' to wear (appropriate appearance). Placed into a position of inferiority, in terms of class, by Lady Tremaine, the hard work that Cinderella must do is how the pauper becomes a princess who is worthy of a prince. It is how she becomes a prize.

Swallowed by sparkles: Reborn the hero's prize

Symbolic death and rebirth – the juncture at which the hero symbolically dies so that he may be reborn as the hero – is the most critical part of any hero's journey. It is the point at which the would-be-hero is 'removed, secluded, darkened, hidden, without rank or insignia' to force a radical break with one state so that he might (re)join the community as a full-fledged (adult) member (Lessa, Vogt, and Watanabe 1979, 234). Conventionally, ritual rebirth is expressed through symbols 'drawn from the biology of death' and those 'modeled on processes of gestation' (Turner 1967, 96). It is often difficult, dirty and disgusting. As a prime example, Campbell cites the Greek hero Herakles (Hercules), who willingly 'took a dive into the throat [of the monster], cut his way out through the belly, and left the monster dead' ([1949] 1968, 91). Of course, Herakles undertook this challenge to save 'Beautiful Hesione, the daughter of the king' ([1949] 1968), and in so doing, he was 'reborn' as the hero. Despite being the object of his quest, the hero's prize also undergoes ritual death and rebirth (or second birth), though with one fundamental change: hers sparkles.

Cinderella is to be the hero's prize, not the hero; the shift to sparkle represents her journey's changed goal and reflects the shape, style and general appearance of the prize she is to be. In the conventional model, the blood, guts and gore (not to mention caves, bellies, and tunnels) produce the hero's rugged, toxic masculinity. Incidentally, his second birth reappropriates the characteristics of first birth, in part to mitigate the threat procreation poses to patriarchal ideology but to also claim its power for men.[6] As I discuss throughout, the body's 'capacity to birth new selves from within the embodied self' is one of the greatest threats to the archetypal hero's selfhood, which is rational, autonomous and unaffected by embodiment (Battersby 1998, 18). As such, the shift to sparkle contains an additional layer of meaning: the sparkles – their shiny, white, reflective nature – disassociate the prize from reproductive potential. For one, no matter how 'messy' sparkles or glitter might be, their 'mess' is nothing compared to menstrual blood. The sparkle encourages girls and women to associate their gender identities with attractiveness and spectacular bodies rather than ones that break, bleed and change, and it is the driving force behind her transformation – or makeover – into the hero's prize.

Cinderella's transformation into the hero's prize begins with Cinderella fleeing to the garden in tatters and tears after Stepmother and Anastasia and Drizella destroy the resourcefully (re)constructed dress that once belonged to her mother. The origin of this dress is important. As Cinderella's only remaining tie to her now-deceased mother and thus Cinderella's position as a child, the systematic destruction of the dress – at the hands of those who would hold her back (from attending the ball) – marks Cinderella's entrance into the liminal period or the point at which transformation, rebirth and change might occur (see, also, Gennep 1960). At this moment, Cinderella is no longer daughter (or servant) nor is she the 'prize'. She is at the point of utter possibility, the point at which the system is either upheld, as it is with Cinderella and her iterations, or disrupted, as it is with female-heroes, as I explore in the remainder of this book.

Cinderella's rebirth begins with Fairy Godmother materializing from sparkles to comfort Cinderella as she weeps atop a bench. As Susan Ohmer notes, the period of transition is lengthy, 'seven minutes, or nearly one-tenth of the film' (1993, 240), evidencing the importance of this rebirth. From there, the sparkles abound: they accompany – alongside 'Bibbidi Bobbidi Boo', which serves as a kind of lyrical sparkle – the transformation of pumpkin, mice, horse and Bruno (the dog) into a coach, horses, coachman and footman respectively. The sparkles peak with the transformation of Cinderella's appearance. In this moment, Cinderella is encompassed by a spiral of sparkles that sweep her hair into a stylish updo and transform her dress into the iconic ice blue, sparkly ball gown, and her shoes into the glass slippers – another kind of sparkle. This is the appearance that makes Cinderella eligible to be his bride.

Admittedly, there is a certain power tied to the sparkle. It is, after all, the driving force behind Cinderella's transformation into the hero's prize. Drawing on queer theories of 'camp',[7] Kearney even attempts to reclaim the sparkle by arguing that it is a 'potentially resistant force': that is, its spectacle can be disruptive to norms and standards (2015, 270). However, the sparkle's link to appearance and its role in the production of heightened, fantasy femininity, which is just as exclusionary as the hero's rugged (toxic) masculinity, limit any positive readings. The sparkle does not produce difference; it erases it while also trapping girls and women within a representational economy refusing depth. This depth, and the reason, rationality, and language associated with it, is integral to female-heroes and, even, to mythopoeic YA, the genre of YA speculative fiction making them possible.

In the Cinderella narrative, the surface is all important. Cinderella is not a prize until she looks like one, and the sparkle as the symbol of her status makes this clear. For example, Rachel Moseley suggests, 'while the sparkle is powerfully spectacular and grabs the viewer's attention, it is also highly ephemeral, drawing the eye to the surface of the text' (2002, 409). Prior to the Fairy Godmother wrought makeover, Cinderella's appearance (rags, cinders) and social situation (servant) ostensibly did not match her inner goodness and kindness (even though Cinderella was pretty before the makeover). This makeover brings those things to the surface and yokes them to her – even prettier and certainly sparklier – appearance, a move that leads to a representational economy equating self (reality) with appearance and using 'wrong' appearances to disenfranchise and exclude those not meeting its ideals, a point that becomes even more clear in the 2015 live-action *Cinderella*.

The 2015 live-action *Cinderella* intensifies and expands the expectations for feminine appearance established by the 1950 feature-length animation in a number of ways. Initially, Cinderella is now Ella. While this is a contemporizing of her name ostensibly making it more relevant to twenty-first-century audiences, it also linguistically erases the 'cinder' usually associated with the figure. In keeping with neoliberal practices dominating this more recent space, Ella also refashions her mother's dress with only a 'little help' from the mice (Branagh 2015). However, the newer film also expands the scope of the makeover to include the Fairy Godmother within its frame while simultaneously increasing the amount of visual or 'textual sparkle' (Moseley 2002, 409).

First, the newer film not only includes the Fairy Godmother (Helena Bonham Carter), typically a crone (a rather round one in the 1950 film), within the makeover sequence, but her makeover also starts the sequence. That is, Ella's ritual rebirth begins with Fairy Godmother 'slip[ping] into something more comfortable' (Branagh 2015). This 'more comfortable' is an overall more youthful appearance, a princess-style ballgown (in white), and blonde hair. It is also incredibly sparkly. Prioritizing the older and more powerful woman's transformation within this sequence speaks to her particularly ambiguous and precarious position within contemporary expectations for feminine appearance (expectations this film depicts). In one sense, Bonham Carter is both more 'at risk' because, especially as the crone, she is older and sparkly femininity requires youth, but she is also a threat to the system owing to her magical powers. Either way, by the cultural space of 2015, even crones must look like prizes.

The increased emphasis on '*looking* the part' – or prioritizing the visual – is significant. Visuality describes a state of being prioritizing superficial appearance over depth, and it dominates contemporary Western culture. While appearances always matter to the hero's prize, they matter even more in this newer version and to the image of 'successful' adolescent girlhood she represents. Aside from Fairy Godmother needing to look like a prize (deeply ironic given Bonham Carter's notoriety for eschewing fashion's norms and standards), this newer film also lessens the auditory sparkle by doing away with the song 'Bibbidi Bobbidi Boo' and increasing the visual sparkle: Ella's transformation into the hero's prize is a surreal, dreamlike sequence in which animated butterflies and birds convey a profusion of glitter, sparkles and sheer radiance. Indeed, it might be better called a sparklemation: swallowed by sparkles, Ella dies to her old self so that she may be reborn appropriately feminine, so that she may be 'clothed [...] in the mantle of' her 'vocation' as the hero's bride, the prize of all prizes (Campbell [1949] 1968, 15).

'Sparkle On, Little Princess': Selling the dream (and rebranding it)

Cinderella's transformation from pauper to princess establishes the kind of behaviours girls outside of the texts ought to be undertaking: to be a successful adolescent girl enjoying all the (relative) privileges that come with existing as the hero's prize, girls must work hard, believe in their dreams and have a certain basic level of (white) attractiveness. They must also undertake appropriate makeover activities (because the above isn't enough). While Linda Parsons and others have demonstrated how folktales, including films working as folktales, undertake this social and cultural work of prescribing gender roles (Parsons 2004; see, also, Walkerdine 1984; Rice 2000), the more expansive Disney Princess franchise, and related consumer activities, takes the modelling a step further. It gives girls the chance to become Cinderella (or one of the adjacent princesses) through purchases. Specifically, a look at the 'culture of princess' – including how a princess becomes a Disney Princess (part of a specific marketing line) – allows a closer look at some of the concepts female-heroes directly engage, including the erasure of difference, the flattening of the body's fleshy materiality and refusal of difference.[8]

Created in 2000 by Andy Mooney (a former Nike executive), the Disney Princess franchise is the epitome of Princess culture, the dominant culture addressing preadolescent or tween girls with profound implications for adolescent girlhood and womanhood.[9] This franchise includes twelve Disney princesses: Snow White, Cinderella, Aurora, Ariel, Belle, Jasmine, Pocahontas, Mulan, Tiana, Rapunzel, Merida and Moana. They are, effectively, a line-up of the ideal princesses.[10] Being a Disney Princess has several requirements, including how the princess must hold the primary role in a Disney/Pixar film (a form of 'god' touched) and how her film should be a box office success (heroes are often 'surrendered to the water in a box'). However, as was the case for Cinderella, ritual rebirth plays an essential role in their existence as Disney Princesses while also speaking to how Cinderella's makeover within the film(s) has proliferated beyond that frame to become a paradigm.

The makeover is an omnipresent face of contemporary Western life, especially if you are a girl or woman. As Rosalind Gill argues in 'Postfeminist Media Culture: Elements of a Sensibility', the 'makeover' has now become a paradigm shaping contemporary Western life. Briefly, this paradigm 'requires people (predominantly women) to believe, first, that they or their life is lacking or flawed in some way; second, that it is amendable to reinvention or transformation by following the advice of [...] experts and practising appropriately modified consumption habits' (Gill 2007, 156). The paradigm is really quite insidious and offers a 'made over' self – and here I mean appearance – as the solution to any number of problems (a changed appearance isn't likely to help). There are countless examples of the makeover paradigm at work in contemporary Western culture and its history is long and complex, but the 1950 feature-length *Cinderella* played a key role as a look at what it takes to become a Disney Princess.

To become a part of the franchise, each princess received a makeover that worked to homogenize the court by making each princess smoother, shinier and sparklier. In so doing, these makeovers, taking place outside of the films, add a requirement to the feminine identity offered by Cinderella: it is no longer enough to be beautiful; you must be beautiful precisely like everyone else. In an article about makeover television, Brenda Weber describes this as the 'economy of sameness' underpinning makeover culture, and while Weber's focus is *Extreme Makeover* (2002–2007), a television programme aimed at adult women, the same principle is at work here in princess culture where it teaches girls 'a form of beauty-by-the-numbers that is narrow, formulaic and dependent on the very cycles of anxiety and desire it promises to transcend' (2005, para. 6), and it does not affect all princesses (or girls) equally. The makeovers are far more radical for Merida, Jasmine, Pocahontas, Mulan, and Tiana, and even for these girls, the treatment is unequal. The princesses of colour fare far worse.[11]

First, Merida, the heroine of Disney Pixar's *Brave* (Chapman and Andrews 2012), offers one very telling example, not least because she foreshadows the exceptional YA heroines saturating contemporary western culture. In *Brave*, Merida is tough and spirited. She prefers riding and archery to the 'elegant pursuits' of a lady, and, ripping her confining princess dress for a better range of movement, she even 'shoot[s] for [her] own hand [in marriage]' rather than becoming a prize (wife). The *A Mighty Girl* blog describes her as '[t]he princess that countless girls and their parents were waiting for – a strong, confident, self-rescuing princess ready to set off on her next adventure with her bow at the ready. She was a princess who looked like a real girl, complete with the "imperfections" that all people have' (2013). The 'imperfections' *A Mighty Girl* seem to cite are a headstrong, independent nature and a fabulously unruly head of red curls (in this light, I suspect I'm imperfect, though my curls aren't red). Merida's induction into the Disney Princess Court included smoother curls, a tinier waist, added curves (feminine contours), and paler skin. Her bow and quiver were swapped for a low-slung belt, and she seems to acquire high heels, or, at least, 'slimmer pointier feet', as Orenstein notes on her blog (2013). The makeover erases what little difference Merida introduced by making her more like the same, a move that is even worse for the princesses of colour.

Mulan, Pocahontas and Jasmine all saw 'their features audaciously whitewashed' in their Disney princess makeovers, as Monika Bartyzel describes (2013). In Mulan's case, the redesign also overtly conflicted with the message of empowerment at work in her film: Mulan cross-dresses to take her father's place in a battle, and her distaste for the 'matchmaker' activities, including the makeup she must wear, is well documented. The makeover prioritizes the franchise's – white, middle-class, 'fit', and sparkly – aesthetic while erasing racial, ethnic and cultural differences, moves that matter deeply. They shape how those who see and hear them understand the world. For example, in 'Kids Meet an Opera Singer', a video produced by HiHo Kids as part of their 'KidsMeet' series, a young white child asks Angel Blue, a Black opera singer, if Blue is 'a princess' because of the ballgown Blue is wearing. Blue responds with a question of her own: 'do I look like one?' (2018). The child responds, '[hesitant] yes, but you don't remind me of one', presumably because Blue does not look like Cinderella. The child eventually offers 'maybe Tiana' – the only Black princess (2018).

The sparkly feminine identity Disney's Cinderella offers is superficial, precarious, exclusionary, and dependent on purchases (bearing in mind that normative white femininity must be present first). In *Cinderella Ate My Daughter*, Orenstein argues that the Disney Princesses (as well as popular culture) present 'femininity as performance, sexuality as performance, identity as performance, and each of those traits is available for a price' (2011, 183). Essentially, it does not matter how you feel, as long as you look the part. It is this 'looking the part', Orenstein argues, in which the Disney Princesses are particularly complicit, not only for their plotlines ('Every single one is the same: it's about romance, love, and being rescued by the prince', as one mother interviewed by Orenstein notes), but it is also the sheer ubiquity of Princess merchandise available for making such 'looking' possible (8).[12] In other words, the Disney Princess franchise participates in consumer culture for children – overwhelmingly for girl-children – that aids in contemporary popular and media culture's insistence that femininity is achieved as performance-through-purchase. Thus, Cinderella's sparkly, heightened, fantasy femininity requires both a rendering of sexuality as performance and the commodification of girlhood specifically and femininity more widely, both of which female-heroes address.

Finally, since the mid-2000s, Disney has been changing the princess narrative, explicitly focusing on the sparkle and trying to reclaim it (and the princesses) as an empowered choice for young girls. As Kodi Mayer details, the princesses themselves have quietly become less sparkly (though they are still quite thus), while marketing has shifted to predominantly 'empowering' messages such as 'Dream Big, Little Princess' and 'Sparkle on, Little Princess' (2016; 2019). While the shift in messaging appears encouraging, these 'empower ads' do little to supplant the culture of pretty at the heart of the myth of adolescent girlhood. The mobilization of the sparkle – it's no longer enough to sparkle; she must also 'sparkle on' – suggests an intensification of the message, rather than a departure, a story the exceptional heroines dominating contemporary YA demonstrate.

Cinderella isn't dead (yet): YA's exceptional and expectational heroines

Cinderella's legacy lives on in the exceptional and expectational heroines dominating YA. This heroine reworks medievalist fantasy's 'exceptional women' trope by adding a layer of expectation and a dash of sparkle (Tolmie 2006). As Jane Tolmie writes, the exceptional heroine must be thus 'to catch our attention, and that of the hero. She often picks the man she wants, eludes the (many) others, escapes rape, lives a life less ordinary. Behind her and all around her is the silent rank and file of women who do not choose, elude, or escape' (146). Her heroism is more evident because she is the only one pushing boundaries, doing things differently. While she escapes, her heroism is unambiguously a product of patriarchal structures, particularly gender-based oppression. In YA, this exceptional narrative becomes one of expectation. Not only must the girl rise above but she must also save the day while doing so – and she needs to look like Cinderella. As Amy Montz says, 'these rebels may tear their dresses when they start their revolutions, but they look exceptional when doing so' (Montz 2014, 12), and while for some this might be empowering, the continued insistence on appearance – and one very narrow one at that – is just an illusion of equality.

Bella Swan and Katniss Everdeen are two of the most well-known YA heroines. Their articulation of the exceptional and expectational formula – essentially looking like Cinderella while saving the day – illustrates how, despite what postfeminism and girl power might claim, even these girls are still the hero's prize. It also shows that while Bella might be criticized for her 'traditional femininity' and Katniss praised as a 'modern feminist heroine', both girls are still trapped in a scheme requiring them to look and act like Cinderella, only Katniss gets to deploy the hero's rugged, toxic masculinity. In other words, I would argue, as Marnina Gonick does of 'girl power' and 'Reviving Ophelia', that instead of seeing Katniss and Bella as 'opposing, competing, and contradictory', as many have, they work together to 'articulate a complex of fiction and fantasy, regulation and persuasion' shaping what it means to be a girl living with Cinderella's legacy (2006, 2).[13]

Bella most easily maps onto the prize's marriage/romance framework. She is an ordinary adolescent girl (white, thin, non-disabled, neurotypical, heterosexual), if not also a little clumsy. Within her story, she undergoes a makeover, a symbolic death and rebirth when she changes into a vampire. In this transformation, Bella not only comes to embody sparkly, heightened, fantasy femininity – in this world, vampires sparkle (Priest 2017) – but she also becomes the porcelain white girl the King decided was an appropriately eligible maiden for Prince Charming. Bella will remain nineteen forever. To be clear, Bella does not just display the sparkle (as the Disney princesses do); she embodies it. In this move, she also loses her humanity: her body can no longer break or bleed, both in the sense of injury as well as reproductively. She literalizes the ideal of symbolic death and rebirth, which is meant to propel a person into a 'relatively fixed or stable condition' (Turner 1979, 234). Bella's sparkle not only upholds the narrow and limiting expectations of feminine appearance but it heightens, intensifies and internalizes it and offers stability in spades.

Katniss, on the other hand, appears to offer an alternative, one that seems to have broken free of Cinderella's legacy, not least because she bears many of the (toxic) traits of heroic masculinity. She regularly hunts to feed her family; they live in the poorest district of Panem, the imaginary world in which her story is set. She successfully enters into the Hunger Games (a life-or-death competition the government uses to maintain control) in place of her sister and she has two young men vying for her affection. Katniss is, in many ways, Maria Nikolajeva's 'hero in drag' (Nikolajeva 2002, 144; 1991, 147–9; see, also, Paul 1990). Nikolajeva argues that this hero is effectively a gender permutation the story allows to ensure its central opposition remains intact. The hero in drag serves as a sort of steam valve, letting 'local' concerns (in this case, girl power) be addressed while the underriding structure (of adversarial, linear, teleological action) remains in place – and often becomes stronger for the release. Tellingly, Katniss' two love interests, Peeta and Gale, exist oppositionally: Peeta is, as Linda Holmes describes, Katniss' 'movie girlfriend', while Gale is her 'movie boyfriend' (2013). Katniss ultimately chooses Peeta, thus confirming her status as a 'hero in drag' or Angela McRobbie's 'phallic girl', a figure who gives the *impression* of having won equality with men by becoming like her male counterparts' (2008, 83).

Despite appearing empowered, Katniss does nothing to address the hero story's system of opposition, which imposes crippling alterity on the nature of 'Not-A' through its relationship to 'A'. She is the archetypal hero inverted. It is worth explicitly stating that my use of archetypes does not see them as universal, timeless, pure or inborn concepts or forms. Indeed, one of this book's tasks is to disrupt that conception inasmuch, at least, as it impacts adolescent girls. As such, I prefer to think of archetypes as the 'model from which copies are made' and to acknowledge the model's cultural and historical implications and any copies (Cuddon 1999, 53). For example, the archetypal hero is the paragon of his people, and the markers describe what it takes to be that paragon. Not all heroes will meet all markers, but there is a tipping point; there is a point at which not-hero occurs. Thus, when an archetypal hero diverges from the model but remains a hero, it is worth paying attention to which markers he fails to meet (or might eschew) and what the divergence might entail or mean. For example, the 'change' might be nothing more than a displacement or permutation that leaves the oppositional structure intact, as with Katniss. Changes will also reflect the shape of cultural norms and expectations when they occur. What does it say about contemporary Western culture when it can stretch to include girl power, but it cannot expand to include darkness, as Thomas describes (2019)? The above discussion of Jasmine, Pocahontas, Mulan and Tiana is also at play here. Replacing a male hero with an ostensibly girl hero is not enough, especially when, in that replacement, the hegemonic expectations around appearance remain and intensify.

Bella and Katniss both undergo makeovers within the stories. These makeovers transform them into the exceptional and expectational heroine. While Bella's transforms her into that sparkly, porcelain white girl and grants her 'shield' abilities (a vampire gift allowing her to protect herself and those around her) (Meyer 2008, 595), I want to briefly focus on Katniss's makeover as it appears to be the least like Cinderella's (but actually isn't all that removed). Before her entrance into the 'Hunger Games', Katniss also undergoes a makeover, one that transforms her into the 'girl on fire'.[14] The fire initially appears to offer a radical break from the sparkle; after all, it does burn. However, her fire requires the transformation of her appearance, as does the sparkle. In the 'Remake Centre', her body is scrubbed with a 'gritty foam' that 'remove[s] not only dirt but at least three layers of skin', and her fingernails are turned into 'uniform shapes' (Collins 2008, 75). Poignantly, the makeover also includes 'ridding' Katniss's 'body of hair' (Collins 2008) and, like Cinderella's, a change in clothing. Indeed, in a move echoing Ella's ritual rebirth in the 2015 live-action *Cinderella*, Katniss's transformation before entering the games a second time in *Catching Fire* (2013), includes a scene in which she is engulfed not in sparkles but fire. In an inversion of the sparklemation, Katniss's fire burns away the wedding dress she would have worn to marry Peeta (at this point it is a ploy to win sponsorship, but Katniss does eventually marry Peeta).

Bella and Katniss are illustrations of how the structure of opposition underpinning patriarchal ideology persists and how it can stretch; despite Katniss being a girl, she is still a hero. Poignantly, neither girl menstruates (or, at least, it isn't depicted). Yes, Bella notes a missed period that results in a pregnancy she first believes to be a 'strange South American disease' (Meyer 2008, 125), but an absent period and a 'monstrous' pregnancy do nothing more than sustain an ideology viewing menstruation and procreation as other. In contemporary Western culture, menstruation, when it is discussed at all,[15] is frequently associated with horror. Moreover, menarche and more generally female adolescence itself has historically been likened to monstrosity, as *Carrie*, both the novel (King 1974) and the film (De Palma 1976) exemplifies.[16] Both have also been linked to a kind of animality, as is also the case with the horror film *Ginger Snaps* and its two teenaged protagonists (Fawcett 2000).[17] These films, and Bella's absent period and pregnancy, literalize the horror associated with menstruation – and the girl's alterity – in contemporary Western culture.

The capacity to procreate, to 'generate new selves from within the embodied (fleshy) self' (Battersby 1998, 13), poses the greatest threat to the archetypal hero's rational, autonomous and unaffected by embodiment mode of selfhood. As such, I discuss menstruation, procreation and the messy, complex relationship between sex and gender throughout this book. Here, it is necessary to note: physical, material bodies exist and there is a corporeality to sex, but how we know, understand and classify bodies, sex and gender is another matter altogether. The heroic romance, and the patriarchal ideology it supports, has been responsible for one very narrow and incredibly dominant way of considering and managing the body since the creation of patriarchy (Lerner 1986; Weigle 1989). Part of the work of female-heroes, perhaps the work of female-heroes, is undoing this myth because until the body is not seen as deviant, different, dangerous and other to the self, it will continue to be the mechanism by which scores of people are othered.

Female-heroes: Reframing myths of adolescent girlhood

Female-heroes intervene in the violent hierarchy, radical alterity, isolating individuality and erasure, particularly of bodily difference, marking what it means to be a self in contemporary Western culture. They do so by occupying the spaces between oppositions foregrounding the body's fleshy materiality, including its procreative potential and demonstrating relationality; that is how seemingly opposing sides might exist in relation to one another without losing their uniqueness. In so doing, they model a version of self 'scored by relationality into uniqueness' (Battersby 1998, 7). This model, which I describe as 'being-hero', combines antithetical states to offer an embodied subjectivity recognizing plurality and change, forming through connection and kinship, and underpinned by a sense of ethical responsibility. Importantly, this model does not preclude violence, but it strategically employs it to right wrongs. It is also not an alternative to, or an inversion of, the archetypal hero's model of rugged, toxic masculinity, as was the case in the above examples. Instead, being-hero is a way of dynamically and actively engaging the space 'in-between'.

As I've mentioned, Western rationality depends on clearly defined oppositional pairs: man/woman, adult/child, mind/body, self/other. Importantly, these states do not describe 'the peaceful coexistence of a vis-à-vis'; they delimit and enact 'a violent hierarchy' (Derrida 1981, 41). The idea can be represented through the form 'A/not-A' in which 'A' man is 'not-a' woman; 'a' mind is 'not-a' body; 'a' self is 'not the other'. The person or concept occupying position A is superior to not-A, and not-A is 'the very antithesis of A'; that is, A defines itself because it is not not-A (Prokhovnik 1999, 25). Briefly but importantly, values occupying position A also relate to one another just as those deemed to be not-A correspond; in other words, all the superior terms are linked in their superiority and all the negative terms are linked in their inferiority: women, children, bodies and others are the same thing, that which A is not, according to this logic.

Owing to this, dichotomy might be a better way of conceiving the hero story's 'conceptual centre' and its impetus to action. In *Rational Woman: A Feminist Critique of Dichotomy*, Raia Prokhovnik argues that dichotomies are shaped by 'four features' (1999, 23). These features are 'an opposition between two identities, a hierarchical ordering of the pair, the idea that between them this pair sum up and define a whole, and the notion of transcendence' (1999). As its goal or quest-orientated focus makes clear, the heroic romance is a playing out of dichotomous thinking. The hero exists in opposition to that which he is not (A/not-A), and not-A is 'the very antithesis of A' (25). The hero is elevated, made more heroic, by the 'shunning, excluding, not being the other', thus demonstrating the implicit hierarchical ordering (26). Finally, the hero's prize offers an excellent, concrete, example of the third and fourth functions: she completes the hero and aids in his 'transcendence'.

However, oppositions or dichotomies do not have to be resolved in this way; the fact that they are is a symptom of patriarchal discourse. The space between A/not-A is interstructural; it is liminal, and it is the point at which the structure might be upheld, as it is with heroes, prizes and exceptional heroines. It is also the point at which the structure might be disrupted and dismantled, as is the case with female-heroes. To be clear, the liminal is absolute neutral (according to the system it doesn't exist); it is utter possibility. Female-heroes use the spaces between oppositions to forge a self that is grounded in embodiment and related to other selves. The body features so centrally because it is the ur-monster: the first and most intimate boundary, serving to preserve the difference between self (hero) and other (monster), but it is also the other within the self, ever-threatening order, stability and control. Dominant models – hero stories, psychological and biological models of adolescent development, and mainstream YA fiction – attempt to allay the body's disruptive potential by erasing markers of difference, enforcing linear, teleological development and insisting on isolating individuality, superiority and success.

Female-heroes intervene in this system of opposition by occupying the spaces between oppositions in ways that foreground the body and its fleshy materiality, especially the body's capacity to produce new bodies. Indeed, they include – instead of repudiating – the body within what it means to be a hero, making spaces for bodies that grow, break, bleed and change. In so doing, they offer a model of selfhood recognizing plurality and change, forming through connection and kinship, and underpinned by a sense of ethical responsibility. To represent the female-heroes' dynamic and active engagement of the space between, I use the figuration 'being-hero'. Recognizing the hyphen's conflicted status in contemporary Western culture, I use this figuration to signify the productive liminality that female-heroes embody and model, to illustrate how – by dynamically and actively occupying the spaces between oppositions – female-heroes disrupt heroic norms and standards. The formulation couples the dynamic 'being' (the action of existing and actively occupying a place or position) with, in this case, hero. The hyphen emphasizes the correlation of 'being' and 'X' while also physically occupying the space between the two terms, thus visually emphasizing their combined meaning; the hyphen fills an otherwise blank space and insists on the relationship between otherwise oppositional pairs.

Incidentally, the 'female' of female-hero performs a similar function to being-hero: it represents the dynamic occupation of a gendered identity, which is then, of course, coupled with hero. Importantly, this female, of female-hero, is not tied to biology in an essentialist way, even as biology, particularly the body's fleshy materiality, is a part of that being. For female-heroes, the body is another kind of hyphen, and rather than a border between self and other, it serves as a threshold: it represents potential connection, it is a conduit for kinship, and it is an important marker of self, even as the female-hero's self is more than just her appearance or body. In *Volatile Bodies: Toward a Corporeal Feminism*, Elizabeth Grosz takes on the Möbius strip, a sort of figure eight with a half twist, as a metaphor for 'rethinking the relations between body and mind', or what I might call A/not-A. Grosz argues, '[t]he Möbius strip has the advantage of showing the inflection of mind into body and body into mind, the ways in which, through a kind of twisting or inversion, one side becomes another' (1994, xiii). As Grosz further argues, it also collapses the difference and distance between inside/outside, surface/depth and self/other.

Finally, female-heroes do not just embody liminality. The journeys these female-heroes go on also disrupt the linearity of the archetypal hero story. The female-hero's journey involves the male, heroic linear developmental pattern or quest-myth and the cyclical, reproductive pattern associated with females. To be clear, female-heroes bring cyclicality into the hero story. They go 'on big adventures' and 'fight external enemies' while also getting their period, learning more about themselves as individuals and members of society, becoming mothers and developing many of the traits Aisenberg associates with the 'new ordinary heroine' (1994, 33 and 13). In other words, female-heroes go on heroic adventures that include many aspects of female initiation (Nikolajeva 1991, 122; Waller 2009, 35). In so doing – by inserting the cyclical into the linear – female-heroes disrupt the linear, teleological trajectory of the heroic romance to offer an alternative and inclusive model of selfhood and a map of how to get there, as a look at mythopoeic YA, the genre of YA speculative fiction female-heroes call home makes clear.

2

Mythopoeic YA: Bringing new worlds into being to conceive new ways of being

First emerging in the early 1980s through, mainly, the work of Tamora Pierce,[1] mythopoeic YA is a speculative, imaginary world fiction initially by women and still for adolescent girls, that is, keeping this discursive group in mind. Beginning as a Tolkienian-inspired fiction, mythopoeic YA draws on the Creative, world-shaping power of myth and YA's liminal potential to envision and articulate new ways of living and being an adolescent girl. In this book, I focus on three key examples – cross-dressing, being-cyborg and shape-shifting of reframed adolescent girlhood. While distinct, each expands the possibilities of what it means to be a self by disrupting the structure of opposition upon which the heroic romance depends. For instance, shape-shifting relates to scrambling the human/animal dichotomy and being-cyborg to the human/machine split, but, at root, both engage the space between oppositions. This engagement allows them to offer a model of selfhood recognizing plurality and change, forming through connection and making space for kinship informed by an ethos of ethical responsibility (Moran 2018). I use the figuration 'being-hero' to signify the productive liminality, the possibility, at the heart of the female-hero's model of selfhood. This figuration couples the dynamic 'being' (the action of existing and actively occupying a place or position) with, in this instance, 'hero'. The hyphen insists upon the correlation of the two terms while also radically and dynamically occupying the space between them. This hero, like mythopoeic YA, disrupts opposition by forming through possibility.

While the female-hero is key to my overall concern with reframing the myths of adolescent girlhood, intervention, in many ways, starts with the world. As Peter Hunt suggests, 'places mean' because a world's place – its shape, texture, temperature, topography and so on – affects the kinds of stories, the kinds of female-heroes, that might emerge from it (Hunt 1987, 11; see, also, Carroll 2012; Dharmadhikari 2009). For example, Meyer's Lunar Chronicles is set in an imagined future in which Lunars, citizens of the moon, are hostile next-door neighbours. The world's modes of transportation include hover crafts and spaceships. In this world, a cybernetic female-hero 'make sense', but a female-hero who cross-dresses to become a Knight of the Realm does not. However, both female-heroes and their worlds push the boundaries of what it means to be a hero. They also demonstrate how mythopoeic YA is not limited to fantasy stories set in the remote past, as myth usually is. However, as this chapter shows, mythopoeic YA is less about generic differences in the traditional sense and is more about building networks of relation to create worlds in which female-heroes are possible.

This proliferation of world-building across media forms is integral to mythopoeic YA owing to how such boundary-crossing frustrates the linearity associated with heroic romance (including 'normal' adolescent development) while also insisting on a relationship between unique instances of story, without sacrificing their individuality. The Grishaverse, for example, is literature's boundaries of form and mode: Three distinct – yet intertextually as well as contextually related – 'series' currently exist alongside a book of fairytales, an immersive website, an array of licensed and unlicensed products, fanfiction, fanart, and the Netflix adaptation pushes the boundaries of YA adaptations. Relatedly, mythopoeic YA is not the one-time experience of a single text. While an individual narrative may demonstrate mythopoeic YA's interventionist stance, stand-alone novels lack the sense of depth and immersive potential necessary for sustained and lasting intervention. The impact of, for example, Tamora Pierce's Tortall Universe is down to, at least in part, the sense that this world is, or could be, real, a feat achieved both by the strength of world-building occurring in individual texts but also, and crucially, between texts. The networks of relation, grounded in the imaginary world, are vital to mythopoeic YA's intervention. These relations allow mythopoeic YA to create new storylines from old ones.

The old storyline mythopoeic YA engages is that of traditional myth and legend, particularly the heroic romance or quest myth, a storyline at the very centre of Western culture. Indeed, this story is responsible for perpetuating the system of patriarchy excluding girls and women from the role of hero. In it, a white, middle-class, 'fit', young man becomes a hero by violently exerting superiority and dominance over that which he is not. In so doing, he renews or restores the world and its 'proper' order. In contemporary Western culture, this narrative appears most visibly in the story of adolescence (how a male child becomes an adult) and in the literature 'for' adolescents. The story functions as it does – violently renewing the world and its order – owing to its 'conceptual centre', its way of seeing and understanding the world (Hourihan 1997, 15). This centre imposes radical alterity on that which is 'not-hero' (monster, darkness, woman, other) to violently ensure the hero's heroicness while setting him above and apart from those 'others'. For this binary logic to function, a clearly defined void, a schism, must exist between oppositional sides lest they risk bleeding into one another. As I have said, if there is no indisputably blank space between hero and 'monster', they might not be so different; they might be the same.

By merely existing, YA – books and beings – complicate binary logic; they are that which exists in-between (adult) literature/children's literature and adulthood/childhood. The liminal is the point of utter possibility, the point at which the structure could change, as it does with female-heroes in mythopoeic YA, or the fulcrum upon which it is upheld, as it is with most instances of YA. This is key: most YA texts serve the system; they acculturate readers into the power structures at play in contemporary Western culture (see, Trites 2000a). Mythopoeic YA functions differently owing to its conceptual centre of possibility. Like all YA, mythopoeic YA is liminal, but it is also formed through the world-creating and shaping power of myth and YA's liminal potential. The hybridity is crucial because the dual perspective gives mythopoeic YA its interventionist outlook. Indeed, where the heroic romance's 'conceptual centre' is one of opposition, mythopoeic YA's is one of possibility. This centre forms in and through the 'betwixt and between', the space between binary oppositions (Turner). It encourages plurality and change and involves relations and relationships that form through equality, kinship and dependence. It also, and most importantly, builds imaginary worlds, which might take the shape of a pseudo-medieval fantasyland or a futuristic (re)imagining of Earth, in which female-heroes break boundaries, blur borders and challenge the necessity of the male hero and all that he represents.

Finally, Mythopoeic YA is an interventionist fiction, cultural work depending on mythopoeic YA's being-YA, a figuration I use to illustrate how this fiction occupies and engages the middle ground to reframe adolescent girlhood. Merely being a work of YA does not guarantee intervention, nor does being a speculative fiction or fantasy text. There are plenty of YA texts in service to the narrow and limiting norms of hegemonic discourse because, rather than engaging the middle ground, they perpetuate the logic of opposition and exclusion upon which hegemonic discourse depends. How mythopoeic YA engages liminality gives rise to a conceptual centre of possibility, not opposition. Through its centre of possibility, mythopoeic YA re-writes hegemonic, binary values, encouraging difference and change. Mythopoeic YA expands and contracts, forges new territory, and nimbly moves across and combines traditional genres (such as science fiction and fantasy) and includes examples from the range of fiction existing between children's and (adult) literature. As such, any 'definition' of the genre must be flexible, and it must be able to cope with fiction this is constantly changing and does not still easily within a single discipline or field. Thus, this chapter, at least partly, maps mythopoeic YA's dynamic existence across the last nearly four decades, a dynamism that is fundamental to the female-hero and her intervention in heroic norms and standards.[2] This approach allows the (changing) shape and nature of mythopoeic YA's intervention and its key features – imaginary worlds, networks of relation, magic and maps – to emerge while also mapping where, when and how female-heroes disrupt binary logic to provide alternative images of living and being an adolescent girl.

Imaginary world speculative fiction

Mythopoeic YA is an imaginary world speculative fiction,[3] a being that describes both the setting, possibly even type, of fiction on offer, while also providing a way – intertextual fields – to conceive the relationship between the various points of entry into its worlds. Indeed, mythopoeic YA's status as imaginary world fiction requires multiple points of entry while also offering the possibility for those points to cross media boundaries (literature, film, television, games, products). As Mark Wolf suggests, 'worlds extend beyond the stories that occur in them' creating a sense of depth and immersive opportunity (2012, 17). These worlds have unique histories, mythologies and religious systems that are often polytheistic. They feature magic or that which is impossible by the standards of 'consensus reality' as well as creatures and modes of transportation not present in our world (Hume 1984, 17). Mythopoeic YA texts also frequently feature literary maps, that is, visual representations of their worlds, as a means of adding depth and verisimilitude to both world and story while also participating in the perception that these places are, or could be, real.

As a term and concept, 'imaginary world' emerges from media studies to account for the world-building occurring in the media franchises of contemporary Western culture: Star Wars, the Marvel Cinematic Universe and the DC Extended Universe (see, for example, Wolf 2012; 2016; 2017). Given this, my naming mythopoeic YA 'imaginary world' fiction is provocative; it is, after all, a literature-based fiction. Moreover, speculative does not necessarily signal fantasy, and the mythopoeic most obviously relates to high fantasy and heroic romance (Alexander 1971; Clute and Grant 1997; Wilkins 2019). However, Mark Wolf also posits 'imaginary world' as 'perhaps the broadest and least technical term' to describe fictional worlds diverging from the world we inhabit (2012, 14). More importantly, he characterizes imaginary worlds as 'realms of possibility [...] that can make us more aware of the circumstances and conditions of the actual world we inhabit' (17). Similarly, speculative implies speculation about the world, its order and what it might be like if the rules changed. Mythopoeic YA's imaginary worlds call attention to adolescent girlhood's narrow and limiting expectations and speculate about what it means to be a hero formed through relation, not opposition.

Imaginary world speculative fiction also intervenes in some common assumptions:

- the literary, especially fantasy, studies' assumption that created worlds are 'secondary' to our mundane one;
- the widely held assumption that fantasy is the primary home of myth or the mythopoeic;
- the assumption that series fiction must progress in a linear, teleological manner or not progress.

While I touch on all three in this section, I discuss two and three in more detail when considering how Meyer's Lunar Chronicles offer 'mythic forms in modern shapes' and how the 'networks of relation' created by mythopoeic YA texts disrupt linearity.[4] These networks are central to the model of being-hero female-heroes offer. Here, I want to focus on worlds, taking a closer look at what Secondary World, Tolkien's term, implies before considering how even high fantasy imaginary worlds, those drawing most firmly on the pseudo-medieval, push boundaries when they are mythopoeic YA.

Mythopoeic YA is fundamentally about featuring female-heroes – heroes who embody the spaces between opposition, a concept conceivable as 'being-hero' – in worlds not beholden to the norms, standards and logic of our consensus reality. The hero stories of mythopoeic YA both draw on and intervene in the heroic romance, a legacy passing directly to the sub-genre through the work of Tolkien and, to a lesser extent, C. S. Lewis and The Chronicles of Narnia. Tamora Pierce, mythopoeic YA's founding mother, frequently declares, 'Tolkien is where' she 'started with fantasy' (Powell's Books n.d.). She also cites Tolkien's Eowyn – who completes one of the most archetypically heroic tasks when slaying the Witch King of Angmar in *The Return of the King* – as one of the first heroines she encountered. However, Pierce also expresses frustration over Eowyn's giving up 'being a sword slinger to become a wife, mother and healer', asking 'why couldn't she do it all' (Cox 2018)? As this chapter demonstrates, Tolkien may have been where Pierce 'started with fantasy', but he is not where she – or subsequent author's writing mythopoeic YA – remained.

As an effect of Tolkien's influence and the heroic romance's conceptual centre of opposition, many consider mythopoeic YA worlds to be 'Secondary

Worlds' (Tolkien 1947, 132). For example, Clute and Grant describe the Secondary World as the 'default [...] venue which underlies the surface appearance of all late-20th-century Fantasylands' (Clute and Grant 1997a), where fantasyland serves to encompass a variety of created worlds that remain literary. About the Secondary World, Tolkien writes:

> He makes a Secondary World which your mind can enter. Inside it, what he relates is 'true': it accords with the laws of that world. You, therefore, believe it while you are, as it were, inside. The moment disbelief arises, the spell is broken; the magic, or rather art, has failed. You are then out in the Primary World again, looking at the little abortive Secondary World from outside.
>
> (Tolkien 1947, 132)

Tolkien's description gives a sense of the immersive quality associated with Secondary Worlds and the reality created 'while you are, as it were, inside'. However, it also reinforces dominant hierarchies and binaries: created worlds are, in this argument, 'secondary' to God's original creation. Therefore, they are also lesser to it, and men, not women, may participate in the creative work of building a Secondary World. Mythopoeic YA shares this creative impulse – the power of 'he makes' – but it disrupts binary distinctions, including Primary/Secondary, man/woman and Western/not.

While the influence on fantasy for children and young adults generally applies to Tolkien and Lewis, Lewis is curiously absent from mythopoeic YA author's discussions of sources – where Tolkien dominates. In part, Tolkien's heightened influence relates to the unparalleled standard set by Middle Earth to which Lewis's Narnia, in its over-reliance on allegory at the derision of myth, does not compare. Tolkien addresses Lewis's issue with myth in his 1988 poem 'Mythopoeia' – incidentally from which I draw the term *mythopoeic*, the act of mythmaking – which he dedicated to Lewis as the 'one who said that myths were lies and therefore worthless, even though breathed through silver' (1988, 97). Moreover, Lewis's most notable contribution to children's literature and fantasy, The Chronicles of Narnia, not only lacks the Creative, world-building impetus informing Tolkien's fantasy and also mythopoeic YA, but the allegory – not just Christian but also 'death is better than life; boys are better than girls; light-coloured people are better than dark-coloured people; and so on', as Pullman so eloquently states – is also fundamentally opposed to mythopoeic YA's ethos of inclusivity (2001) (see, also, McSporran 2005; Mills 2011; Cecire 2019).

Given Tolkien's influence and as an effect of the 'conceptual centre' of binary opposition under which Western/not is included (Hourihan 1997, 15), mythopoeic YA's imaginary worlds are frequently pseudo-medieval and

European. They also frequently, but not always, emerge as 'high' or 'epic' fantasy (see, for example, Alexander 1971; Clute and Grant 1997). As an expression of the West's distant past and the time of heroes (Beowulf, Sir Gawain, King Arthur), the pseudo-medieval occupies the privileged position inscribed by the binaries at the heart of fantasy (an iteration of myth). Of the pseudo-medieval, there are many examples of mythopoeic YA: Kristin Cashore's Graceling Realm, Susan Dennard's Witchlands books and Tamora Piece's Tortall Universe, which I discuss through. Alison Croggon's The Books of Pellinor offer another excellent example. A high fantasy imaginary world with a highly developed religious system, deeply held beliefs and lore, Edil-Amarandh is home to Bards (have 'magical' abilities), Hulls (corrupt Bards), Elidhu (elemental creatures) and Maerad – the female-hero of this world. Set predominantly in Annar and the Seven Kingdoms, The Books of Pellinor follow Maerad as she is rescued from slavery, discovers she is a Bard and saves the world, following Campbell's basic patterning of separation-initiation-return. However, Maerad stands in stark contrast to the exceptional heroine dominating YA, even though she is, in many ways, exceptional.

Maerad is fated to save her world, but she relies on the support of those around her – she cannot fulfil the terms of the prophecy without her brother, and she would not have made it to the necessary time and place were it not for the help of many, many others. Maerad is also not entirely human. She has Eldihu heritage, which gives her the ability to 'be wolf' (Croggon 2005, 426). In this way, Maerad's version of being-hero includes the woman and animal within the heroic frame. Maerad's boundary-pushing example of being-hero is possible because of the unique articulation of Edil-Amarandh. In this 'high' or 'epic' fantasy world, Maerad would not be a cyborg, but she can 'be wolf' – once she learns how. Maerad's status as woman-bard-Elidhu depends on the shape of her world, and on that world giving the impression that this world, at least, could exist, despite how it diverges from our world (adolescent girls do not shape-shift into wolves).

Mythopoeic YA employs various tools to create a sense of depth and verisimilitude. In the case of Edil-Amarandh, this includes the claim that these books are translations of lost historical documents. For example, The Gift, the First Book of Pellinor, claims to be a translation of 'one of the key legends of the lost civilization of Edil-Amarandh', specifically the 'Naraudh Lar-Chanë (or Riddle of the Treesong)' (Croggon 2004, vii). Subsequent stories continue this translation work. The world-building worked so well that Croggon issued an 'Author's Note' on her website 'confessing' the world's fictional status ('The Books of Pellinor' 2008). The first four novels (publication order) also feature appendices, such as 'A Brief History of Edil-Amarandh' and 'Of Annar and the Seven Kingdoms', that aid in creating this imaginary world (Croggon 2004, 473–9 and 480–91). There are also fragments of lays and poems included before, and often within, many chapters. Two narratives also exist outside of the primary 'translation': *The Bone Queen*, telling Cadvan's story before the Riddle of the Treesong and 'The Island', a short story in which Maerad is pregnant with her first child. These novels, short stories and paratextual materials develop the world of Edil-Amarandh beyond the primary narrative, with literary maps, the visual representations of imaginary worlds, playing a pivotal role.

Each of the Books of Pellinor, as is common in mythopoeic YA, also includes a pretextual map. These graphic maps contribute to a world's authenticity in several ways, most notably appealing to the sense that the world is – because it is mapped – 'real' (Muehrcke and Muehrcke 1974, 318). These maps also often deepen that sense of 'real' by insisting, through notes or titles, that they are a product not of the author-creator but of the world itself. The maps of Edil-Amarandh, Tortall (Pierce) and Menos, the island world of Maria Turtschaninoff's Red Abbey Chronicles, employ this method of world-building. Turtschaninoff's Maresi, the first book of the Red Abbey Chronicles, demonstrates this method of world-building through two pretextual maps: the first depicts the layout of The Red Abbey, where most of the story occurs. The second is Menos, the island location of The Red Abbey. On the island map, there is a note indicating it was '[d]rawn by SISTER O in the second year of the reign of our thirty-second Mother. Based on the original by GARAI OF THE BLOOD in the reign of the first Mother' (2016, 9, formatting original). Both that Sister O drew this map and that it is not the first map of Menos contribute to a sense that this world existed before the glimpse into it we receive in Maresi. The note also suggests that the world has, at least, the potential to continue after we leave it, even if 'our island is very small and difficult to find' (14). Attributing the maps of a place to characters from within the text draws readers into the story's world as they contribute to the world's depth and indicate the potentially enormous size and scope of imaginary worlds.

In naming mythopoeic YA 'imaginary world speculative fiction', I recognize how the genre disrupts the structure of opposition at the heart of fantasy and myth, a disruption this chapter considers exploring. Importantly, 'imaginary' also reflects how these worlds are sites of, and for, imaginary activism. In *Digital Citizenship in Twenty-First-Century Young Adult Literature: Imaginary Activism*, Megan Musgrave uses 'imaginary activism' to describe 'a variety of activities that are depicted in fictional contexts and designed to instigate real-world discussion, engagement, and action' (2016, xi), a sentiment certainly applying to the female-heroes populating mythopoeic YA. However, it also applies to their worlds and to the genre's outlook or ethos of re-framing what it means to be a girl.

Mapping sensibility

Mythopoeic YA's defining feature is resistance to dominant discourse, and how in charting new territories, it offers new ways of being. Part of how mythopoeic YA undertakes the cultural work of reframing myths of adolescence, especially adolescent girlhood, is through demonstrating what I call a 'mapping sensibility', one integrally tied to mythopoeic YA's status as imaginary world fiction. In *The Dark Fantastic: Race and the Imagination from Harry Potter to the Hunger Games*, Ebony Elizabeth Thomas begins theorizing what she terms an 'imagination gap' (2019, 6), which is an inability to see, envision or imagine characters of colour as anything apart from 'the Dark Other', the antithesis of the hero (25). The imagination is powerful. If works of fiction cannot imagine girls as heroes, girls cannot be heroes – and as Thomas illustrates here, this alterity impacts Black girls even more. These girls cannot be heroes or, as I discussed in the previous chapter, the hero's prize because Cinderella's normative white femininity is impossible for them to achieve.

Mythopoeic YA intervenes in this 'imagination gap', by offering female-heroes who are not beholden to the body and its shape, size, colour or ability to function. Their intervention in the hero paradigm is about re-shaping the 'cartography of [our] imagination' (Thomas 2019, 17), changing its landscape, the images available within it. It is a structural change, and it involves a mapping sensibility. Quite broadly, the sensibility describes mythopoeic YA's creative impulsive and its proclivity to change as well as its tendency to push boundaries and blur border. The mapping sensibility directly relates to the literary maps (graphic presentations) participating in world-building, and it describes how mythopoeic YA disrupts the logic of cartographic theory and practice story and opens a space through which to conceive ambiguity and change. This fiction does so by engaging blank spaces, accounting for the disjunct between a map and that which it maps – particularly considering how mapped things change (while maps often do not or do so slowly) – and foregrounding the topography (hills, mountains, rivers) and the general unevenness the land.

First, cartography, the theory and practice of mapmaking, rests on the assumption that 'objects in the world to be mapped are real and objective', that they are 'independent' of the mapmaker and that they can be, through systematic observation, measurement and math, mapped (Harley 1989, 4). The motivation to map stems from an impulse to know and understand 'there' – that which is unknown (and possibly unknowable) – by converting it into the signs and symbols understandable to 'here' (Bachelard 2014, 228). By necessity, this process flattens and condenses the reality of 'there' as it structures and organizes it. Most commonly, maps depict places and imagine communities related to those places (Anderson 2006), but as I discuss elsewhere, the processes and practices of mapmaking also apply to bodies and to the imagined community of adolescence (Phillips 2018). Importantly, the results of cartographic processes and practices can be independently verified. As such, maps make truth claims – from the perspective of the mapmaker, and they are political and, like the hero story, no less violent (Ross 2009, 10). As Tarek Osman notes, maps refuse and erase 'distinctions on the ground' when they codify and legitimize social rule. Thus, while cartographic maps can be useful tools (2013),[5] they refuse ambiguity and change, erase difference and flatten materiality. Literary maps, on the other hand, open 'here' to the possibility of 'there' – even, possibly, working to make 'here' a little more like 'there'.

In mythopoeic YA, there is no physical, objectively verifiable 'there'. These worlds are primarily created by and through story. They are imagined. As I discussed above, literary maps, graphic illustrations, play a central role in world-building because they appeal to a world's existence – the place, it would seem, is 'there' to be mapped – as they participate in creating it (Muehrcke and Muehrcke 1974). The move from 'object exists in the world to be mapped' to 'object maps world into being' is paradigm-shifting. It disrupts the binary logic of mapmaking and opens a space through which to conceive ambiguity and change. For example, pretextual maps, maps coming after any publication information and usually immediately preceding the story, are one of the first 'windows through which the world is seen' (Wolf 2012, 7), and 'more than a boundary or a sealed border', according to Gérard Genette, pretextual maps are 'threshold[s]' offering readers 'the possibility of either stepping inside or turning back' (2010, 1–2). Anna Juan Cantavella suggests literary maps can 'locate the reader at a midway point between the real and the imaginary' (2017, 41). Literary maps, especially pretextual ones, are the threshold between 'here' and 'there', and mythopoeic YA capitalizes on that liminality to engage blank spaces, account for change and offer three-dimensionality.

First, Jonathan Crowe argues that literary, especially fantasy, maps rely on a convention of blank spaces, that is by their very nature literary maps include that which is unmapped within their frame. Admittedly, the role of blank spaces on maps is somewhat contentious: Mendlesohn (2008) and Ekman (2013) contend that because literary maps are about 'making known', about bringing into being that which does not exist within our world, blank spaces on literary maps foreclose the possibility of the unknown and serve to threaten the stability of the story world. Alice Broadway's Skin Books trilogy makes this logic clear – before showing how female-heroes undo it. In this instance of mythopoeic YA, bodies are transformed into maps: Staintstone comprises 'marked' citizens and 'blank' others. The blank's alterity within this world is profound: to be marked is to have your 'life story etched on your body'; to be blank is to be 'formless and void', to be exiled and damned (2017, 1). The blanks threaten the stability, structure and order of the marked world, until Leora – an adolescent and the child of a union between marked woman and blank man, though Leora does not know this until the novel's end – begins to 'wonder [...] if the blanks are really so terrible?' (27). From her doubly in-between positioning (adolescent and marked/blanked), Leora disturbs the borders and boundaries of her world.

In mythopoeic YA, however – and as Leora demonstrated – blank spaces 'encourage reader-map interaction' (Zähringer 2017, 10). Cantavella further argues that 'gaps are [...] for the reader to fill' (2017, 50), to place themselves into the story, to combine elements of story into new and exciting ways. Readers do fill these, as well as other, 'blank' spaces, as countless examples of fanfiction and fanart depict.[6] One notable example: Kae Marie, known on Instagram as 'dragonbookchic', has taken reader-map interaction to a heightened, and particularly embodied, level by having the maps of Pierce's Tortall and Circle Universes tattooed on her body.[7] In Pierce's corpus, these two worlds never interact; they are separate universes. This tattoo then fills in a blank space – it engages the unknown – by connecting these two worlds, even potentially creating a new imaginary world. Indeed, this tattoo-map changes not only the boundaries and proportions of the world – 'the Endless Ocean look[s] a bit like the Quite Large Inlet', as friend and colleague Aishwarya Subramanian pointed out (2018) – but also forges the connection between worlds on and through the reader's body, changing that body as the body changes the world. These kinds of moves are imperative to how mythopoeic YA reframes adolescent girlhood.

Engaging change and recognizing and making space for the disconnect between map and that which is mapped is the second aspect of mythopoeic YA's mapping sensibility. In Mastiff, the third book of Pierce's Beka Cooper trilogy, a conversation about maps offers the opportunity to question the 'truth' or accuracy of maps in the face of a changed landscape:

> Lady Sabine shook her head. 'Do we look like coneys to you? Cooper's map says the distance round this end of the marsh is forty miles back to the Rivers Road. It's a map by the Crown's own cartographers.'
> [...]
> Ormer said, 'A Crown what' s-it, you say. Mapmaking cove, he is? And he walked the ground himself in his pretty court slippers?'
>
> (Pierce 2011, 229)

There is an issue of authenticity – of the 'real' – at stake in this exchange: a map should represent the 'real' land. As this map was made by the 'Crown's own cartographer', there is a heightened expectation regarding its authority – at least according to Lady Sabine. As a lady Knight of the Realm of Tortall, Lady Sabine is charged with protecting and defending the land, but in over-relying on the sanctity and truth of maps, she has lost touch with the land, the physical, material place. When the map of a place, or I would argue of a body, becomes more real or true than the place itself, a radical break occurs, creating a situation in which the land (or bodies) is seen as lacking.

While this reading is bound up in issues regarding the 'real' and the naming of things (cartographer and mapmaking cove), I am, here, concerned with the text's preoccupation with illustrating the disjuncture between the map(s) of a place and the reality of it, as a further narration makes clear: "'When was it [Cooper's map] done?' Ormer asked […] 'We've had that much flooding these last three year. If your map be old, mayhap it's missing as much as thirty square mile of marsh, give or take'" (Pierce 2011, 230). Landscapes change, and while maps can also change, there is a gap between the physical, geographical land and its map (an image, a representation), and in these gaps, change occurs. By calling attention to the provisionality of maps, this exchange offers the possibility of not just questioning the narrow and limiting authority of hegemonic maps but also of creating new maps and new ways of mapping. Mythopoeic YA suggests maps do not have to be static or sacrosanct in their depicting of truth, in part because they embrace, in this case, the temporality of 'truth'.[8] I return to these issues in Chapter 4's discussion of the Lunar glamour and in Chapter 5's concern with the names of things.

The third feature of mythopoeic YA's mapping sensibility is how these maps also intervene in the flattening that occurs during mapmaking by modelling the importance of topography and how the curves, contours and general unevenness of the land and by extension worlds cannot be fully accounted for using flat maps. In Pierce's *Squire* (2001), book three of the Protector of the Small quartet (henceforth Protector), Raoul (Kel's knight master and commander of the army, known as the King's Own) uses a map to track bandits that have attacked, burned and robbed a small village. Through magic, the flat, two-dimensional map transforms to reproduce in miniature the 'actual' terrain of this fictive place.

> Using the key, he drew a circle around the dot labelled *Owlshollow*. It included the bandits' last known location. When he closed the circle, the map vanished. They were looking down at real terrain, forested hills, streams and rivers, marshes. Owlshollow appeared as a small town at

the junction of two roads and a river. It was situated on rocky bluffs, protected on two sides from raiders who came by water.

(Pierce 2001, 75, emphasis original)

The magic charm (the key) transforms that which is encircled, in this case, Owlshollow, into 'real terrain'. Not only does the narration make it clear that a shift has occurred – because the map vanished – but the removal of italics suggests a shift from 'the dot labelled' to the 'real' Owlshollow (not italicized). This magical map quite literally (re)creates Owlshollow and its surrounding terrain within the narration.

Finally, according to conventional logical, the map of a place can only ever appeal to the reality that it maps. Maps of imaginary worlds, however, create that which they claim – by being maps – to map. There is no 'real' Owlshollow, apart from the one(s) created by, and within, narration. Thus, this narration, crucially using the device of a map, participates in world-building, but it also offers a new kind of map (even if only through language, another representation), one that allows the topography of the land to be realised in three dimensions. As such, this map is also particularly key to this book's overall concern with refusing the superficiality associated with the selfhood offered by Cinderella (the ideal image of successful adolescent girlhood). The magically heightened topographical nature of this magical map contests the flatness of conventional, two-dimensional maps and, by extension, the flatness of the images by which the adolescent girl in popular and media culture constructs herself, a possibility that begins in 1983 with the publication of Tamora Pierce's *Alanna: The First Adventure*.

Tamora Pierce: Mythopoeic YA's founding mother

Tamora Pierce's role as mythopoeic YA's founding mother and her influence on several generations of, especially but not limited to, women cannot be understated – it is also not yet fully understood. Nevertheless, Pierce's Tortall Universe is one of the most well-developed and long-standing examples of mythopoeic YA. Existing in our world since 1983, Tortall officially comprises eighteen novels, with, at least, two forthcoming, a book of short stories and 'a spy's guide'. These stories offer portals into the world of Tortall.[9] Pierce's Circle Universe, a world with 'roots in the medieval Middle East and Central Asia', is also impressive (Pierce 2019b). However, quantity and duration are not the only reasons for Pierce's influence. Her commitment to open and honest discussions of topics ranging from hazing, puberty, sex, consent to animal rights alongside how she undertakes the complicated process of changing the way people think about sexuality, gender, class, race and ethnicity are a driving force behind her influence.

One way to understand Pierce's influence is through book endorsements, praise from popular or well-respected authors within your field. Book endorsements are an important part of publishing and book culture, and they play an amplified role in YA, especially YA speculative fiction (Wilkins 2019, 47–9). In the case of Pierce, they play two roles. They speak, as I discuss here, to her influence on the field of mythopoeic YA and, as I discuss below, linking texts published years apart. In fairness, both occur simultaneously (and to more authors than just Pierce), but I find it useful to separate them. Speaking to Pierce's influence, in a blurb endorsing her *Tortall: A Spy's Guide* (2017), Leigh Bardugo offers, 'Pierce didn't just blaze a trail. Her heroines cut a swath through the fantasy world with wit, strength, and savvy. Her stories still lead the vanguard today. Pierce is the real lioness, and we're all just running to keep pace' (2017). Bardugo's statement demonstrates Pierce's lasting influence ('still lead' and 'keep pace') on the field of YA fantasy while also speaking to her intervention within it ('blaze a trail' and 'cut a swath'). In the cultural milieu of the early 1980s, Tamora Pierce's fantasy 'for teenagers' was doing something different, especially in its interest in teenage girls. Pierce's commitment to what could be called a feminist project, one that is becoming – through the doors she opened and the work of others – increasingly intersectional in its scope, is the foundational root of mythopoeic YA.

Where Bardugo's comment speaks to Pierce's role within mythopoeic YA, Sarah J Maas pushes Pierce's influence further by including both the craft of writing and being a girl within a commendation for Pierce's *Tempests and Slaughter* (2018). In this blurb Maas claims, 'Tamora Pierce's books shaped me not only as a young writer but also as a young woman' (2018). While the quote is specific to Maas, the same applies to many, now adults, who read Pierce's books as young people. For example, columnist and activist Lindy West (Al-Sadi and West 2018), Guardian Books editor Alison Flood (2018) and I, alongside many of Pierce's fans, credit Pierce and her female-heroes as vital parts of their growing up. *The Queen's Readers: A Collection of Essays on the Worlds and Words of Tamora Pierce*, edited by Amanda Diehl and Holly Vaughn (2014), evidences this impact, as does the ever-increasing list of academic work focusing solely, or in part, on Pierce. On Facebook, groups such as 'Tamora Pierce's Unofficial Fan Community' demonstrate much the same while also showing how Pierce's fiction has saturated the lives of a generation (or two) of people. Of note, these groups and the essay collection do not just include women. Men, and people travelling under positions not represented by the gender binary, also play an active role in these spaces.

Indeed, from naming pets and children after characters from Pierce's worlds to hairstyles (Alanna's chin-length bob) and tattoos (of characters, quotes and maps), the saturation of Pierce's fiction and its impact on the lives of her readers is profound.

Pierce's 'trail', to use Bardugo's phrase, begins with Alanna: The First Adventure, the first book of the Song of the Lioness quartet (henceforth Song). Song is, ostensibly, the first point of entry into Tortall, though this is not guaranteed.[10] Featuring a cross-dressing female-hero who trades places with her twin brother (Thom) to gain access to the conventionally male space of knighthood (see Flanagan 2008), this portal into the world of Tortall complicates the hero paradigm by inserting a female into the role of hero to question the gender binary: '[g]irl, boy or dancing bear, you're the finest page – the finest squire-to-be-at Court' (Pierce 1983, 215). Despite her female sex, Alanna proves her abilities at tilting, fencing, archery and combat – the activities associated with training to become a knight (or the archetypal hero) in this world. Indeed, Alanna's abilities as Alan, her cross-dressed persona, exceed those of the boys at Court. In so being, she, as he, is a hero.

Initially, Alanna's narrative appears to be a straightforward replication of conventional hero stories, particularly in that she cross-dresses to join the male world of knighthood.[11] In so being, Alanna appears to offer little more intervention, which is to say none with any real depth, than do YA's 'exceptional heroines' (Wilkins 2019, 19). In fact, she seems to reaffirm Lissa Paul and Maria Nikolajeva's argument that female characters as heroes are nothing more than a 'simple gender permutation, creating a "hero in drag"' (Nikolajeva 2002, 44). As I have discussed, these heroines leave the heroic romance's plot – a linear transition from boy to man – in place by either remaining androgynous, which requires rejecting or abjecting body and gender, or by exiting the story and resuming their position as the hero's prize. Alanna's cross-dressing is, however, more complicated, and it becomes a 'transgressive and provocative act', with personal and political ramifications, as the following chapter discusses in more detail (Flanagan 2008, xv).

Crucially, Alanna's cross-dressing involves borrowing her twin brother Thom's appearance – his signification – before she takes on the subject position of Alan, her cross-dressed persona. As a twin and a child, Alanna enters the heroic romance, and she becomes Alan, a boy in his, or her, own right. However, becoming Alan is not enough for Alanna because she does identify as a girl, but it does make intervention possible. Borrowing her brother's signification and becoming Alan affords Alanna the opportunity to disrupt the story from within its frame. Specifically, when Alan(na) experiences puberty, including breast development and menarche, on the road to hero, the plot and trajectory of the heroic romance – the structure – changes.

Circularity, repetition and the capacity to 'generate new selves from within the embodied (fleshy) self' enter the heroic romance (Battersby 1998, 13). From within the story, Alanna disrupts and deconstructs the heroic romance, leaving an alternative, inclusive model in her wake, a model I describe as being-hero: a relational model of self that combines antithetical positions to offer an embodied subjectivity recognizing plurality and change, forming through connection and making space for kinship. For Alanna, this means engaging the masculine and feminine as well as the woman and warrior parts of herself, as the following chapter considers.

Alanna's disruption also opens doors for further such acts. For example, Pierce's Immortals quartet features Daine, a demigoddess with the ability to shape-shift because she is both human and 'of the People – the folk of claw and fur, wing and scale' (animals) (1992, 70). Daine's bond with the animals, despite her demigoddess status, offers an avenue for interrogating the hierarchal and dominating impetus of hero stories: as Chapter 5 explores, it is not until she listens to the thoughts and perceives the smells, sounds and feelings of her animal friends (as opposed to using her 'will' to direct them) that Daine learns to shape-shift, thus fully coming into her powers. Moreover, Kel, also known as 'the protector of the small', can try for her shield without disguising her sex and gender as Alanna did (Pierce 2002, 355). Daine and Kel – and the countless female-heroes emerging since Alanna's story – would not have been possible without that (or a) first intervention.

Through writing and publishing 'teenaged girl heroes', Pierce and Atheneum Books (now a part of Simon and Schuster) imbued mythopoeic YA with the subversive tendency still at work in contemporary iterations of the sub-genre (Pierce 2019a), as Pierce's continued presence demonstrates, both in the frequency with which contemporary YA authors, like Bardugo and Maas, cite her and also in how publishers situate new mythopoeic YA fantasy as working within the tradition begun by Pierce. For example, *Inkmistress* (2018) – the most recently published story set in Audrey Colthurst's Northern Kingdoms – features Asra, a demigoddess and bisexual female-hero with the ability to change the future through writing about it with her blood. Part of the publisher's marketing strategy for *Inkmistress* includes the 'X meets Y' formula that Kimberly Wilkins cites as integral to YA and, especially, YA fantasy (2019, 2). Here, the formula defines *Inkmistress* as 'perfect for fans of Tamora Pierce and Kristin Cashore', placing this new instance of mythopoeic YA text firmly in the tradition begun by Pierce and continued by, in this case, Cashore, one the YA authors citing Pierce as influential. As this chapter, and indeed the remainder of the book, demonstrates, the 'currency for conversation' forming around mythopoeic YA is different from the more unilateral transmission occurring in, for example, the Disney adaptations and proliferation of Cinderella (Geronimi, Jackson, and Luske 1950). It also laid the foundation for a genre of YA speculative fiction, pushing the boundaries of what it means to be YA.

Being-YA

As a field, YA is deeply concerned with supporting the child's transformation into an adult and most YA texts exist in service to dominant, patriarchal norms and standards. By enculturating readers into prevailing power structures, they help to maintain the status quo and perpetuate dominant ideologies (Trites 2000a; Pattee 2010). Unlike most YA, mythopoeic YA complicates and disrupts the system of opposition at the heart of hegemonic, patriarchal discourse by, centrally, featuring female-heroes, heroes who break boundaries and blur borders to offer a relational model of selfhood combining antithetical states to offer an embodied subjectivity recognizing plurality and change, forming through connection and kinship. The model does not invert the archetypal hero's rugged, toxic masculinity; it disrupts that model by occupying the liminal ground – the blank space between hero and monster. The being-hero model of selfhood offered by and through female-heroes is also present in the genre where it takes the shape of being-YA, a dynamic and ever-shifting occupation of the ground between (adult) literature/children's literature. As such, mythopoeic YA continually insists that its border and boundaries be re-evaluated, especially in terms of what it means to be YA.

First, what is YA typically believed to be? The answers are many and usually inaccurate and frequently dismissive. YA is commonly considered children's literature, a genre, reading level, age range, marketing category, woman's writing, contemporary realism, problem novels, issues fiction and 'blockbusters', especially *Twilight* (Meyer 2005). (In all the times I have posed 'what is YA?' to non-specialist audiences, *Twilight* is invariably a response, often the first.) Within the challenge of describing or defining YA, questions of merit also arise: Is it 'real' literature? If it is, what makes it meritorious? Too often, the answer to this question restricts YA to its usefulness in American high school classrooms (Robinson; Stephens). This is not to say that it isn't useful in those spaces but that to relegate YA to being nothing more than a bridge *From Hinton to Hamlet*, for example, is to limit its scope and potential (Herz and Gallo 2005). Indeed, while each of these depictions offers a unique set of problems – reinforces dominant binaries, degrades the literature, focuses on readers at the expense of the books, focuses on marketing categories at the expense of readers and refuses depth and complexity – they all perpetuate a cultural conversation that belittles YA and those who read it. How then can we define or describe YA without inflicting the radical alterity of binary oppositions?

I describe YA as a liminal field of literature, media and culture. It exists between that which is 'for' children and 'for' adults, although it is experienced and consumed by a far wider range of people. I also contend that it has a poetics, aesthetic and philosophy, that is both inherently tied to the audience it hails (the 'young' adult) but that is also more than or different from that relationship. YA is, in other words, more than just a marketing category, age range or reading level. As a literature, it is intimately related to both children's and (adult) literature, though the latter is less recognized. However, YA is also more than literature in the sense of books. Many instances of YA, mythopoeic YA included, push literature's boundaries of form and mode. Moreover, YA also includes films, television programmes, websites, social media texts (YA Booktok is just as much a part of YA as is the most literary of YA novels) and more. This plus the genres present within YA – romance, realism, science fiction and fantasy, contemporary, historical and literary fiction – are way I refer to YA as field.

Drawn from sociology, the concept of field is a useful mechanism for thinking about cultural products and practices.[12] Field describes a position-taking, a stance, a viewpoint or an outlook. Medicine is a field. Politics is another. These fields describe ways of relating to the world while allowing for a multitude of positions or stances within their frame. There are numerous specialities in medicine and politics each enveloping countless positions and smaller fields. Incidentally but with less-than-incidental consequences, the fields of medicine and politics also overlap, as the politicalizing of women's healthcare in the United States is demonstrating as I work on these revisions. Like these fields, YA is a position-taking. It offers a particular view and specific ways of understanding and interacting with the world at large (fields, upon fields, upon fields). Within this conceiving, relationality plays a key role. For example, field accounts for the similarities between contemporary YA and mythopoeic YA – two genres at opposing ends of a spectrum according to mainstream discourses (which see everything as oppositional) – while also making space for their divergences: both are YA, feature adolescents and consider the kinds of issues adolescents face, but the setting and handling of those issues differ. In effect, they offer different perspectives on what it means to be an adolescent (with implications for adulthood and childhood).

Briefly, I could use 'adolescent literature' to describe mythopoeic YA, as Trites and others have done to describe the literature existing between children's and (adult) literature. In that view, YA is a part of 'adolescent literature' or literature for adolescents. In some ways, the designation makes sense and is, even, appealing. For example, Trites identifies the 'possibilities of adolescent literature' in her introduction to the 1996 'Special Issue' of the *Children's Literature Association Quarterly* on 'Critical Theory and Adolescent Literature' (1996, 3).[13] Mythopoeic YA forms through possibility (not opposition). In this way, Patricia Head's description of adolescent literature as a 'border country' is equally attractive (1996, 32) as is Anna Lawrence-Pietroni's argument that 'adolescent fiction undercuts fixed categories' (1996, 34). Lawrence-Pietroni's further claim that, at least some, instances of adolescent literature 'destabilize expectations of character and genre as self-contained and complete' is especially appealing. However, adolescent literature does not, for me, offer the same ambiguous potential as does YA, even if YA is increasingly associated with a particular marketing category (linked to a demographic).

Adolescence is deeply tied to the psychological and biological developments occurring at puberty and other age-related categories (that are used to impose norms, expectations and order) (Lesko 1996; Waller 2009, 32; Phillips 2018). YA, on the other hand, has always been somewhat of a misnomer and an unstable signifier, as I discuss below. Here, adolescence carries a sense – owing to the associated biological 'truths' – and is or can be quantifiable, measurable, verifiable and determinable. Even if, in reality, adolescence is just as unstable a signifier as is YA: most commonly, an adolescent is someone between the ages of twelve (or thirteen) and eighteen (or twenty-five) (Hall 1904a; 1904b; Arnett Jeffrey 2014; Stetka 2017). However, adolescence might also refer to someone between the ages of ten and nineteen as the World Health Organization claims (n.d.), or, perhaps, it is a person between the ages of ten and twenty-four as four medical professionals mark it to be in an article about 'The Age of Adolescence' in *The Lancet Child and Adolescent Health* (Sawyer et al. 2018). Of course, if the adolescent isn't white, these numbers shift yet again and are even more contingent and political (Syed and Mitchell 2015). Nevertheless, adolescence carries a sense that adolescents are 'real' and knowable in ways that YA does not, and mythopoeic YA uses that instability, which might also be called liminality, to include a wide range of stories, worlds and female-heroes within its frame.

Liminality is central to my construction of YA just as it is to the female-hero and the model of relational selfhood they offer. Above, I mentioned that, as a body of story, YA relates to both children's literature and (adult) literature and that the latter is less recognized than the former in this characterization. YA relates to both because it exists between them because YA is the liminal field between the 'relatively fixed or stable' states literature and children's literature (Turner 1967, 93; see, also, Gennep 1910). In so being, YA displays characteristics of both sides of the oppositional pair it disrupts, even if YA's relationship to (adult) literature is less recognized. Binary oppositions require a radical break between opposing pairs (therefore YA as a distinct field both should not and cannot exist). Moreover, the system privileges one term or side in the oppositional pair over the other. In this case, YA is conflated with children's literature in an effort to maintain the illusion of opposition between adult/child and the adult's superiority (literature is 'better' without the quantifier children's). Each of these moves refuses the liminal's creative, albeit destructive to binary systems, potential. Existing outside of the mainstream (though this is changing) and as a hybrid fiction drawing on the world-creating and shaping powers of myth while also directly engaging YA's in-between status, mythopoeic YA complicates the structure of opposition at the core of its source material and by extension hegemonic discourse. In so doing, mythopoeic YA offers a conceptual centre of possibility through which it re-writes hegemonic, binary values, encouraging difference and change.

In mythopoeic YA, the possibilities of the liminal are engaged rather than foreclosed. Incidentally, this also speaks to why I use imaginary worlds and speculative fiction to describe mythopoeic YA and the worlds it builds rather than the more common secondary worlds. It also addresses how mythopoeic YA can include, as I discuss in the following section, science fiction and fantasy texts (as well as theoretically many other speculative fictions) under the umbrella of a term that usually denotes high or epic fantasy. Finally, liminal potential also disrupts the 'progressive' demands of literary series by forming networks of relation. Together these features offer a model of being-YA steeped in flexibility and responsiveness with the potential to collapse dominant and dominating binaries. Before turning to those two final features, I want to focus on what being-YA means in terms of age ranges and marketing categories using Tamora Pierce's fiction.

Mythopoeic YA began, as I have argued, in 1983 with the publication of Tamora Pierce's Song of the Lioness Quartet, but that quartet, alongside most of Pierce's corpus, is now considered by many, though not all, to be middle grades fiction (MG). Over the last thirty-five years, YA's borders and boundaries have shifted.[14] At mythopoeic YA's formation, YA more strongly engaged the early stages of adolescence, hailing a 10- to 14-year-old demographic through its themes and content.[15] For example, both Pierce's Alanna and Kel experience menarche, or their first periods, within their narrative arcs, as does Croggon's Maerad in The Books of Pellinor.[16] First periods are now too young for YA's frame, as current cultural preoccupations are not centred on what could be called the emerging adolescent but, rather, on the 'emerging adult', a phrase coined by Jeffrey Arnett (2006). As the transition from childhood to adulthood is increasingly becoming an attenuated process, especially for dominant cultural groups (i.e. white and middle-class), the YA market has shifted older, a shift to which mythopoeic YA, despite its marginal position within a marginal field, has not been immune.[17] However, it is also complicated, as a closer look at the trajectory of Pierce's fiction reveals.

While many consider Pierce's books MG, amusingly (and also poignantly), Pierce originally wrote Alanna's story as a '732-page' (adult) fantasy novel (Pierce 2019a), but in the early 1980s, fantasy was so dominated by (white) men that publishers weren't willing to take a risk on a fantasy series by a woman and about a teenage girl. Claire Smith, Pierce's to-be agent, suggested Pierce transform Alanna's story into YA, giving birth to mythopoeic YA and, crucially, aligning the story with YA-at-the-time. While the exact nature of the changes Pierce made are unclear (she claims to have destroyed the original version), a few have been recorded. First, in an article on 'Growing up Female' for the LA Review of books, Josephine Wolff recounts, 'the only fight Pierce recalls with her first editor, Jean Karl at Atheneum, was over a scene in *Lioness Rampant* (1988) in which Alanna drinks wine as medicine' (2017). Unlike the YA of today, alcohol was out. Interestingly, the shift from wine to tea will have occurred after Pierce's initial redrafting of Alanna's story. Prior to editing the manuscript, Pierce had been telling Alanna's story to the girls living in the group home where she worked. Pierce writes, 'our director felt that parts of that adult novel were inappropriate (it was a very strict home)', so she 'told the girls Alanna's story, edited for teenagers' (2019a). While I do not know what 'edited for teenagers' precisely means, Alanna sleeps with three different men across her quartet, and all three are integral to her being-hero, as I discuss in the following chapter. Here, it's probably safe to assume that sex was at least part of that editing (although it's still pretty fascinating – because Pierce was writing fantasy and not contemporary realism – what stayed in!).

For most of its history, Alanna's series has been YA (see, for example, Rosenberg 2011; Aasi 2012; Stacks 2013; Kelly 2015). It was only with the birth of middle grades fiction (MG) in the early 2010s that the quartet, owing to its concern with puberty and its 'chaste' handling of birth control and intercourse, became MG.[18] Having said that, Pierce won the Young Adult Library Services Association's (YALSA) Edwards Award in 2013. YALSA is a division of the American Library Association, and their award 'honors an author, as well as a specific body of his or her work, for significant and lasting contribution to young adult literature' (ALA 2012). The committee cited Pierce's Song as well as her Protector quartet in their rationale for giving Pierce the award. In other words, the borders and boundaries of

Pierce's Tortall have shifted in the years since its publication, and this change is integral to mythopoeic YA, as it contributes to the genre's conceptual centre, its way of seeing and understanding the world through possibility, not opposition.

Finally, in this book, YA serves a theoretical framework, even as it engages very real marketing categories increasingly niche-driven along age lines, from which to consider the range of fictions engaging the in-between. This framework, which I call being-YA, makes it possible to include, rather than exclude, different forms of mythopoeic YA and books that no longer or do not yet appear to be YA. Indeed, since 2010, YA has seen a steady 'ageing up' with many recently published YA novels, including mythopoeic YA ones, occupying a hazy ground between YA and adult fiction – or a yet to be fully substantiated additional market space.[19] In mythopoeic YA, one of the first most notable shifts occurred in 2012: Leigh Bardugo's Grishaverse began with the publication of *Shadow and Bone*, as did Sarah J Maas's (not unproblematic) Erilea with *Throne of Glass*. Kristin Cashore's Graceling Realm seemed to conclude with Bitterblue, a book offering a complex commentary on the nature of reality and epistemological truth (how we know what we know).[20] This world recently expanded with the publication of *Winterkeep* (2021), and it will grow still (2022). Also 2012 saw the publication of *Cinder*, the first of Marissa Meyer's Lunar Chronicles, an imaginary world in which Cinder(ella) is a cyborg, Lunars (citizens of the moon) are hostile next-door-neighbours secretly engaging in biological warfare against Earthens, and hovercars and spaceships are the most common modes of transportation.

Mythic forms in modern shapes

Given that mythopoeic YA draws on myth, particularly the quest myth or heroic romance, both of which are usually associated with 'high fantasy' (Alexander 1971; Sullivan 1992), it would be easy to assume that mythopoeic YA is YA fantasy. Indeed, my editors insisted on fantasy in the book's title and the examples I have discussed fall within that genre. However, mythopoeic YA is not about generic differences in the traditional sense, as being imaginary world fiction demonstrates. Instead, mythopoeic YA describes an ethos or outlook – a commitment to difference, a mapping sensibility – more than it delimits a specific generic label. As such, the form or shape of the fantastic is less critical to mythopoeic YA than how that fantastic intervenes in what it means to live and be an adolescent girl. In this way, Marissa Meyer's Lunar Chronicles is mythopoeic YA, despite its ties to science fiction.

To many, science fiction and fantasy are diametrically opposed; they are oppositional poles within the field of speculative fiction. Fantasy features motifs, modes of thought, and narrative patterns utilising the logic of myth, magic, and sometimes religious beliefs. It, as Michael Levy and Farah Mendlesohn argue in the 'Introduction' to *Children's Fantasy Literature*, 'is the realization of the impossible' (2016, 3). Science fiction, on the other hand, 'attempts to realise a possible' (2016), and it engages technology, innovation, and the promises of the future. While a full definition of both is outside the scope of this section, chapter, and book (and is considered to be both an impossible task as well as an unproductive one), the general differences are important, especially the privileging of science fiction within the binary pair science fiction/fantasy. More widely, contemporary realism is overwhelmingly seen as the more valued and valuable form of fiction, a distinction mapping onto high/low culture debates, literariness, and other value judgements disenfranchising a range of people and stories. Fantasy – as unreal, impossible, and, more damningly still, escapist – is othered because it is not realism and then, again, because it is not science fiction, and, at first glance, The Lunar Chronicles appears to be science fiction.

Set sometime after World War IV, *The Lunar Chronicles reimagines our world:* Cinder(ella) is a cyborg, and she lives in New Beijing, which is part of the Eastern Commonwealth, one of the six nations of Earth. The moon has been colonised and hovercars and spaceships are the most common modes of transportation. Each of these things – future orientation, intergalactic living, advanced science and technology – are markers of science fiction, and many do identify The Lunar Chronicles as science fiction (see, for example, Insenga 2018; Merrylees 2018). Yet, it has also been called a YA dystopia (Coste 2020; 2021; Gilbert-Hickey and Green-Barteet 2021), an instance of steampunk (Doughty 2015), and a 'Young Adult science fiction fairytale romance series' (Didicher 2020, 49). The variation is, I believe, a symptom of The Lunar Chronicles' liminal, hybrid status; its existence as mythopoeic YA. Thus, while this imaginary world may seem more closely aligned with science fiction, its concern with reframing what it means to be an adolescent girl and its blurring of the boundary between technology and magic and science fiction and fantasy make it mythopoeic YA.

The primary way The Lunar Chronicles intervenes in adolescent girlhood is by featuring a cybernetic Cinderella. As I discussed in the previous chapter, Cinderella is the hero's prize or the model of successful adolescent girlhood, according to dominant, patriarchal discourse. As the prize, Cinderella serves as a mirror by which the hero secures his rugged, toxic masculinity. She reflects – to the hero – that which he is not (sparkly, fantasy femininity). Through this image, he is able to anticipate or imagine himself as a whole, rational, autonomous being.[21] By portraying the mirror as a cyborg, a human-machine hybrid whose body is fragmented and scared, The Lunar Chronicles disrupts the dominant model of what it means to be a girl, as I explore in the following chapter. Here, it also begins to show how The Lunar Chronicles is not simply science fiction. For one, Meyer's Lunar Chronicles may well feature advanced technology that is only not yet possible within our world, but Cinderella's existence as a cyborg is a realisation of the impossible, according to the heroic romance (which radically excludes the machine because it isn't human and, ideally wants girls to be prizes).Importantly, Cinder is not the only female-hero in this world; she is part of a systematic, collective interrogation of the archetypal hero story (or patriarchy), particularly the specular economy underpinning it. Briefly, this economy describes how man (the hero) projects his view of the world onto it so that it he can see himself in it, so that his 'self' as whole, rational, autonomous and not bothered by embodiment is available to him. It also describes 'how we present ourselves and how others perceive us' and is increasingly tied to the images of ourselves we share with others (Marshall 2010, 488–99). Effectively, it is the misguided but ever present belief that 'you are who you appear to be', and it traps girls and women (especially but not only) in their appearance. The system uses Cinderella's flat, shiny, sparkly appearance to regulate disruption. Cinder's intervention is important, but it is strengthened by the women around her. Scarlett (Little Red Riding Hood) not only rescues her grandmother with help from Wolf – a genetically modified human-wolf hybrid – but is also curvy, depicting a female-hero whose body is not the ideal thin of hegemonic expectations. Cress (Rapunzel) is five feet tall and is the world's most renowned hacker, demonstrating a female-hero who is shorter than 'average' but also one who excels in a field traditionally dominated by men. Winter (Snow White) is Black and has 'three scars on her right cheek' (Meyer 2014). Throughout the quartet, Winter refuses to use her 'magical' ability, as I discuss below. Here, the choice profoundly affects her physical and mental health, thus including disability with the heroic frame. Cinder and the other girls expand what it means to be a hero by pushing the boundaries of their folktale counterparts and foregrounding the body. However, there is one more female-hero in this world, and she pushes the boundaries of what it means to be human even further.

Iko, Cinder's friend and android side-kick, is also a female-hero owing to the sustained way in which she disrupts what it means to be a girl/who gets to be a girl. Iko is a machine, and in *Cinder* (the first published novel set within this world), she appears as a one: Iko has a 'bulbous head', wheels and 'pronged hand[s]', an appearance not only signalling her non-human status but one that is also radically unlike the ideal Cinderella demonstrates

(Meyer 2012, 193 and 11). However, Iko is consistently coded as female and feminine, even when appearing the least like a girl (whatever that looks like), and she is not limited to this one body. In subsequent books, Iko briefly inhabits *The Rampion* (a spaceship) before existing within, and as, Darla, an escort droid. These moves are made possible because androids have 'personality chips'. These chips are, effectively, the android's mind, self or soul. It would be easy to assume this chip reaffirms the mind/body split at the heart of the heroic romance and that Iko's movement towards Darla's escort-droid body with its 'perfect symmetry and ridiculously lush eyebrows' reaffirms appearance expectations associated with girlhood (Meyer 2014, 355). However, as I show in the following chapter, Iko's movements across bodies and her coding as female and feminine, even when she appears the least so and despite never having the requisite biological anatomy, offer a powerful deconstruction of heroic norms and standards.

Iko's transformations are possible because of the advanced technology available in this world, and such technology usually serves to mark science fiction. It is also opposed to the magic of fantasy, along the lines of real/not-real (Reynolds 2007, 163; Waller 2009, 146). However, Laurence Yep argues that the shift from fantasy to science fiction merely requires 'a series of transformations: the magical steed into a rocket ship, the knight's armor into a white lab coat, the enchanted sword into a slide rule' (1978, para. 10). I suggest, therefore, that the science fiction elements of Meyer's world – hovercrafts and spaceships, cyborgs and androids, as well as futuristic medical technology – are differences of degree not of kind, a point that Campbell (1991) also makes regarding *Star Wars* (1977–). For Campbell, Star Wars is myth(ic) because it is concerned with the questions of myth: what does it mean to live and be in this world? How did we get here, and where do we go when we're gone? The same questions mythopoeic YA asks but for girls, that is keeping the discursive group in mind. As such, texts like Star Wars – and Meyer's Lunar Chronicles – are merely mythic forms in modern shapes.

Technology is not the only form of 'magic' in this world. Most Lunars can manipulate 'bioelectricity', which gives them the ability to make others 'see what the Lunar wishes them to see, and even feel what the Lunar wishes them to feel' (2012, 172). As 'bioelectricity' suggests, this ability is a blurring of the distinction between 'science' and 'magic', one the text continually navigates. For example, 'Well [...] the Lunar gift is nothing more than the ability to manipulate bioelectric energy – the energy that is naturally created by all living things. [...] it is the same energy that sharks use to detect their prey' (176). This 'gift' is both a natural talent or ability but it also manipulates nature. In this passage, Dr Erland is attempting to demystify the Lunar ability, arguing, to Cinder, that it is 'not magic' and that 'claiming it to be magic only empowers them' (2012, 176). However, to Cinder and others, the Lunar Gift does appear to be magic. Poignantly, Pierce's Tortall Universe identifies to the 'all purpose' magical ability as 'The Gift' (Pierce 2003, 48), as I discuss in Chapter 5. Here, The Lunar Chronicles text takes something scientific – some research suggests that animals both produce bioelectricity and use it to communicate (see, also, Quantumbiologist 2010) – and makes it magical.

With this gift, Lunars are able to construct a 'glamour [...] what they call the illusion of themselves that they project into the minds of others' (Meyer 2012, 172), and it is about power and controlling that image through which selves are known. It illustrates the disjunct between appearances and reality, or the fleshy material of the body. For example, Queen Levana (a wicked stepmother) uses her glamour to disguise a 'disfigured' appearance because in her world, the world of the Lunar, beauty is power (Meyer 2015a, 692), and the ideal appearance is even more spectacular than Cinderella's: 'She [Levana] was indeed beautiful, as if someone had taken the scientific measurements of perfection and used them to mold a single ideal specimen' (2012, 183). The important part: Levana, like most Lunars, can manipulate this appearance to continually suit changing norms and expectations offering the illusion of perfection, only to dismantle it, as I discuss in Chapter 4.

Finally, the form of magic occurring in a Secondary World speaks to the shape of the world: places mean, as I mentioned above. The Lunar ability, depicted as scientific and genetic, could not logically occur in Pierce's pseudo-medieval universe, just as spells, sorcery and wild magic (that is specifically linked to nature) could not logically occur in Meyer's futuristic re-envisioning of the world. However and as is a theme with mythopoeic YA, the boundary between this division is complicated. Not only does The Lunar Chronicles engage the tension between science and magic through a science that works like magic but Daine's 'wild magic' in Pierce's Tortall Universe is another 'genetic trait' (Meyer 2013, 52) – passed to Daine from her father, Weiryn God of the Hunt (Pierce 1992). Both 'magics' also operate outside of language (i.e. not through spells) and are strengthened through the strengthening of one's mind. These two iterations of magic, or perhaps the fantastic, do not logically occur in our world but they do in theirs, setting the tone of the fantastic bodies and selves available within that space as well as contributing to the space itself.

Networks of relation

Mythopoeic YA status as imaginary world fiction also provides a way to conceive the relationship between distinct texts. In literary terms, mythopoeic YA is considered 'series fiction'. In this view, the various quartets and duologies forming Pierce's Tortall universe are series fiction, but they also potentially contribute to a larger Tortall 'series' (see Appendix 1). Three of these groups are quartets, one is duology, and two are trilogies. Within this terminology, they are all also 'progressive' as each tells a 'continuous and developing story' over time (Watson 2004, 532). However, the networks of relation formed by mythopoeic YA texts extend beyond the individual series – a series is but one portal into a world (Ryan 2003, 91) – and mythopoeic YA's series develop in multidirectional ways across time: sometimes moving the world's timeline forward and, at others, returning to previous points within the world's history to 'fill in' a gap left (or created by) a previous window. Thus, rather than linear publication order, mythopoeic YA's imaginary worlds are bound by a mythic mindset manifesting as a mapping sensibility, which is a concern with re-shaping the narrow and limiting expectations of adolescent girlhood in contemporary Western culture.

The texts comprising Pierce's Tortall Universe, in particular, do something more than this categorisation 'progressive series' entails: they each exist independently but also interdependently. The category of progressive series cannot, in its focus on a single developmental line, take this multiplicity into account, just as the singular, linear developmental trajectory of adolescent theory cannot take female adolescence into account, as I argue elsewhere (Phillips 2018). To illustrate: Pierce's Tortall universe currently exists as three quartets, a duology, trilogy and seven short stories. Each text exists independently but also interdependently, first within its quartet and more widely within the Tortall universe. Imperatively, this interdependency is not at the expense of individuality; instead, the linked nature of these texts allows individuality to flourish by deepening the specific through its engagement with the many. In other words, twelve distinct storylines construct the universe; yet, each storyline and each quartet (duology and trilogy) also participates in the construction of the universe, each contributes to the whole, while the arcs are wholes themselves. In this way, the Tortall universe acts as an additional series, or – and I believe more importantly – seventeen novels create and develop a single imaginary world. In other words, the uneasiness of definition that I read concerning YA is echoed here in resistance to categorisation.

These stories provide portals into Tortall, spanning 234 years, through the adventures of Alanna, Daine, Kel, Aly, Beka and Numair (Arram). They also extend and expand our view of the Tortall Universe through both time and space. Developing the world's history by filling in a gap left by a previous story, the events of *Tempests and Slaughter* (2018) take place concurrently to most of The Song of the Lioness quartet (1983–8), while Beka's story, published between 2006 and 2011, takes place a century beforehand.[22, 23] *Tempests* also, in its focus on Numair's (Arram's) first years at the University of

Carthak geographically expands the Tortall universe: previous stories focused primarily on the Tortallan continent, while also including a male-hero within mythopoeic YA's frame. The collection of short stories and the Spy's Guide do much the same – while the latter, in its presenting of 'artefacts' from the world, gives the impression that these portals were collated and created, not by Tamora Pierce, but by characters from Tortall.

Pierce's Tortall Universe is especially preoccupied with establishing its collective existence. For example, the aforementioned Beka Cooper Trilogy – published two decades after The Song of the Lioness quartet's first foray into this world but set two hundred years before it, according to the world's timeline – comprise 'A Tortall Legend', or so the front cover declares. Moreover, the paratextual 'blurb' to Tempests and Slaughter – the newest portal into Tortall – positions it, the first of the Numair Chronicles, as where 'THE LEGEND BEGINS' (Pierce 2018, formatting original). This particular legend concerns how Arram becomes Numair and 'the most powerful sorcerer in Tortall' (1992, 68). Legends are often called the 'folk history' of a people and are part of the mythic milieu (Brunvand 1998, 196), while chronicle appeals to a 'record', a chronicle, as it were, of events that 'really' happened. Isobelle Carmody's The Obernewtyn Chronicles, Marissa Meyer's Lunar Chronicles, and Melina Marchetta's Lumatere Chronicles also employ this method of world-building. In both cases (legend and chronicle), though more strongly with legend, the histories offered by these mythopoeic YA stories are not the 'legitimate' history of textbooks; that is, they are not mainstream discourse. They are the people's history told through the stories they share.

In its focus on a single, linear developmental line, 'progressive series' cannot take this multiplicity and multi-directionality into account (Hassler-Forest 2017), just as the teleological and linear trajectory of adolescent development is problematic for many adolescents. For this reason, I argue that portals into mythopoeic YA's imaginary worlds – in whatever form – constitute intertextual fields. Wolf would call much of what I consider mythopoeic YA's intertextual field the 'narrative fabric' of a world (Wolf 2012, Loc 4617). The weaving together of all the various narrative threads (a character's storyline, for example) and braids (when storylines overlap) constituting and providing access to a world. While Wolf is quite liberal in his view of narrative, suggesting for example that 'even maps can imply' such (Loc 4625), the insistence on story refuses the material, a problem I discuss throughout this book. Here, framing imaginary worlds strictly in terms of narrative (or story) only re-figures their otherness, setting up an opposition between our 'real' world and the fictional world, refusing 'the wider body of relations influencing the creation and consumption of storyworlds', as

Colin Harvey points out (2015, 46). I draw on Harvey because he argues that these relations should also be considered as 'emplaced and embodied' (46), linking imaginary worlds more firmly to our 'real' world and the 'imaginary activism' (Musgrave 2016) – changing perceptions of adolescent girlhood – they can inspire.

While imaginary worlds are created by and through narration, they also have a very real physical, material existence within our world. Not only owing to the objects – like clothing, jewellery and food – participating in their construction but also through how readers embody elements of the world. For example, cosplaying (dressing as) specific characters. For these reasons, I believe mythopoeic YA's imaginary worlds constitute intertextual fields. Jenkins defines intertextuality as 'the relations between texts that occur when one work refers to or borrows characters, phrases, situations, or ideas from another' (2006, 287). Numair's appearance in multiple 'series' demonstrates this intertextuality, while field describes a position-taking, a stance to account for how these worlds work within contemporary culture. Tamora Pierce's influence on the sub-genre and the 'network of relation' formed by contemporary authors citing, especially, her older work in The Song of the Lioness, Immortals and Protector of the Small quartets is one such way this fantasy works within contemporary culture.

* * *

Mythopoeic YA is an interventionist fiction, cultural work depending on mythopoeic YA's 'being-YA', a figuration I use to illustrate how this fiction occupies and engages the middle ground to reframe adolescent girlhood. Simply being a work of YA does not guarantee intervention, nor does being a speculative fiction or fantasy text. There are plenty of YA texts in service to the narrow and limiting norms of hegemonic discourse because, rather than engaging the middle ground, they perpetuate the logic of opposition and exclusion upon which hegemonic discourse depends. The way in which mythopoeic YA engages liminality gives rise to a conceptual centre of possibility, not opposition. Through its centre of possibility, mythopoeic YA re-writes hegemonic, binary values, encouraging difference and change. Indeed, mythopoeic YA tells new stories, featuring unorthodox heroes (e.g. not the archetypal white, able-bodied, attractive male) set in unconventional imaginary worlds (e.g. not the prototypical Western, pseudo-medieval world), while also now taking full advantage of digital opportunities available in the twenty-first century. Mythopoeic YA offers unparalleled avenues for increasing diversity and inclusivity through not only the stories and characters set within its imaginary worlds but also through the boundary-pushing ways in which it affords access to those worlds, access and intervention that has shifted over the years since mythopoeic YA formed. Specifically, this Chapter has explored how mythopoeic YA has moved from Alanna's 'doing as I did [becoming a knight …]' to more complex engagements of race, gender and sexuality, and (dis)ability that offer readers – adolescent and more broadly – alternatives to hegemonic norms and standards (Pierce 2003, 18).

Beginning as a white feminist project, mythopoeic YA's growing intersectionality speaks to the needs of contemporary society. Indeed, while it began as a sub-genre tied to the pseudo-medieval and featuring female heroes quite literally interested into the heroic narrative by cross-dressing (Pierce's Alanna) or taking on a masculine persona (McKinley's Harry), mythopoeic YA is now much broader in scope and outlook. Moreover, mythopoeic YA's intervention into dominant paradigms is increasingly complex as Leigh Bardugo's Grishaverse demonstrates, but, also, Pierce's Tortall, as Chapter 5 considers. In short, mythopoeic YA, as Pierce says of fantasy and science fiction, is 'a literature of possibilities' (Pierce 50), but what are the next possibilities? In 'Theory Rises, Maginot Line Endures', Caroline Hunt suggests the future of YA is 'largely digital', declaring that we, as critics, avoid considering e-texts and 'alternative' methods of reading at not just our peril but also to the detriment of readers, especially those who do not align with the imagined 'uniformly affluent "normal" teen reader' (2017, 211). While YA fantasy does not typically address issues of literacy – Tracie Chee's extraordinary Sea of Ink and Gold (*The Reader*) is an exception – mythopoeic YA's transmedia imaginary worlds offer significant opportunities for taking up Hunt's call. Indeed, 'by expanding the range of narrative possibility rather than pursuing a single path with a beginning, middle, and end', mythopoeic YA offers 'new story structures' (Jenkins 2006, 119) thus countering the narrative of white, male, able-bodied superiority dominating mainstream, hegemonic discourse alongside how we approach knowledge and information and also the communicating of both to all manner of people.

Finally, while mythopoeic YA offers a counter or subcultural space to popular and media culture, the relationship between the two is not binary. Rather, the two discourses – hegemonic fantasies of being a girl and fantastical narrations of being a girl – are interwoven and overlapping. In short, where contemporary Western culture offers illusions of choice, impossible ideals and silences, mythopoeic YA – because it is speculative – offers bodies that express multiplicity and difference, thereby offering frameworks for living and being a body that challenges the dominant, hegemonic fantasy of adolescence. This reconfiguring of the body is essential. Because the body is that by which she is excluded, the body must be mapped differently for inclusion – of difference, change and multiplicity – to occur. Thus, the remainder of this book (re)maps these frameworks, speaking from the silenced position within, and between, the binary oppositions (mainstream YA/mythopoeic YA, male/female, mind/body, human/animal, human/machine, abled/disabled) underpinning the dominant discursive construction. I do so by drawing on the work of material feminists such as Susan Hekman and Stacy Alaimo and a tradition of feminist ethicists such as Nel Noddings, Virginia Held, Diana Tietjens Meyers and Mary Jeanette Moran, and ask: what happens to the self and its relationship with other selves when it is conceived of as both embodied and relational?

3

Disrupting the myth: Alanna becomes a warrior-maiden

Alanna's hero's journey begins when the Lord Alan of Trebond (her father) declares that his two children, Alanna and her twin brother Thom, are to 'leave for the convent, and [...]the palace' to begin preparing for their adult roles in life (Pierce 1983, 1). At the palace, Thom will train to be a Knight of the Realm of Tortall. At the convent, Alanna will learn to be a 'lady', which denotes a rank and gender position in this world. In other words, Thom and Alanna are to leave their parental home to become the hero and his prize. However, Alanna has other plans: 'Tomorrow he gives us the letters for the man who trains the pages and the people at the convent. You can imitate his writing, so you can do new letters, saying we're twin boys. You go to the convent [...]. And I'll go to the palace and learn to be a knight!' (2). For Thom, the plan is quite simple: he will pretend to be Alanna until they have left the family grounds. As 'younger sons [...] could go first to the convent, then to the priests' cloisters, where they studied religion or sorcery', his deception is minimal (7). Alanna, however, will remain disguised or cross-dressed for years. During this time, she does not just pretend to be Thom. Instead, she becomes Alan, a boy training to become a Knight, before finally becoming a warrior-maiden, a gendered identity between the poles of opposition. In so doing, she threatens the whole system.

Undoing the 'horror of the blood' sits at the core of this disruption (Irigaray 1974, 228). Menstruation, particularly its procreative potential, is at the centre of women's othering within the heroic romance; it makes her '*more* biological, *more* corporeal, and *more* natural than men' (Grosz 1994, 154, emphasis original), a move that also links women with the Lacanian Real. Naively, this Real can be associated with the 'real' properties of a thing: the flesh, blood and bone of a body, for example. It is that which language necessarily mediates and is thus outside of or prior to discourse/language. Woman's conflation with the body (that is perceived as Real) prevents her from entering the Symbolic – the heroic romance or discourse – because this phallogocentric system lacks an Imaginary (model) capable of accounting for, or taking into, account the fleshy material body and its potential multiplicity; indeed, it repudiates both (Irigaray 1974; Cixous 1976; Kristeva 1982). Importantly, I do not aim to set up an alternative female Imaginary; instead, following Luce Irigaray, I am to speak from the silent spaces, the gaps within patriarchal discourses. Moreover, my concern with menstruation and reproduction is not to exclude girls and women for whom neither is – either by choice or biology – possible. Rather, I speak the unspeakable because the story refuses to do so, because it radically excludes the blood, and because until that refusal, until the horror, is neutralized, the story will leverage it against everyone.

To undo the horror of the blood, we must employ a sort of 'shameless speech', speaking about the body that includes the body, about the blood. Shameless speech is a two-part process, and it is encapsulated by Marta Weigle's 'birthing speech' (1989, 163–9). For Weigle, birthing speech, or the speech that happens during birth, 'is substantive – verbally and bodily – involving mouth and vagina, words and blood' (167). This speech is of the body, and it includes the body's speaking, an articulation outside language according to patriarchal systems. This speaking brings new bodies into being. In this sense, and this is the second part of the process, it is also about giving birth to speech, meaning and signification – in a way that does not radically exclude the body because, instead of being abject, it is a part of the self and of the sign-system producing that self. It is a speech that creates a space for identity to form through plurality, connection, kinship and ethical responsibility. Briefly, I return to the capacity to become more than one through the processes of reproduction throughout. My concern with menstruation and procreation is not to exclude those for whom this potential is not – by choice or biology – possible. Instead, I do so because the ability to 'generate new selves from within the embodied self' is at the centre of woman's exclusion from the hero paradigm (Battersby 1998, 18). As such, including this potential – because it requires a self that is formed and forming through relation instead of opposition – within what it means to be a self radically destabilizes isolating individuality and radical alterity.

Admittedly, Alanna has been criticized for appearing to reconfirm isolating individuality and for participating in the 'exceptionalism' dominating contemporary and YA fantasy (Wilkins 2019, 19). In 'Decolonizing Childhood: Coming of Age in Tamora Pierce's Fantastic Empire', Sarah Sahn argues, 'while Alanna breaks down the barriers that would keep her from her vocation as a knight, she does so for herself, not for anyone else' (2016, 147), and while this is ostensibly true, in the sense that Alanna does not set out to change the system for others, her 'provocative act' has more than personal ramifications (Flanagan 2008, xv). Subsequently, girls are allowed to try for knighthood without hiding their sex or gender, and Alanna becomes the

King's Champion, a political appointment usually held by men (because only men can become knights). She also makes her daughter possible, both in the sense of giving birth to her and making a space in which, as I discussed in Chapter 2, Aly 'could do something else, if [she] wanted to' (Pierce 2003, 18). Thus, and agreeing with Alexandra Garner, I believe Alanna ultimately works to make 'knighthood more inclusive while simultaneously destabilizing its authority as a patriarchal institution' (Garner 2020, 370). However, while Garner restricts that work to the final two books of Alanna's quartet, *The Woman Who Rides Like a Man* (1986) and *Lioness Rampant* (1988), I believe it starts sooner – as soon as Alanna decides to trade places with her brother. More importantly, it also stems from her story's conceptual centre of possibility – that is, the story's way of seeing and understanding the world through connections, repetitions and kinship.

Finally, this chapter argues that while Alanna may appear to offer a girl hero shoved into the role of a hero, her story, her way of 'being-hero', actually radically expands the possibilities of what it means to be a woman – 'who rides like a man'. It does by deconstructing the problems women face in a man's world, by showing how the fleshy material body must be refused or silenced. I argue that Alanna's cross-dressing to become a Knight of the Realm of Tortall in Tamora Pierce's Song of the Lioness quartet offers a lens to explore the effects of the heroic romance on girls and what happens to that story when the gender binary breaks down. As such, Alanna's being-hero is more complicated than a straight portrayal of 'tomboyishness', 'female masculinity' (Halberstam 1998; Wulandari 2019), or cross-dressing. Her trading places with her brother is also not 'a simple gender permutation, creating a "hero in drag"', which Maria Nikolajeva says is the result of centring female characters in 'mythical or romantic narratives' (2002, 44). Alanna is also not one of YA's 'exceptional heroines', though she is extraordinary – particularly in her drive and determination to forge her own path (Wilkins 2019, 19). Instead, owing to the complex ways it destabilizes gender and sexuality as naturally cis and heterosexual, Alanna's cross-dressing 'ruptures […] straightjacketed heterosexuality' (Saxena 2012, 39). It disrupts the point and purpose of the heroic romance to reveal the queer, ambiguous possibilities of adolescence and adolescent identity (Stockton 2009; Matos 2020; Owen 2020).

Alanna is a twin (and a child)

Alanna and Thom can trade places – Alanna can slip into the heroic romance – owing to their status as twins, children and the complex and sometimes conflicting ways the text codes Alanna as masculine and Thom as not. Indeed, and as is common in twin narratives, especially twin narratives for children, Alanna and Thom appear to comprise a single self that has been split across two bodies. In this sense, Alanna is Thom's 'counterpart' or 'double', as Caroline Hunt (1986) and Robyn McCallum (1999) respectively term such figures (see, also, Waller 2009). As McCallum notes, 'a primary effect of the double is to destabilize notions of the subject as unified, or coherent, or as existing outside of a relation to an other' (1999, 75). The heroic romance's goal (which is identical to mainstream YA's) is to produce a unique, rational, autonomous, self-sufficient individual who is not troubled by embodiment; the double must be resolved. Thom's death, at the end of Alanna's quartet, would appear to offer this closure, especially as she is coming into the fullest sense of herself at the time of his death. However, as I discuss in the book's Conclusion, Thom's death does not offer a resolution, and, more importantly, Alanna uses her counterpart status to destabilize the linear, teleological trajectory of the heroic romance and the unified, coherent and individual (heterosexual) identity it exists to produce. Here, I want to explore how Alanna functions, before trading places with Thom, as his *'living mirror'*, a heightened version of the hero's prize's role (Irigaray [1974] 1985, 221, emphasis original).

The heroic romance offers a model of selfhood that requires the hero to find wholeness or completeness by overcoming that which he is not, and as I've shown, the most fundamental 'that-which-he-is-not' is his body. In some cases, the hero's overcoming means radical exclusion: the hero kills the monster. In others, he uses 'that-which-he-is-not' to complete himself through a process of containment. The hero cannot have the body within himself or even his sense of self, and so within the story, women serve as that body. This is not to say women are 'his' body but, rather, body, fleshy, material, prone to change and capable of producing new bodies/selves. The heroic romance contains this threat – and uses it to complete the hero – by containing it within a heterosexual union, effectively perpetuating patriarchy through the slaying of monsters and marriage. When entering into this story as the hero's prize (as Cinderella does after her sparklemation), women also become a mirror or that which allows the hero to see himself more clearly. Specifically, the hero's prize – the picture of sparkly hyper fantasy femininity – allows the hero to see himself as an individual who is whole, rational, autonomous and not affected by embodiment and secure in his masculinity.

In the case of Alanna and Thom, Alanna serves as Thom's living mirror. The twins are identical: 'the only difference between them – as far as most people could tell – was the length of their hair. In face and body shape, dressed alike, they would have looked alike' (Pierce 1983, 1). In the present of narration, she is his mirror image. Their bodies are the same; the things (clothing and the length of their hair) that differentiate them are superficial and can be changed. In fact, once Alanna's hair is cut and she changes into a 'shirt, breeches, and boots', she 'look[s] enough like Thom to fool anyone but Coram' (one of the children's caretakers), who presumably knows her too well (8–9). In the 'normal' course of things, Alanna would allow Thom entrance into the Symbolic, which is the point and purpose of the heroic romance. Alanna's supporting role positions Thom as the would-be hero, the person to whom signification is available, and it is always Alanna's similarity to Thom, never Thom's to Alanna. Without Thom, Alanna would not be able to enter into the heroic romance as she does. She would not be able to become Alan and certainly not a female-hero. However, Alanna and Thom will not always be children.

The foundation of similarity that initially makes Alanna's cross-dressing possible also depends upon Alanna and Thom being children. At some point on this journey, Alanna will become 'a girl – you know, with a chest and everything', as her brother points out (2). While this claim taps into essentialist notions of what it means to be a sexed and gendered self, I would argue that it also speaks to a common assumption about what it means to be a girl: that until puberty and the development of secondary sexual characteristics (breast growth, rounder hips, no facial hair) the little girl is, as Freud declares, 'only a little man' (Freud [1933] 1973, 151). This is not to say that little girls do not exist; that would be an impossibility along the lines of Jacqueline Roses's impossible child (1994). No, this is about how – according to dominant patriarchal structures – little girls do not exist because there is nothing to see; until the body visibly differentiates itself from the default male norm, little girls *could be* little boys because there is nothing to mark them as different.[1] Here, Alanna doubtlessly is a girl – her cross-dressing depends on it: if she were not, this endeavour would just be wearing Thom's clothes. However, she is also not yet recognized or recognizable as a girl, a reading I develop in the following chapter through Iko, an android who identifies as and is coded as a girl. Unlike Alanna, Iko will never develop, at least naturally or biologically, a 'chest and everything'; nevertheless, Iko is a girl. Girl-child and girl-android deconstruct hegemonic assumptions about what it means to be a girl.

Here, Thom's maleness, his being a boy despite being a child, is assumedly a visible presence; the marker of Alanna's being a girl – her 'chest and everything' – has not yet developed (or appeared), so she is not yet 'a girl' (Pierce 1983, 2). In her critique of Freud, Luce Irigaray suggests that hegemonic discourse (heroic romance, Western philosophy) recognizes 'the little girl' as 'only a little man' because her body lacks a visible marker of its sexed state: 'She has nothing you can see. She exposes, exhibits the possibility of a nothing to see. Or at any rate she shows nothing that is penis-shaped or could substitute for a penis' ([1974] 1985, 47). In exhibiting nothing, there is nothing for representation. The girl-child's body does not mean; it is prior to our outside of signification, which is why Alanna 'look[s] enough like Thom' and not the other way around. The specularization of the body (how its sex is judged through sight/seeing or not seeing a penis) elides sex and sexual differences. Yet, Alanna's being a girl is the very thing that establishes the need for this cross-dressing. Her story pushes against hegemonic expectations (the girl child that should not exist, but she does). Through being a girl-who-is-not-yet-a-girl and twin, Alanna can borrow her brother's signification to become Alan, a boy in his (or her) own right – because Alanna also identifies as a girl,[2] it also opens a pathway for disrupting the binary opposition between men and women and exposing the flaw in representational economies; it gives the girl a sexual history before puberty.

This perceptual absence of a gendered body is not unusual in understandings of childhood. Rose suggests that the child's body is erased because childhood sexuality – 'bisexual, polymorphous, perverse' ([1984] 1992, 4) – threatens the stability of adult 'normal' heterosexuality. Yet, it is not that the child's fleshy, physical body does not exist – that would be another kind of impossibility – it is, instead, how this discursive production, in its binary nature, requires that the child's body have no sexual meaning. Thus, while at birth children are immediately marked male or female, it is both a biological sexing of the body that lacks sex and depends on a visual apprehension of having/not having a penis. In this way, the female-child's body is, perhaps, not so much erased as it is omitted or silenced. While it is an elision that adolescence disrupts – as Alanna's body will demonstrate through becoming a 'real girl' – it is also the possibility of becoming a 'real girl' that makes Alanna's cross-dressing possible (Pierce 2000, 125). Thus, while the statuses 'boy' and 'girl' are precarious, it is also precisely because Alanna is a girl who identifies as one that she may cross-dress. However, her cross-dressing is also made possible (or desirable) because Alanna's aptitudes and desires align more with those coded as male and masculine than those skills coded as feminine – and because they do so more than Thom's.

Alanna is skilled at hunting and fishing, and as Coram muses, she has 'a feel for the fighting arts' (Pierce 1983, 15). He also notes that she is 'as stubborn as a mule' (Pierce 1983). Alanna has what it takes to become a knight, a hero. Crucially, Alanna possesses the skills to become a knight – coded as masculine by both the text and the hero paradigm – and her brother does not. In *Into the Closet: Cross-Dressing and the Gendered Body in Children's Literature and Film*, Victoria Flanagan argues that the absence of strong male and masculine characters is what allows cross-dressers to 'carve [their] own gender niche' (2008, 104). For example, Disney's Mulan, which Flanagan cites alongside Alanna, can take up her father's call to arms because of his frailty; indeed, she does so out of a sense of duty to him and her family. Thom's lack of interest in the fighting arts and his 'finicky' status opens a space in which Alanna can perform hegemonic masculinity, and Alanna does use it to create her own 'gender niche' (2008), but she also uses it to deconstruct the gender binary and the quest romance.

On the road to Alan

The journey, or being 'on the road', is the central part of the heroic romance (symbolic or ritual death-rebirth sits at its core). It is, theoretically, where anything could happen, but, usually, at least according to the stories that get told and retold, the hero's movement follows a straight and narrow path securing a heterosexual, single, stable, heroic identity in the process. Alanna borrows her brother's signification (his appearance) to slip into the heroic romance. Ultimately, she disrupts the story's linear teleological impetus to offer an alternative developmental model, taking plurality and change into account, forming through connection and making spaces for kinship informed by an ethos of ethical responsibility (Moran 2018). However, the road to warrior-woman is long, and Alanna's becoming Alan is the first step on it. While being a child and twin made the cross-dressing possible, Alan requires something more: first, Thom must write him into existence, second, Alanna must change her appearance and, third, she must perform heroic masculinity (better than the boys who aren't girls). While all three are distinct, each requires the silencing or disavowal of femininity and her (female) body. To become Alan, Alanna must sacrifice her female or feminine self.

Symbolically, Alanna's lack of access to the Pages' wing is a lack of access to representation and subjective agency – to being a hero, entering language and being recognized as a human being. Moreover, Alanna's exclusion is a symbolic representation of the fate of all women under patriarchal regimes. As Irigaray suggests, 'it is not that she lacks some "master signifier" or that none is imposed on her, but rather that access to a signifying economy, to the coining of signifiers, is difficult or even impossible for her because she remains an outsider, herself (a) subject to their norms. She borrows signifiers but cannot make her mark, or re-mark upon them' ([1974] 1985), 71). Alanna's lack of access to the signifying economy of the heroic romance and her femaleness is a lack that always already affects women because signification is the purview of man; Alanna's 'looking like' Thom merely makes this lack explicit. Moreover, this 'borrow[ing] signifiers' is crucial. The ability to deal in signification positions Alanna as reliant on her brother, further securing his agency (a subjective position) while denying hers.

As a female, Alanna must borrow Thom's signification to gain entrance into the hero story. As a male, Thom can also supply her with a new origin story as Alan; Thom can write Alan into existence.[3] Thom's ability to deal in signification is central to Alanna's becoming a hero. It is one of the things making it possible: Thom 'can imitate his [the father's] writing' (Pierce 1983, 2), and in being so able, he has access to Irigaray's 'coining of signifiers' ([1974] 1985, 71). He, unlike Alanna, can deal in signification, and thus it is Thom who provides Alanna with the discursive status of 'twin boy' (Pierce 1983, 2). He writes Alan into existence: 'Thom was expert at forging his father's handwriting. He wrote two new letters, one for "Alan" and one for himself. Alanna read them carefully, relieved that there was no way to tell the difference between Thom's work and the real thing' (7). This letter creates Alan, and Alan-as-letter must be equivalent to the 'real thing' for this discursive construction makes everything that follows possible. It takes both this reading of discourse – Thom's having access to discourse, language and signifiers – coupled with the change to Alanna's appearance for her to gain subjectivity as Alan, for Alanna to enter into the heroic romance as a 'twin boy' (2).

The discursive shift is essential, not least owing to how discourse and language mediate our world, but Alanna still looks like Alanna after Thom writes Alan into existence. While discourse is crucial, there must also be a material change in Alanna's case. The discursive shift is not enough. After Thom writes Alan into existence, Alanna changes clothes, and Maude cuts her hair. After which, Alanna can depart her family grounds on the road to Alan. Importantly, this journey also begins with a look in a mirror.

> Alanna stared at herself in the mirror. Her twin stared back, violet eyes wide in his pale face. Grinning, she wrapped herself in her cloak. With a last peek at the boy in the mirror, she followed Maude out to the courtyard. Coram and Thom already mounted up, waited for them. Thom rearranged his skirts and gave his sister a wink.
>
> (Pierce 1983, 9)

Thom's letter writes Alan into existence, but this look in the mirror actualizes – for Alanna – the discursive shift, and it is provocative. As Thom's 'living mirror' (the role Cinderella plays for the hero), Alanna should not be able to see herself in a mirror ([1974] 1985, 221); she is the mirror. However, after the discursive creation *and* the physical transformation, Alanna can look in a mirror, and when she does, she sees 'herself' in it – with her twin's 'pale face'.

In one sense, Alanna's mirror moment literalizes Irigaray's suggestion that women must 'borrow[…] signifiers' (71). Alanna borrows Thom's appearance, the very core of his signification. In so doing, she undergoes the 'the symbolic castration' – despite Alanna's lack of a penis – that 'all subjects must suffer to enter the Symbolic' (Chappell 2007, 93; see, also, Lacan 2001). This castration applies to Alanna because, as Chappell adds, it is the symbolic 'loss of corporeal jouissance' that occurs 'with entry into language and social laws' (2007, 93). Alanna is dissociated from her body and the pleasure of her body (a kind of castration) to become Thom and then Alan. In other words, Alanna is the maternal body – or at least, as a woman, she has the potential to be – thus, her castration under the Symbolic is a kind of death to her self, at least her female one. Crucially, while this is happening in narration, it is also a symbolic playing out of that which happens to all women and anyone not meeting the heroic ideal.

For Alanna, becoming Thom means a dissociation from her body (it is 'his pale face' she sees, not hers), a rift that becomes even more profound (as I discuss below) when existing as Alan. Flanagan explores this becoming-subject-through-castration and argues that Lacan's system of subjectification (of becoming a subject) is divided into two parts: 'either "having" or "being" a phallus' (2008, 31; see, also, Butler 1990, 55–73). Men symbolically always already have the phallus in the form of the penis, but women can be the phallus. Flanagan further explains

> the determining factors of this system of gender difference are the possession, or lack and absence, of a phallus. Lacan envisions femininity as a subject position characterized primarily by lack, but female cross-dressing heroines victoriously claim the cultural signifier of masculinity as their own while disguised as men.
>
> (2008, 31)

Through cross-dressing, Alanna claims 'the cultural signifier of masculinity', but she does not become a man. Alanna remains a girl throughout her cross-dressing and is frequently concerned about having to 'lie' to everyone she knows (see, for example, Pierce 1984, 226). In this way, Alanna's becoming-Alan is an articulation of the (male) subject coming into being; as Judith Butler suggests in *Gender Trouble*, this becoming rests 'on the condition of a primary repression of the pre-individuated incestuous pleasures associated with the (now repressed) maternal body' (1990, 57). The female body is 'pre-individuated incestuous pleasures'. It could always potentially be the maternal body, and the subject coming into being must repress his mother's body to become subject, to become a man. Alanna, then, does not just suppress her mother's body; she also refuses her own (potential) mother's body. However, Alanna's mirror moment – an instance of ritual death and rebirth in heroic terms – also opens possibility, the chance of disrupting the hero story, because it begins to destabilize the specular economy underpinning subject formation.

Through this mirror moment, Alanna becomes both the mirror (prize, not-self) and that which is mirrored (hero, self). She collapses the oppositional and dialectical relationship between brother/sister, mirrored/mirror, 'A'/'not-A'. Alanna is neither mirror nor mirrored, a point the 'violet eyes' make explicit. She and Thom share these eyes, and in this moment of transformation, the eyes – not his, not hers – become theirs. They are the link between the girl she was and the boy she is becoming. The eyes literalize her liminality. Thus, while the refusal of the body it requires is problematic, Alanna's seeing her brother in the mirror starts her subject formation as a gendered identity between the poles of opposition. It confirms her status as 'on the road to Alan' and a foreshadowing of how they will disrupt that structure by occupying the middle ground. Finally, and if only because it gives a certain weight to Alanna's transformation, Thom shares no such moment of self-identification; 'his skirts' signify differently than do Alanna's breeches. Thom is temporarily disguised. Alanna is cross-dressed, and this cross-dressing is integral to the gendered, subjective self she becomes, but as is the case with most hero's journeys, the road is long and fraught – and it includes the radical disavowal of identity as Alanna and her body.

Finally, my reading is underpinned by a material feminist approach to the body. As Susan Hekman argues, material feminism is a call 'not to privilege the discursive over the material, but to understand the material in discursive terms' (Alaimo and Hekman 2008, 88). As the following chapter explores in more detail, if the discursive is solely responsible for mediating the world (a material reality), the ensuing radical break between, for example, embodiment and appearance refuses difference, flattens materiality and sparkles a situation that has a very real, physical and material effect on individuals. However, inverting the system and solely privileging the material also does not work (if such a thing could ever be fully achieved given our world is mediated through language). For one, inversion changes nothing. It is a theoretical cul de sac, leaving norms and standards in place. Here, biological essentialism (privileging the material) would deny Alanna her existence as Alan; the unique expression of her gender identity and the complicated ways in which it is neither boy nor girl but, rather, both, as the remainder of this chapter explores.

Alan: Alanna silences her body

To become Alan (a hero), Alanna must disavow her identity as Alanna, repress the materiality of her female body and perform heroic masculinity. While the performance is important – and the training she undertakes is difficult – hiding, concealing as well as silencing her body takes centre stage at several points, especially once she 'turns into a girl – you know, with a chest and everything' (Pierce 1983, 2). Once this happens, Alanna's journey begins to shift, and, once again, a mirror plays a key role: 'suddenly she froze before her long mirror. Watching the glass closely, she bounced up and down. Her chest moved. It wasn't much, but she had definitely jiggled. Over the winter, her breasts had gotten larger' (106). In one sense, this implies her breasts were always already present, at least in as much as they 'had gotten larger'. It is a subtle but valuable shift, given how mainstream patriarchal discourse would disavow those breasts until their appearance. Nevertheless, these breasts, the physical material body, must be sacrificed for Alanna to be Alan.

Briefly, it is also worth calling attention to the linguistic 'death' Alanna experiences on this journey. Names (and, as I discuss in the following chapter honorifics) are important. They confer rank and identity while also granting access to history or lineage. Alanna's entrance into the heroic romance includes a name change. She becomes Alan. This linguistic death – the removal of the diminutive 'na' – is symbolic of the bodily elisions Alanna's becoming hero also requires, as I discuss in the following section. It also echoes the change Cinderella's name underwent between Disney's 1950 feature-length animation and the 2015 live-action film. In both cases (Cinderella's and Alanna's), these elisions represent the norms and expectations of the system at a particular time and place. Here, Alanna cannot enter the hero story, but Alan can – if he looks and acts the part.

In the main, Alanna's body must be suppressed for her signification as Alan to be achieved, and this suppression speaks to the bodily suppression that all women face. In other words, more widely than this cross-dressing, Alanna's becoming Alan (hero) is a playing out of what must happen to the fleshy materiality of all bodies under the law of the hero story, which is the patriarchal, hegemonic law of the father. Alanna achieves this by cross-dressing; women in contemporary Western culture, through the frames of selfies and through continually working to meet hegemonic ideals of appearance. For example, 'It wasn't easy to live with the binding on her chest. For one thing, her growing breasts hurt, though luckily, they remained quite small. She was twice as careful now about how far she opened her shirt' (Pierce 1983, 107). The female body is refused; the text makes this clear with the 'binding'; however, it also reinforces how difficult this is by suggesting 'it wasn't easy' and how the 'growing breasts hurt', a fact many girls and women can attest to. Indeed, it is important to note that this refusal of the body does not apply only to Alanna. As the hero's prize and the model of ideal adolescent girl, Cinderella's 'heightened fantasy femininity' is also repression or silencing of the body, and it is one that adolescent girls redeploy in their quests for perfection. In other words, while Alanna's disguise necessitates it, anyone who has ever worn an underwire bra, Spanx or heels can attest to how those things contain the fleshy material body, albeit to different ends and aims.

Poignantly, Alanna is never narrated as padding anything; it is always about 'binding' her body or, later, wearing a 'bandage' to 'stop the red flow' (Pierce 1983, 132). Alanna's cross-dressing is never about creating the male body underneath her clothes; it is always about suppressing the fleshy materiality of the body. Although the text does also offer a 'bodily' marker of maleness – a changing voice, 'his [Prince Jonathan's] voice was beginning to boom and crack' – that Alanna must also affect through her body, 'soon Alanna would have to start faking the voice-change herself' (118). Here, the narration offers a physical property – in as much as the voice change is a bodily occurrence – that Alanna must perform. Yet, this is also not the same as constructing a bulge in trousers or binding breasts, acts that alter the body's contours. In other words, I have been concerned with how Alanna bodily creates herself as male, a construction that depends on the suppression of her female body, not on the creation of a male body underneath her clothes; yet, the distinction is complex, and in offering this example of a male bodily change that Alanna must perform, the text illustrates the complexity to the relationship between the performance of gender and the physical, fleshy body behind and within those performances, and one – learning to use and using a sword – warrants a closer look.

Swords are symbolically laden and overwhelmingly associated with heroic, toxic masculinity; they are integral to knighthood and sword work is central to Alanna's becoming a hero. For example, at the end of *Alanna: The First Adventure*, Alanna and Jon face a group of Ysandir, known to most as The Nameless Ones. These immortal beings existed before humans, and they are stealing the spirits or souls of the young people living near the city in which they were long-ago confined. Jon and Alanna fight them, ultimately destroying them all but not before they command Jon to '"see your companion for what she really is!"' (1983, 199). They make Alanna's clothes disappear using magic, leaving her wearing just 'her belt and scabbard' (199). While this does reveal the body beneath Alan's clothing thus prompting Alanna to reveal her identity to Jon, the scene is more about confirming her masculinity than it is about constructing her as a girl; not only does she prove her fighting skills in the battle that follows but the belt and scabbard suggest a strap-on. She has claimed the phallus.

In all the ways that matter to the heroic romance (which is the symbolic structure of Western discourse), Alanna has become Alan. She has claimed the phallus and become Nikolajeva's 'hero in drag' or the 'phallic girl' in Angela McRobbie's terminology (Nikolajeva 2002, 44; McRobbie 2008, 83). For McRobbie, the phallic girl 'gives the *impression* of having won equality with men by becoming like her male counterparts' (83, my emphasis). In becoming Alan, Alanna becomes 'like her male counterparts' – in fact, she becomes better, at least being a Page, than most of them: 'you're best at archery and tilting and staff fighting and weapons. And you're a good student', Douglas (a fellow Page) declares (Pierce 1983, 171). Importantly, the phallus is not the organ to which it is contingently linked; the phallus is a structure, the structure of Western discourse, the Symbolic order (see Coats 2004, 97–101). It is an ordering principle, a way of seeing and understanding the world, as Alanna's learning to use a sword demonstrates. After a lengthy lecture on the importance of a sword and instruction on making and caring for a sword, Alanna is one of the Pages chosen to spar, and it is a disaster. As she describes, 'It – it was like – my body wouldn't do anything I told it to. My mind was saying, "Do this! Do that! Do something!" And my body just wasn't connected' (1983, 130). Alanna has not yet mastered the phallus, but as Coram assures her, it's only because 'Master Alan' is 'just not a natural with a sword' (1983). Alanna may not have been born a boy, but she can become Alan.

She – representative of non-signification – becomes Thom, the 'boy in the mirror' (1983, 9), and in doing so, she is on the road to becoming an 'I', or self, capable of 'coining of signifiers' (Irigaray [1974] 1985, 71). Thus, where Alanna cannot use the symbols of writing, Alan can; 'he' can write to the father: '"You [Alan] may go. Don't forget to write to your father yourself"' (52). While Alan cannot copy the father's writing (that's Thom's ability), he can now coin signifiers. He can write to the father. Moreover, Alanna has not become, and cannot become, the father (this possibility also belongs to Thom). For this reason, the mirror moment and the cross-dressing – the wearing of masculine clothes and taking on, or borrowing, a masculine subjectivity – are not enough for Alanna. While the mirror moment provides the possibility of subject formation and the collapsing of the dialectical distance between the brother and sister makes heroic selfhood possible, the subjectivity Alanna gains is, for her, only partial. For Alanna, in the unique position of occupying a male space while being a female and identifying as a girl, there must be more. Indeed, the above markers of her 'heroism' only account for part of her journey across the Song of the Lioness quartet. She also uses her powerful healing magic to save Prince Jonathan from a sweating sickness sent to destroy the Royal family (1983, 99–103), learns to weave, which is traditionally considered 'women's work' (1986, 117), dresses 'like a girl' (1984, 137), and Alanna gets her period – and these things must be included within her hero story.

Finally, Alanna only gains a sort of pseudo-signification as Alan, one that – while valuable for problematizing woman's exclusion from discourse or signification, which occurs because of, and through, her body – does not offer an alternative because it elides or refuses the body. In many ways, it is a mirror problem. According to Irigaray, 'really successful femininity cannot lay claim to being ideal or confer an ideal upon itself. It lacks a mirror *appropriate* for doing so' ([1974] 1985, 105, emphasis original). This is why Alanna's subject formation, as a metaphor for the subject formation all women experience under hegemonic regimes, includes her seeing Thom in the mirror. There is no Imaginary for the female subject, for an embodied female subject, so Alanna must borrow his appearance at the expense of hers. In the following chapter, Cinder breaks this mirror as a cybernetic Cinderella. In this chapter, the inclusion of Alanna's first period within her heroic romance disrupts the discourse, particularly its linear, teleological thrust.

Un-horror-ing the blood

When Alanna gets her period in the middle of her hero's journey, the trajectory of that journey irrevocably shifts. It sets in motion a journey within the journey, disrupting the story's linear teleological path by including cyclicality, repetition and relation within its frame. However, when menarche occurs, Alanna is at the palace training to be a Knight of the Realm of Tortall, and in all the ways that matter, she has become Alan of Trebond, the son of Lord Alan and the younger twin brother to Thom. Alanna's discursive situation creates a scenario in which menstruation is horrifying: 'She got out of bed – and gasped in horror to find her things and sheets smeared with blood' (Pierce 1983, 132). As Alan, Alanna 'remains an outsider', the epitome of being 'subject[ed] to their [masculine] norms', and in this time of crisis, the physicality of the body is not enough: she lacks the ability to read, to understand, its signification (71). To neutralize that horror, a re-articulation of the body must occur. We must speak the unspeakable, the taboo. Before turning to that neutralization through a telling of the bleeding, I want to consider the shape and nature of the horror of the blood, both in terms of Alanna's 'gasp[ing] in horror' and, more widely, the silence and horror with which the blood is approached in popular and media culture (as representative of a hegemonic space).

In contemporary Western culture, it possibly seems like the blood is no longer horrible – even if it clearly is for Alanna. Cher did, after all, announce in the film *Clueless* way back in the mid-1990s that she 'was surfing the crimson wave' and 'had to haul ass to the ladies' (Heckerling 1995). Cher's proclamation, while offering a certain kind of visibility and one that was unavailable to girls in previous generations also masks the depth, even as it appears to offer something new (see, also, McRobbie 2008). According to Lydia Kokkola, 'the abject [...] is the primal fear that cannot be expressed through language [...] and so it is expelled or repressed within the subconscious [...] but it cannot remain repressed; it re-emerges as disturbances in language' (2013, 64). For Kokkola, Cher's 'crimson wave', a euphemism, is such disturbance, a rupture in the dominant language and, thus, potentially disruptive. However, euphemisms can also be erasures, ones that often serve to perpetuate and entrench shame.

More often than not, menstruation is elided – even in YA, a field of fiction featuring people of menstruating age. In these instances, the refusal to acknowledge the blood perpetuates the shame associated with bleeding, as I discussed in Chapter 1's consideration of Bella Swann and Katniss Everdeen neither of whom are seen to menstruate (Bella's absent period is not the inclusion of menstruation within her story. Indeed, the expectation of her menstruation heralded by its absence is entirely the problem.)In other words, by neglecting the topic, the literature both reinforces and constructs the shame around menstruation, and in so doing it continues to other girls and women. To counter the stigma associated with menstruation, I believe we must undertake a kind of 'shameless speech'. Here, at the time of Alanna's first period, a conversation between Alanna and an older woman illustrates the process.

> 'You poor child', she chuckled. 'Did no one ever tell you of a woman's monthly cycle? The fertility cycle?'
> Alanna stared. Maude had mentioned something, once –
> 'That's what this is? It's *normal*?'
> The woman nodded. 'It happens to us all. We can't bear children until it begins'.
> 'How long do I have to put up with this?' Alanna gritted.
> 'Until you are too old to bear children. It's as normal as the full moon is, and it happens just as often. You may as well get used to it.
> (1983, 136–7, emphasis original)

Alanna is a 'poor child' because of the absence of this telling, though, as the narration makes clear, Alanna had heard something 'once' regarding 'the woman's monthly cycle'. But, that hearing was both incomplete (like a euphemism or a shameful speaking). It was also without the weight of experience. Thus, Alanna, the child, needs a telling about this 'woman's monthly cycle' now (1983, 136). Until told, the child does not know the body. That is, the bleeding happens, the body, you could say, articulates (Haraway 2004, 106), but Alanna does not understand. The physical, material bleeding has given new meaning to that which 'Maude had mentioned', and in this way, the narration makes explicit the link between the bleeding (the physical, bodily occurrence) and the telling of it (the discursive production). Understanding takes both.

In other words, there is a difference between the bleeding (as a physical occurrence) and its meaning of it. For Alanna, this bleeding will happen, and it did, regardless of what she knows about it, but what she comes to know about it has a direct impact on her being. The meaning is that which Alanna lacks access to, as the child and as Alan. 'Tell you of the woman's monthly cycle' serves as both the naming of this thing, this physical occurrence, and its making normal (1983, 136). Without the telling, Alanna does not understand the bleeding. Thus, prior to this telling the bleeding at once exists and yet does not, and it is the telling that allows, makes possible, the transition into knowledge: "'That's what this is? It's *normal*?'" (136, emphasis original). Crucially, in this making normal, the telling links this 'woman's monthly cycle' (what Alanna refers to as 'it') to the 'full moon'; not only is this an instance of relationality ('woman's cycle') but it is also repetition. Moreover, the making normal depends on a link to nature; there is a suggestion that both these things are natural, and thus normal because they occur in nature issues that I take up in both the following chapters: Cinder's (Chapter 4), by coupling the human with the machine, particularly replicative/reproductive potential, and Daine's (Chapter 5), by explicitly taking woman's association with the real, Daine is a shape-shifter, into account.

As Alanna is cross-dressed and has taken on the subject position of Alan, this telling is complicated: 'again Mistress Cooper raised her eyebrows, "you're female, child, no matter what clothing you wear. You must become accustomed to that"' (136). This is about the 'obviousness' of the body. Alanna is 'obviously' female, but she is also not. She is just as obviously Alan. Despite the heightened physicality of the femaleness through this 'bleeding' – despite the body's insistence upon its own obviousness – 'clothing' and performance have obscured it, changing its borders and boundaries. Therefore, discourse is so important; discourse has the power to change our perceptions of things, and while our perceptions of things cannot offer absolute truth, they do shape our world. Specifically, new understandings of the body 'are to create a new version of the social, a more ethical social world which does not insist upon framing the self through repudiation of the other' (Vint 2007, 27). In Alan's case, this new understanding of the body begins a process whereby she becomes neither Alanna nor Alan but someone in-between, and while this is a personal journey, it has political implications. As such it is important that this conversation about the bleeding is not the only conversation within Pierce's Tortall (or even mythopoeic YA; Alison Croggon's The Books of Pellinor includes another excellent example).

In the Tortall Universe, Kel – a girl training to be a knight without having to disguise her sex and gender, owing to Alanna's 'provocative act' (Flanagan 2008, xv) – also needs a telling of the bleeding. While Alanna's conversation was required because of her masculine subjectivity, the text insists that Kel, even as an obvious girl, requires the conversation. First, in the 'remember[ing] of several talks she'd had with her mother' and second with the conversation accompanying the first bleeding.

> Lalasa opened the dressing room door. Looking at Kel, she saw the problem immediately. 'Do you know what this means?' she asked opening a dry-goods chest and drawing out linen and a fresh loincloth.
> Kel nodded, still scrubbing.
> […] Have you cramps?'
> 'An ache, like.' Lalasa patted her abdomen.
> Kel nodded.
> 'Willow tea will help. Here.' She showed Kel how to fix a linen pad inside her loincloth, to catch the blood. 'We can change that at lunchtime.'
> (Pierce 2000, 98)

Kel, thanks to her mother, already knows what this bleeding is, as the 'nodded' suggests and as I discussed above. Yet, as this is the first bleeding, a conversation still occurs, and it focuses on the practical, thus expanding the work of Alanna's telling.

Again, this conversation is about making the bleeding, using the text's term, 'normal' and modelling that normalcy for others. Admittedly, I am hesitant to use the term 'normal', even as the text uses it for all the ways 'normal' has been deployed to police that which is abnormal as 'the process of feeling or being normal fundamentally requires … constant comparison with others' (Waller 2020, 6). Indeed, following Alison Waller, 'ordinary' might be a more productive term. As Waller argues, 'ordinary actions or behaviours are those that can be identified as part of the usual order of things' (3). The practical – scrubbing hose, resolving cramps and how to use a linen pad, including when to change it – are part of including this bleeding within the 'usual order of things'. Moreover, ordinary (instead of normal) offers a valuable intervention in the 'extraordinariness' often associated with girl heroes in YA fantasy. Indeed, while there is a temptation to read Kel's first bleeding in opposition to Alanna's and as the more ordinary menarche – most girls have not become, through cross-dressing, boys – the text refuses that distinction.

Despite knowing what this bleeding is, the above conversation between Lalasa and Kel is prefaced, in narration, by 'She had a dull ache in her abdomen. Was that normal?" (2000, 97), contrasted with Alanna's earlier exclamation of "'That's what this is? It's normal?"', and this use of 'normal' in both situations suggests that these texts are very much concerned with making normal of this bleeding. Critically, the making 'normal' occurs in language – through narrations of conversations, which are, in fact, a double layering of language: the narration itself and the dialogue shared between two women, to which that narration appeals. Moreover, this making 'normal' does not just end with the conversation surrounding menarche. Instead, the text also writes it into the girl's everyday existence: 'As Kel washed her face, cleaned her teeth, and combed her hair, Lalasa put out her clothes, including a fresh breastband and loincloth, and one of the cloth pads Kel wore during her monthly bleeding. It had begun the day before' (Pierce 2001, 39). The repetition of the stories within Pierce's work, alongside the inclusion of menstruation into the girl's daily life, is imperative to changing the discourse. In other words, the open, honest and frank discussions of menstruation, birth control,[4] sex and pregnancy are vital to reframing the myth of what it means to be a girl.

On the road to Alanna

From the world-shifting position of having experienced menarche as Alan (a hero) and re-signifying that experience (horror to ordinary), Alanna begins the process of becoming a gendered self between the binary pairing of man/woman, and in so doing, she begins to re-shape her world. In other words, after menarche, Alan's hero's journey radically shifts. As he(ro), she is no longer on the linear path to conquering hero. Instead, her journey includes two interwoven journeys: the hero's linear one threaded through with the cyclical patterns associated with womanhood. This additional journey, or a journey within the journey, frustrates heroic masculinity by including the body within the heroic frame and disrupting linear, teleological development. As such, Alanna requires a second ritual rebirth.[5] Briefly, ritual rebirth is the point at which the would-be hero (initiate, neophyte, adolescent) dies to his old self to be reborn as the hero, and it is essential to the hero's story; it signifies the radical break between self and is the vehicle of transfer between the two stages. Crucially, this makeover – despite Alanna's 'being Alan' – has little to do with announcing her true sex or even her 'true' self. It is certainly not about transforming her into the hero's prize. Instead, it is a shift in the order of things that offers the possibility of change.

In her quartet's second book, Alanna returns to Mistress Cooper and asks the older woman to teach Alanna how "'to dress like a girl'" (1984, 137). Just as she had to learn to be Alan, Alanna must learn to be a girl. Importantly, this desire has little to do with announcing her 'true' sex. Coram and Maud, the children's caretakers, know that Alanna is a girl, as they both assisted in the deception; both Mistress Cooper and George (Cooper's son, king of thieves and Alanna's friend) know that Alan is 'really' Alanna since her first menstruation; Alanna sought George's help to find the healing woman. Sir Myles, one of Alanna's teachers and ultimately her adoptive father, has suspected since witnessing Alanna healing Jon from the 'Sweating Fever' in Alanna's first year of Page training (1983, 82). While Alanna is socially Alan at the time of her request, it has little to do with revealing a deeper truth about herself, especially one that might upend her social truth. Instead, it is about exploring the possibilities of self. In many ways, Alanna's makeover – and the subsequent girl disguise that she adopts to venture 'into the city, getting used to her skirts and learning about things most girls her age took for granted' (1983, 144) – becomes an additional instance of cross-dressing.

Initially, Alanna's learning to dress like a girl functions textually as Alan learning to dress like a girl, a reading the text makes explicit at Alan's first dress fitting: not only does Mistress Cooper suggest that s/he is 'worse than a city lad getting fitted with his first pair of long breeches', but Alanna also complains, once the dress has been fitted, that "'it [her feminine appearance] doesn't look right [...] It looks like Squire Alan in a girl's dress'" (1984, 138). Reinforcing my view that Alanna has become Alan, Alanna not only fails to meet expectations of feminine performance – she is acting 'like a city lad' – but she also fails to meet expectations of feminine appearance – 'it doesn't look right'. Her hair is too short, and her stance is too masculine. Where the makeover of popular and media culture is about becoming more, or better, feminine (Cinderella's 'sparklemation' is the ideal example) and about possessing a certain self-determination through such activity, Alanna's makeover does something else – because it is Alan's. Rather than a neoliberal moment of self-actualization through bodily self-improvement, this makeover offers another instance of cross-dressing: male-to-female cross-dressing. This makeover offers Alan-in-drag as its result, and in so doing, it provides a re-articulation of the makeover narrative. It offers a mode of being female that, rather than being dependent on the body's appearance, is open to interpretation.

Before exploring the ramifications of this makeover-as-drag, it is useful to consider what it does take – a change to her hair – for Alanna to appear feminine, for her to not look 'like Squire Alan in a girl's dress' (183). First, hair played a crucial role in Alanna's transformation into Thom, as the 'length of their hair' was one of the only differences most people could see between the twins (1983, 1). In Alanna's world, at the time of her cross-dressing, men wore breeches and women skirts, a sumptuary law contributing to the strict gender rules barring Alanna from becoming a knight simply because she was a girl. Briefly, the quality, design and material of that clothing signified class and rank. Here, changing clothes was essential to her becoming Thom and then Alan, but the clothing alone wasn't enough. Maud cutting Alanna's hair is what allowed Alanna to look into the mirror and see Thom/herself-as-Thom. In this new instance of cross-dressing, Alanna looks like squire Alan '"because we've done nothing with Squire Alan's hair"' (138). As she did before, Alanna must change her hair, in this case, donning 'a black wig' when 'she went into the city (usually in Mistress Cooper's company), getting used to her skirts and learning about the things most girls her age took for granted' – even as she continues on the road towards knighthood.

Hair plays a pivotal role in Alanna's hero story, but it is only one kind of hair that does: the hair on top of her head. Body hair is curiously absent, despite how this hair plays a crucial role in masculinity. In his conceiving of the 'normal' adolescent (one of the hero's 'thousand faces'), G Stanley Hall argues that attaining a beard as central to the 'normal' adolescent's developmental trajectory (his narrative pattern) and that to be beardless is to be abnormal. Hair is complicated, and it plays a fundamental role in Alanna's cross-dressing. However, in all this preoccupation with Alanna/Alan's hair, the absence of narration regarding body hair is striking. Only once in the entire quartet is Alanna referred to as a 'beardless youth' (1988, 1). Ironically, this is after she has revealed her 'true sex' and at the start of the final book of her quartet. In *The Last Taboo: Women and Body Hair*, Karin Lesnik-Oberstein opens by calling attention to how 'the hair on the top of women's heads is valued and admired', while they 'remove the hair on their bodies' (2007, 1). Lesnik-Oberstein also suggests that body hair is never seen, even 'when there are references to women shaving, such as in some American sitcoms' (1) – the parallel to my reading of menstruation and the invisibility of its blood is provocative. Here, in a narration of cross-dressing – in which hair plays such a pivotal role – the absence of (body) hair reinforces Lesnik-Oberstein's view that female body hair is taboo.

Returning to Alan's cross-dressing and her subsequent girl disguise, the hair remains integral. On her seventeenth birthday, Alan goes for a walk in the palace gardens as a girl, as s/he is narrated as thinking 'there was no law that said she had to be a boy on her seventeenth birthday' (1984, 153). To do this, s/he first retrieves her 'pretty clothes – a lace-trimmed chemise, delicate silk stockings, tiny leather slippers, a purple silk dress' from 'the wooden chest she kept at the foot of her bed, locked and magically protected' (152). While it is interesting enough that this whole endeavour is described in such furtive and evocative/sumptuous terms – lace-trimmed, delicate, tiny and silk – the fact that it is 'thinking of Delia' that sends her there is even more so, as this thinking offers a complicated portrayal of desire. In one sense, it offers the possibility of Alan being sexually attracted to this 'beautiful' woman, but it also simultaneously posits Delia as an example of femininity that Alanna should emulate: 'she [Alanna] wasn't a beauty like Delia, but she wasn't a hag either' (152). Not only is it now impossible to separate, at least, this cross-dressing (Alan as a girl) from issues of sex and sexuality, but it also simultaneously posits Alan–na as in between. She is neither Alan nor Alanna, just as she is neither 'beauty' nor 'hag'. Alanna/Alan is on the road to a gender position between the poles of opposition.

Owing to this liminality (the biggest threat to the system underpinning dominant ways of being), it takes – even with these clothes that are heavily coded as feminine – 'the black wig she normally wore in public' because 'there weren't enough violet-eyed redheads around' for Alan to appear as a girl (152-3). The clothes – again – are not quite enough, so much so that Alanna wears a wig as 'some kind of disguise' (153) when leaving her rooms as a girl. In other words, Alanna, crossed-dressed as Alan, must wear a disguise in order to be – to appear as – the girl she already is and always has been, even if she once looked like her brother. As such, this makeover is not about Alanna coming into appropriate femininity, but it might be Alan in drag. Alanna's gender and sexuality have not shifted. Thus, while this narration of Alanna masquerading as a black-haired girl on her seventeenth birthday opens a space for a queer reading – if only in the initial ambiguity as to what about 'the sight of Jonathan dancing with Lady Delia' makes Alanna 'too restless to socialize, and too nervous to sleep' (1983, 152) – the queerness is ultimately not Alanna's but Jonathan's, the quartet's archetypal hero (who must learn to live with a Lady Knight). Jon is the object of Alanna's desire, not Delia: 'Alanna's lips quivered. She wanted Jonathan's love. To be honest, she had wanted it for a long time' (156). In this way, it is not Alanna's (homosexual) desire for Delia that is at play here, but, rather, some mutual desire between Alanna, Jonathan and Alan-in-drag, so it is perhaps his.

Warrior-woman

Heterosexual closure is the central aim of the heroic romance; the hero wins his prize and they live 'happily ever after'. In *Lioness Rampant*, Alanna is nearing the end of her hero's journey. She has encountered 'fabulous forces', won a 'decisive victory' and returns home with a 'boon' (Campbell [1949] 1968, 35). Owing to her long absence and Jonathan's impending coronation, Alanna is to be (re)presented at court. It isn't quite that this ball is being thrown for her, as the ball was thrown for Prince Charming in *Cinderella*, but it's a near thing. The seamstresses hired to dress Alanna for the occasion believes Alanna ought to wear a dress: '"Ye can't show your legs to the whole court and his Majesty that's to be"' (Pierce 1988, 213). Alanna rebuts this position, arguing 'I'm not a lady – I'm a knight [...] and I'm making my bow to court as one. Dresses are fine sometimes, but not tonight' (214). The seamstress's position aligns with heroic norms and standards which also map onto sex and gender assumptions within Tortall and Western consensus reality; women wear dresses (as a lady being presented at court Alanna should wear a certain kind of dress, like Cinderella's ball gown). However, Alanna – who has rightfully earned her shield (and who has proved that earning over and over) – is not 'only' a lady nor is she 'only' a knight; Alanna is a warrior-maiden.

To represent Alanna's hybrid status, Thayet (the exiled princess of Sarain, stunningly beautiful, and ultimately Queen of Tortall) suggests an alternative outfit: 'It was a shirt and tunic, with soft, full breeches instead of hose. The tunic was longer than usual, coming to the knee, yet splits in the sides to the waist ensured the wearer's freedom of movement' (1988, 214). The shirt and tunic serve as a mediating option between breeches/gowns, and it represents the gender identity and subject position Alanna achieves through her hero's journey. Importantly, this is not the end of Alanna's journey, despite this scene taking place in the final book of her quartet. As an adult warrior-woman, Alanna appears in Pierce's Immortals quartet and (complicatedly) the Protector of the Small quartet. She also features in the Tricksters duology; Aly, its female-hero, is her daughter. In many ways, the ending of Alanna's quartet is only the start of what it means to be a female-hero. Nevertheless, this outfit is important, and not only because clothes played such an important role in her cross-dressing. The tunic with splits to ensure freedom of movement certainly isn't 'brass tits on the armour' (Altmann 1992), and in so being it serves as a powerful metaphor for the female-hero.

In this chapter, I have argued that Alanna slips into the heroic romance as the hero by borrowing her brother's identity (signification) before developing a heroic one of her own. Becoming-Alan offers a certain kind of intervention, but it is limited. Indeed, Alan is Maria Nikolajeva's 'hero in drag' (Nikolajeva 2002, 144; 1991, 147–9; see, also, Paul 1990). For Nikolajeva, and I would agree, the heroic romance, owing to a host of reasons, refuses girls and women entry into its system as women who are not merely there to support the hero. The 'hero in drag' is a gender permutation allowing the central opposition to remain intact, as Alanna demonstrated when silencing her body to become Alan. Had, Alanna stayed as Alan, her cross-dressing – for all that it was a 'transgressive and provocative act' (Flanagan 2008, xv) – would not have deconstructed the gender binary; she would not have become a female-hero. As Angela McRobbie argues, 'the phallic girl' (Nikolajeva's hero in drag) 'gives the impression of having won equality with men by becoming like her male counterparts. But in this adoption of the phallus, there is no critique of masculine hegemony' (2008, 83). For this reason, Alanna required something more. Above, I considered how Alanna's period kick-started a journey within the journey. Importantly, Alanna didn't have to follow the trajectory initiated by menstruation; she had proven herself to be Alan, and she could have continued down his heroic path. However, for Alanna, Alan wasn't enough; being the archetypal hero wasn't enough, as is the case for many people.

Alanna's female-hero's journey (as is the case with all female-hero's journeys) includes both the linearity of the hero's and the cyclicality of the patterns associated with women, especially repetition and the potential for reproduction. Above, I discussed Alanna's relationship with Jon, and, rightly, questioned whether she was sleeping with him or he was sleeping with Alan. Laying that aside, Jon is the Crown Prince, and he becomes King of Tortall. Had Alanna stayed with him – and Jon does propose – she would have become the hero's prize. Flipping that script and pairing Alanna with, for example, Lady Delia, the court beaut, Alanna was 'thinking of' just before sleeping with Jon, also doesn't suffice (1984, 152–7). It would either cement Alanna's status as a hero in drag or function as an eschewing of heterosexuality and heroic norms and standards. Alanna isn't limited to Jon or even the musing about Lady Delia. During her female-hero's journey, Alanna also enters into a romantic and sexual relationship with Liam Ironarm, an important step on her journey. While the pair fall for one another quickly and passionately (as passionately as you can in a YA novel now considered to be MG), Liam fears magic and can never fully accept Alanna for who she is, teaching her more about herself. The person who can accept Alanna for herself – all of herself – is George Cooper, King of Thieves-cum-Spymaster.

Finally, in 2019, a fan posed a question about Alanna's sexuality to Pierce on Twitter. In response, Pierce (@TamoraPierce) tweeted: 'Alanna has always defied labels. She took the best bits of being a woman and a man, and created her own unique identity. I think the term is "gender-fluid", though there wasn't a word for this (to my knowledge) when I was writing her' (2019c). While Pierce's affirmation of Alanna's gender ambiguity is refreshing and fans certainly appreciated it – the tweet has received nearly five thousand likes and over a thousand comments and retweets – the ambiguity is present in the text, offering readers the chance to see themselves in the hero story whether they identify as a girl, boy or any identity in-between. Within the world of the story, her intervention in what it means to be a hero does not just change things for Alanna. Crucially, it opens a space in which Keladry of Mindelan, in a later series, might try for her shield without disguising herself, without hiding her sex/gender. Alanna's 'disruptive act' – trading places with her twin brother, becoming Alan and ultimately becoming a female-hero – sets the stage for further disruptive acts both within and without Tortall.

4

Breaking the mirror: Cinder(ella) is a cyborg

Two screws once held my left hip together; that hip is now a combination of metal, (disintegrating) polyurethane, ceramic and a couple of screws. It will need replacing (again) in the future. Before receiving that artificial hip (which has now been a part of me for longer than the 'real' one), I spent a year, when I was thirteen, in an abduction brace and a wheelchair; there were many wires, screws and mechanical parts. There were also many screws and wires in the braces that straightened my teeth, including dental amalgam and composite resin (fillings to repair cavities). I need glasses or contact lenses to see clearly, and both of my 'big' toes consist of three metal pins alongside muscles, bones and other organic parts. In other words, my body has been 'cut and sewed and pieced […] together', and I bear the scars of those actions (Meyer 2013, 320). In being so fragmented and scarred, I cannot achieve the sparkly, heightened fantasy femininity modelled by Disney's Cinderella – as is also the case for Cinder, the cyborg female-hero at the heart of Marissa Meyer's Lunar Chronicles.

Cinder's cyborg body refuses the shiny, sparkly, flatness that Cinderella models, and in doing so, she breaks the mirror by which the hero forms himself and in which girls and women are trapped. In fact, opening with '[t]he screw through Cinder's ankle had rusted' (Meyer 2012, 1), *Cinder*, ostensibly first foray into the world of The Lunar Chronicles, wastes no time demonstrating that Cinder's appearance – her way of being a girl – is not Cinderella's while also giving some clues as to how it as a female-hero's. As I discussed in Chapter 1, Cinderella is the hero's prize or ideal image of adolescent girlhood. This opening sentence undoes all of Cinderella's pretty, shiny, sparkly requirements: 'the screw through Cinder's ankle' suggests her body is not whole and indicates that it is not entirely human. Her body is not fit, as in healthy, because this screw has 'rusted'; it has failed. Her body is also not 'fit' as in pretty because, at a foundational level, 'pretty' requires the first kind of fit. Cinder's body is not the fit and able body produced by the makeover paradigm, which is the predominant framework for becoming a woman (prize) that I discussed in Chapter One using Walt Disney's *Cinderella* (Geronimi, Jackson, and Luske 1950). Cinder's body is not only fragmented and scarred but also radically includes inorganic, mechanical parts. In so being, Cinder is unfit for the selfhood Cinderella models; instead, she offers an alternative model, one I call being-hero, a way of being a hero steeped in flexibility and responsiveness with the potential to collapse dominant and dominating binaries. The hyphen visualizes how, by radically occupying the space between oppositions, female-heroes intervene in heroic norms and standards to offer their alternative model.

Cinder's model of being-hero involves the dynamic coupling of the human and machine, which usually comprise a binary pair; humans are not machines. Cinder, however, is the ironic homogenization of the two in the Harawavian sense (1991). She is neither one nor the other; she is both, and being human-machine hybrid forms the centre of Cinder's being-hero. As such, posthumanism plays an integral role in this chapter.[1] Moreover, posthumanist approaches to The Lunar Chronicles are typical. For example, Victoria Flanagan includes Cinder in *Technology and Identity in Young Adult Fiction: The Posthuman Subject* (2014), and Ferne Merrylees (2018) and Angela Insenga (2018), both have chapters on The Lunar Chronicles in *Posthumanism in Young Adult Fiction: Finding Humanity in a Posthuman World*. The 'Introduction' does an excellent job of outlining posthumanism's critical debates and linking them to YA.[2] In different ways, Flanagan, Merrylees and Insenga are all concerned with the posthuman potential for disrupting 'humanist concepts of subjectivity' by 'endorsing a more expansive and de-hierarchized understanding of selfhood' (Flanagan 2014, 187). Merrylees, for example, draws on posthuman theory to show how Cinder pushes the boundaries of the autonomous (heroic) individual, further arguing that 'adolescents need to cultivate a form of hybridity to negotiate our increasingly technological world' (2018, 76). This 'hybridity' is very much the work of female-heroes, and in this chapter, it takes the shape of what Alexandra Lykissas describes as a 'cyborg-erella' (2020).

Importantly, Cinder is not the only female-hero in this world. Cinderella as a cyborg is integral to this chapter and my overall interest in reframing what it means to be a girl, but, perhaps even more importantly, Cinder is part of a systematic, collective interrogation of the specular economy at work in contemporary Western culture. The Lunar Chronicles does so by questioning the implicit one-to-one relationship between self and appearance, the relegation of 'femininity [what it means to be a woman] to a bodily property' (Gill 2007, 149) and the requirement of 'fixed' (shiny and sparkly) perfection including the concomitant flattening and erasure of the body's fleshy materiality. Indeed, in The Lunar Chronicles, the body (woman) is not merely a surface; it is the boundary between surface and depth and a site of amalgamation and potential relation. It also models a form of 'collectivity' or collaboration that is a vital avenue for addressing the heroic romance's isolating individuality and its narratives of dominance, an issue that the following chapter specifically engages (Lykissas 2018). Here, Cinder's cyborg status – her hybrid, ironic, plural and fragmented existence between human and machine – forms the 'conceptual centre' of The Lunar Chronicles. Still, her intervention would be incomplete without considering, for example, the Lunar Glamour and how it complicates the reliability of appearance as a marker of one's self or identity. It would also not be complete without Iko's pushing the boundaries of what it means to be a girl (Iko is an android who identifies as a girl and is coded as a girl but has none of the requisite biology 'necessary' to be a girl, let alone a human). The Lunar Chronicles' collective interrogation of the heroic romance's specular economy adds depth and weight to Cinder's intervention. It also opens a space for considering relationships, an issue I pick up in the following chapter.

This chapter takes on the objectification women face within the heroic romance – specifically, the prize's existence as a mirror and the concomitant representational economy dominating contemporary Western culture. In other words, how girls and women are trapped within the body and a scheme requiring that body, which is to say, girls and women because, according to the story, they are the same, to look at act like Cinderella. In contemporary Western culture, woman's superficiality has reached a heightened depthlessness. Images are paramount in our increasingly digital culture. Through Facebook timelines, Instagram feeds and other social media and online platforms, human beings create their 'self' by editing and curating images. They do so to an unprecedented extent (even before the Covid-19 pandemic forced us to live more and more of our lives online). Frederick Jameson identifies the shift to 'image' – or increased visuality – as marking a 'new kind of flatness or depthlessness, a new kind of superficiality in the most literal sense' (1991, 8). Explicitly, the homogeneity of images, their 'fixed' perfection and how they conceal their constructedness turn surfaces into surfaces of surfaces. For adolescent girls, this turn to the image is especially harmful because the kinds of things these images hide – the fleshy materiality of the body – and the way they police standards of appearance are the very thing marking adolescent girls as Other. The Lunar Chronicles intervenes in this narrative by offering a 'girl full of wires' as a female-hero: that is, by insisting that depth matters.

Cinder(ella) is a cyborg

Cinder is a 'girl full of wires' (Meyer 2012, 82). However, she is not *just* a girl full of wires. Yes, Cinder is a cyborg, but she is also a 'teenage girl', the 'best mechanic in New Beijing' (2012, 10), a Lunar (citizen of the moon) and a revisioning of Cinderella. As a girl, and especially as a Cinderella figure, Cinder should be the hero's prize, and in many ways, her narrative maps onto the 'persecuted heroine' framework just as much as Perrault's, the Grimm's and even Disney's Cinderella's do: Cinder's story takes place in 'once upon' albeit a future 'time'. Her stepmother, Adri, is wicked (as is her Aunt Levana). Cinder has two stepsisters, though one of them, Peony, is kind. Iko, a plucky android, stands in for the Disney versions' mice, while Dr Erland functions as Cinder's fairy godfather. As a twenty-first-century Cinderella, Cinder took herself to the ball in an orange 'gasoline car' she repaired (hover crafts are the usual mode of transport in this world, not pumpkins turned coaches or even petrol-driven cars), much like Ella makes her dress in Disney's 2015 live-action Cinderella. There is also a Prince. However, despite all the ways she merits the role, the chance to be his prize was taken from Cinder when her Aunt Levana set fire to the child's nursery. The attempt on Cinder's life left her with a missing left leg and hand, burned right arm, shoulder and cheek, and injuries to her spine, heart and eyes, thus making her unfit to be the hero's prize (2013, 320 and 324).

Ironically, the attempt on her life places Cinder within the heroic romance as the hero: an early attempt on the hero's life resulting in his being 'reared by foster parents in a far-off country' is a common feature of hero stories, according to Lord Raglan in 'The Hero of Tradition', one of the most well-known patterns delineating the archetypal hero (Raglan 1934; 1936, 178). With a few minor shifts to account for her sex and gender, Cinder's 'hero story' adheres to fourteen of the twenty points of Raglan's model. Her score rises to fifteen if her engagement to Prince Kai results in marriage (plenty of fanfiction depicts that wedding, and Meyer just released a 'choose your own adventure novel' in which, at least theoretically, Cinder gets married in some options).[3] At fifteen (of twenty-two), Cinder is just as much a hero as the Greek hero Jason or the god Zeus; both share her score. However, Cinder is also a girl whose body is unfit to be the hero's prize, which means it is also unfit to be the hero. In so being, she also cannot be the 'exceptional heroine' YA favours, as that model requires heightened forms of the previous. These frameworks cannot account for Cinder's existence as a girl who is also Lunar cyborg mechanic, and it is not a benign insufficiency.

The centre of opposition underpinning the hero/prize relationship and accounting for the appearance and actions of both pairs radically excludes Cinder because she is a cyborg, part human, part machine. In so being, Cinder's body cannot be erased in the way the heroic romance requires. As Donna Haraway describes, cyborg bodies 'do not resolve into larger wholes, even dialectically' (1991, 149). Rather, this body is 'about the tension of holding incompatible things together because both or all are necessary and true' (1991). For Cinder, the tension includes not just that which is human and machine – she is '36.28 percent not human' and, presumably, 63.72 percent human (Meyer 2012, 82) – but also that which is masculine and feminine and replicative and reproductive. In her world, this hybridity or liminality makes Cinder, at best, a second-class citizen and, at worst, an object to be owned.

Briefly, Cinder's left hand and a portion of her left leg (from foot to mid-thigh) are metal. She has 'four metal ribs', 'metal vertebrae along her spine', and 'metal splits along the bones in her right leg' (Meyer 2012, 82). There is also 'synthetic tissue around her heart', 'wires in her brain' and 'optobionics behind her retinas' (2012, 82; 2013, 320). Cinder is both human and machine, and to many, her 'cyborg' parts matter more than her human ones; the 36.28 per cent of Cinder that is not human is enough to make her property: '[l]egally, Cinder belonged to Adri [Stepmother] as much as the household android and so too did her money, her few possessions, even the new foot she'd just attached' (2012, 24). This new foot is a 'steel-plated' one that Cinder purchased with money earned through her job as a mechanic. However, Cinder, foot and earnings belong to Adri, and Adri leverages that power to radically disempower Cinder.

Upon discovering Cinder's purchase, she forces Cinder to disconnect the 'new foot', thus divesting cinder of agency. On principle and in pride, Cinder does not immediately reconnect her old foot, which was 'four years' too small (mechanical inorganic parts do not grow with the body) (Meyer 2012, 3). Instead, she uses homemade or makeshift crutches until she needs to '"pass" as a noncyborg human' to attend the ball, as I discuss below (Coste 2021, 66). Illustrating the depth of Cinder's othering, Adri also volunteers her for the cyborg draft a vaccine testing programme that uses cyborgs as 'guinea pigs' (2021, 29).[4] Cyborgs clearly are not fully human within this world, and while the Lunar Chronicle disrupts this narrative in a number of ways, I want to focus on Cinder's being-cyborg makes her a female-hero, particularly how Cinder disrupts the human/machine, masculine/feminine and replicative/reproductive binaries with implications for linear teleological development patterns.

Across The Lunar Chronicles, Cinder is coded as masculine and feminine, girl/not-girl and machine/not-human in many ways, but her status as 'not-girl' initially comes to the fore, particularly in terms of her clothing and her work as a mechanic. First, as Meyer describes on her website, Cinder usually wears 'comfortable and utilitarian' clothes. These clothes, including 'cargo pants' (2012, 14), are appropriate to Cinder's work as a mechanic. For example, she can store a 'wrench' in one of the pockets (97). ('Women's' clothing rarely has such useful things as pockets, especially dresses.) In the opening pages of the first novel, Prince Kai assumes that Linh Cinder is a man because he cannot imagine a girl, let alone a teenage one, as 'the best mechanic in New Beijing'. Cinder's body also does not present as feminine, which directly influences Cinder's perception of herself (10). For example, in a passage during which Cinder's stepsisters Pearl and Peony are being fitted for ballgowns, the narrator (focalized through Cinder's perspective) comments, 'at fourteen, Peony had already developed curves that Cinder couldn't begin to hope for. If Cinder's body had ever been predisposed to femininity, it had been ruined by whatever the surgeons had done to her, leaving her with a stick-straight figure. Too angular. Too boyish. Too awkward with her heavy artificial leg' (34). While Cinder identifies as a girl, she has internalized hegemonic norms and expectations, much as girls outside of the text do when they do not meet norms and standards.

There are two issues at work in this construction of Cinder as not feminine: this not being a girl until her 'curves' develop relates to both essentialist notions of what it means to be a woman and the erasure of woman's sexual history prior to adulthood. Like Alanna in the previous chapter, Cinder is not yet a real girl because, here, she has not developed Peony's 'curves'; there is no visible marker of her womanhood (see Freud [1933] 1973, 151, Irigaray ([1974] 1985, 47). In exhibiting nothing, there is nothing for the specular economy to recognize as 'girl' thus – in hugely exclusionary and problematic ways, as Cinder's sense of alterity demonstrates – Cinder is not a girl, or at least girl enough (ironically, she is also too much, but I return to that). To compound the issue, Cinder's body also presents as 'boyish', 'stick-straight', 'angular', 'heavy' and artificial.[5] Despite these moves, Cinder is a girl, and the texts use a range of strategies to make this clear: Cinder refers to herself as a 'teenage girl' (Meyer 2012, 10) she uses feminine pronouns (she/her) and others identify her by those pronouns and the honorific miss. Moreover, despite her cybernetic operations, Cinder's 'reproductive system is almost untouched' (116).

First, reproductive anatomy, the processes of reproduction and reproduction itself are not requirements of adolescent girlhood. Indeed, the conflation of the two and how procreative potential 'others' women is part of what female-heroes work to undo. Like my discussion of periods and menstrual blood in the previous chapter, until 'we take seriously the notion that a "person" could normally at least always potentially, become two' (Battersby 1998, 2) and find a way to conceive identity formed in relation instead of opposition, the story will leverage procreative potential against everyone, particularly girls and women as they are the creatures it associates with procreation. For girls and women for whom – by choice or biology – procreation happens outside the 'norm', the story is worse.

At first glance, Cinder's untouched womb seems to recapitulate essentialist beliefs about what makes a woman, especially when it links that 'naturalness' to reproduction: the doctor making the above observation about Cinder's reproductive system also rather enthusiastically points out that while "'lots of female cyborgs are left infertile because of the invasive procedures'", he does not "'suspect [Cinder] will have any problems'" (Meyer 2012, 116). Pointing to this passage, Nicky Didicher, for example, argues that the 'untouched reproductive' system allows 'Meyer to resubscribe to an older version of femininity' (2020, 54). However, on closer inspection, the potential for procreation within a cyborg body, which is usually associated with replication or 'ectogenesis (conception outside of the womb)', reveals a deep ambiguity (Flanagan 2014, 126), one with the potential to reframe ontological assumptions around what it means to live and be in this world.

In the west, creation is privileged over procreation, which western discourse positions as 'elemental or physical or biological' while it construes creation as 'spiritual or metaphysical or symbolic' (Weigle 1989, 61). Owing to the structure of binary oppositions underpinning this story, women procreate while men create. For Haraway, the emancipatory potential of the cyborg lies in it being 'uncoupled from organic reproduction'; it does not have an 'origin story in the Western sense' (1991, 150). In this view, the cyborg is outside of the myth and is thus able to rewrite the Western 'myth of original unity' (that we began as a whole autonomous self but with entry into language and the Symbolic (Lacan) unity fragmented (1991). It is worth remembering that the archetypal hero story works to restore, however incompletely or impossible, that unity. Haraway's cyborg offers an alternative mythology, but in doing so, it does away with the very thing (the naturalness of her body and its procreative potential) that others women. The cyborg is a powerful metaphor, and female cyborgs have the power to disrupt the dominant view that science is rational, masculine and another discourse from which women are excluded. However, as Battersby writes, 'women are not clones; and neither do they reproduce like amoebae. The reproductive work of bearing and rearing children involves necessarily non-equal power relations, as well as a body that is messy, fleshy and gapes open to otherness – with otherness "within", as well as without' (1998, 59).

Procreation, the capacity to birth new selves, and the flesh, mess and gapes required by that process pose the biggest threat to the Western 'myth of original unity' (Haraway 1991, 150). Thus, for me, like Battersby, reproductive, procreative potential – and the threat it poses to unified conceptions of the self – must be considered, must be included within what it means to be a person if violent hierarchy, radical alterity, isolating individuality and erasure are to change. The cyborg, particularly the processes of ectogenesis, or babies in bottles, and the science, technology and disavowal of the blood, is the ideal of patriarchy. It represents birth that can be controlled.[6] Still, once again – and clearly – this is not to say that being a girl requires such capacity of even the begetting of children or the begetting of children 'naturally' (if there is such a thing). Instead, it is about finding ways to conceive the self through multicity, change and relation. It is about pushing the boundaries of what it means to be a hero, girl and human, and it is why Cinder's existence as a cyborg with an untouched womb is vitally important.

As a cyborg, Cinder embodies the ironic homogenization of the 'human' and 'machine'. As Donna Haraway describes, cyborg bodies 'do not resolve into larger wholes, even dialectically' (1991, 149). Instead, this body is 'about the tension of holding incompatible things together because both or all are necessary and true' (1991). Cinder has the cyborg potential to replicate, to reproduce 'uncoupled from organic reproduction' (1991) – especially because she is a mechanic – and the potential and the capacity to become more than one, to 'generate new selves from within the embodied (fleshy) self' and the threat that poses (Battersby 1998, 13). Cinder can detach and reattach her cybernetic limbs changing the shape and boundaries of her body, and she can repair other cyborgs, androids and machines, giving them new life. Cinder also has biological reproductive potential making her truly disruptive to patriarchal systems. Tellingly, despite the 'untouched' state of Cinder's reproductive system – which the text, she is not represented within The Lunar Chronicles as menstruating, a common occurrence in YA. However, Meyer confirmed on Twitter that Cinder does get her period, 'But they hardly seem to slow her down!' (2015c). The absence of menstruation, despite the presence of an 'untouched reproductive system', indicates how the fleshy materiality of the female body is silenced in patriarchal regimes and how mythopoeic YA isn't immune to those narratives, intervening in some areas even as it remains tied to the discourse in others.

Finally, contemporary Western culture is dominated by what Rosalind Gill describes as a postfeminist media 'sensibility' (2008).[7] This sensibility describes a way of living and being in the world significantly affecting girls and women and is underpinned by a neoliberal choice biography – the notion that one's biography (that is, identity) comprises the choices, often purchases, made (Gill 2008; Gill and Scharff 2011). It is the rendering of the self that is founded on the premise that the (correct) choices an individual makes form his/her identity while also granting agency. In other words, the makeover paradigm is created by the continual (re)presentation and (re)framing of the self within a narrower and narrower ideal, while being fuelled by neoliberal narratives of choice that are given extraordinary scope by the seemingly limitless options available in the modern, technological

West. Within this sensibility, the body is a key site of concern. It is where those choices are evidenced, and it is also the location of femininity. As Gill notes, 'Instead of regarding caring, nurturing or motherhood as central to femininity (all of course highly problematic and exclusionary), in today's media, possession of a "sexy body" is presented as women's key (if not sole) source of identity' (2008, 149). This 'sexy' body is not about sex – desire, pleasure, or reproduction. This 'sexy body' – that Cinder does not possess (or which is not a part of Cinder) – is a superficial facsimile. Sex-y bodies, bodies that are capable of sex, pleasure, and reproduction are radically excluded from the model, and a consideration of the Lunar Glamour allows the impact of this superficiality to emerge.

The Lunar Glamour: Appearances May Be Deceiving

The Lunar glamour – 'what they [Lunars] call the illusion of themselves that they project into the minds of others' (Meyer 2012, 171) – offers an opportunity to consider the relation between surface/subtext, discourse/materiality in more detail, while also considering the implications of not 'measuring up' to the surface requirements. Furthermore, the nature of this glamour – its interest in appearance, femininity, and 'glamour' in the ordinary sense of the word – invites comparisons with makeover culture, with its cosmetic surgery and selfie filters. The Lunar glamour is the makeover in its ideal form: instant, ever changeable, and without scars; that is, the Lunar glamour is a sort of perpetual, real-time, filtered selfie, and it produces Cinderella's, if not sparkly, luminous, heightened, fantasy femininity. The Lunar glamour is also intensely about beauty, power, and control. Shells – Lunars without the ability to manipulate bioelectricity – androids and mirrors (because they do not have bioelectricity) are immune to the Lunar ability, while Cinder – owing to her liminal perspective – can see through it. As this ability is about power and control, shells, androids, mirrors, and Cinder are threats to that control.

Superficially, there is no visible difference between humans and Lunars. Indeed, Cinder is a Lunar but is unaware of that aspect of her being until she is revealed as the missing Princess Selene at the end of the first book of her quartet. While there is no visible difference between humans and Lunars, most Lunars can manipulate bioelectricity, or 'the energy that is naturally created by all living things' (Meyer 2012, 176). They can do magic, even as this world goes to great lengths to argue the Lunar gift is not magic. Nevertheless, Lunars can create a glamour, effectively a real-time, filtered selfie with this ability. They can also manipulate the world in such a way as to make 'people see what the Lunar wishes them to see, and even feel what the Lunar wishes them to feel' (171). Effectively, Lunars project their view of the world (and of themselves) onto others, changing the way the world is seen and understood; gifted Lunars shape their world to their will. In principle, this ability does not affect physical, material reality; it is a perceptual shift, a discursive reshaping – so it seems. However, as I will argue, the Lunar glamour (a discourse) has a material weight and presence at odds with its elusive nature.

First, the Lunar glamour, like Alanna's cross-dressing, questions the connection between appearance and body, a questioning deeply implicated in contemporary assumptions concerning gender. Specifically, the Lunar glamour questions the contemporary Western belief that femininity depends on a body that appears feminine. After encountering two Lunar 'ladies' (Meyer 2015b, 591), the following exchange occurs between Thorne and Cress, a shell. In this exchange, 'Thorne let out a low whistle. "Holy spades. The women in this place". Cress bristled. "You mean the *glamours* in this place. One of them was a man". Stumbling, Thorne looked down at her. "You don't say. Which one?"' (591). The Lunar glamour is powerful enough to erase those secondary sex characteristics that were, for example, so integral to Alanna's becoming a girl, a potentially empowering ability – for those who have it. Shells, like Cress, are unable to participate in this appearance-altering behaviour (but they can see through it). For those who can wield it, the glamour does not create an even playing field; it does not improve the situation people face when not physically meeting norms and standards. Instead, it heightens and intensifies expectations. These women are not just women; they are 'holy spades' women.

This twofold construction of glamour – a magical ability and an ability concerned with beauty – speaks to glamour as conceived in Western consensus reality. The Lunar glamour unites the original and contemporary uses of the word, an issue at stake for Rachel Moseley. Moseley suggests, 'in the history of the usage of the word [glamour], the primary meaning – "magic, enchantment, spell" – has been displaced by the idea of surface or physical feminine allure' (2002, 404).[8] This is the Lunar glamour, or, should I say, the Lunar glamour is both 'magic, enchantment, spell' and a creating of 'allure'. Interestingly, while both male and female Lunars construct glamours, the descriptions of Lunar appearance often tend toward the feminine: 'He [Jael] was willowy and lean, with wavy dark hair and near-black eyes that burned in the candlelight' (Meyer 2013, 278). Within this world, a gendered appearance is mutable. In the quest for pretty or beauty, the glamour aligns women and men with the feminine, as 'one of them was a man' indicated above (Meyer 2015a, 591). Here, the attributes 'willowy' and 'wavy dark hair' speak to conventional markers of femininity. While it is unclear if this is Jael's glamoured appearance or his 'natural' one, it does describe the kind of appearance preferred by Lunars.

The central aim of Moseley's article is to unite glamour's two definitions – magic and appearance – to trace, through the figure of the 'teen witch' (403), shifting discourses of feminism. Moseley states, 'in reinstating the primary meaning of the word, a profound but contradictory link is posited between femininity and magic in which femininity is produced as superficial and deceptive charm, mysterious and unknowable essence, and as power' (2002, 404, emphasis original). Within The Lunar Chronicles, this 'link' is manifest in the figure of the glamour-wielding Lunar, and this Lunar, as I discussed above, has significant implications for femininity. The Lunar glamour is power, but it is also about heightened fantasy femininity: Cinderella's femininity. As such, it offers femininity as an illusion, as powerful and persuasive, but an illusion. With the glamour, there is no depth – femininity is only performance – but there is also a profound rift between the glamour and the body's materiality, what the text posits as a kind of 'truth', and what I refer to as materiality.

The glamour also illustrates the unreliability of appearance if only because it erases difference while also expressing bodily unrealities, as Scarlet (a refiguring of Little Red Riding in The Lunar Chronicles) is narrated as musing: 'Stupid Lunars and their stupid glamours. Anyone could be an enemy. Anyone she passed could be a thaumaturge or one of those lousy aristocrats or the queen herself', and Scarlet wouldn't be able to tell the difference (2015c, 541). It is not just that anyone could be an 'enemy', 'thaumaturge', 'aristocrat' or 'the queen'. It is that, given the glamour, anyone could be anyone. Appearance is not enough to determine who someone really is. The Lunar glamour aside, there is a distancing implicit in appearance; there is a space between the viewer and the viewed, and in this space, misapprehension can occur. The dissonance between self and appearance that always already exists is heightened through this glamour; however, the novels also refuse to posit the body as the only truth.

Known as the 'endless lie', Levana's glamour not only masks a body that is thoroughly 'disfigured' (Meyer 2015b, 692) but the glamour becomes 'so real that she [Levana] had no use of her true skin anymore' (2015a, 96). Crucially, as with all glamours, Levana's 'endless lie' – despite its extenuated existence – does not change the physical body. Indeed, it offers a disjuncture between the body appearance more profound than any of the glamours I mentioned above.

> Beneath the glamour, her face was disfigured from ridges and scars, sealing shut her left eye. The destroyed skin continued down her jaw and

neck, disappearing beneath the collar of her dress. Her hair was thinner and a lighter shade of brown, and great chunks were missing where the scars had reached around to the back of her head. More scars could be seen on her left arm where her silk sleeve didn't hide them.

(2015b, 692)

These 'ridges' and 'scars' are Levana's 'true skin', and it is their truth that the glamour conceals, not only from others but also from Levana herself: 'after so many years of wrapping herself in the glamour, it was nearly impossible to let it go' (Meyer 2015a, 191). This use of 'truth' concerning the 'true skin' does not posit the fleshy body as more 'true' or 'real' than the glamour. The glamour is its own kind of truth, the 'truth' of the way Levana wishes to be seen. Thus, this notion of 'true skin' appeals to the physical materiality of the body that is posited as a kind of truth.

Poignantly, Levana relies so heavily on her glamour instead of taking advantage of surgery that would materially improve her body (as opposed to the transience of the glamour) because with surgery 'there would always be scars no matter how faint' (2015b, 206). This is the power of the Lunar glamour and the photoshopped selfie. There are no scars with either of these mechanisms, yet they still transform the body. The 'makeovers' they afford represent the ideal form of bodily improvement, a better body without evidence (scars) of the body that came before. The transformations wrought through the glamour and selfie also speak to the ephemeral quality of a 'perfect' appearance. Ideals do not last, so new changes, new makeovers, need always be enacted. The temporary nature of the glamour and the selfie allow – because they are illusions of (temporary) perfection – for this perpetual making over, reinforcing the mandate to work embedded in makeover culture.

Still, despite the transience of this magical makeover and the fact it is only a perceptual change, for Levana, it is much more profound. Her glamour has become reality now: 'by now, so many had forgotten what she truly looked like', and 'her glamour was the reality now, no matter what Evret thought, no matter what anyone thought' (2015a, 206). While there is a tension here – perhaps, a desire on Levana's part for the glamour to be 'real' and not just the 'reality now' – the glamour's dominance is clear. The glamour's hold is strong: 'after so many years of wrapping herself in the glamour, it was nearly impossible to let it go. Her brain struggled to release her grip on the manipulation' (2015a, 191). While this shows another way in which the texts refuse to posit the 'truth' of the body (physical shape or glamour) definitively, this reading of the glamour also and more importantly crystallizes the insidious nature of the selfie: it – glamour or selfie – may be an illusion, but it is a powerful one, not least owing to its pervasiveness. After all, how many girls have stood before mirrors unable to 'see' anything other than the 'flaws' dictated by popular and media culture's pervasive images of perfection?

Androids: Iko is a girl

The dominant myth of adolescent girlhood relegates femininity to a bodily property. Indeed, this is one of the elements Rosalind Gill identifies as contributing to the postfeminist media sensibility dominating contemporary Western culture (see 2008). Essentially, Cinderella is, at least in part, the hero's prize (and thus a woman) because she looks the part. Equating femininity with the body comes at the expense of other possible ways of being a woman and radically excludes anyone not being a woman in this way or without the 'correct' body. The Lunar Chronicles disrupt this view of womanhood in several ways. For example, in how Cinder is still a girl despite the mechanical, inorganic things (coded as masculine) that are a part of her body and, thus, her self, and the complex interrogation of appearance made possible through the Lunar Glamour. Androids, especially Iko – Cinder's android friend who functions much like Cinderella's mice – further complicate the attribution of femininity to a body property by doing away with the (fleshy, organic) body. In so doing, these androids also demonstrate how the representational economy traps women by constructing the body as something that can never fully, or permanently, meet the ideal.

First, there are several kinds of androids in the world of The Lunar Chronicles, ranging from designer escort-droids with 'tauntingly ideal feminine shapes' to models that are clearly machines 'with a spherical head atop a pear-shaped body' (2012, 287 and 8). While male escort droids do exist within this world, escorts are 'mostly girls', or, at least, female escort droids are more overwhelmingly discussed (2014, 406). The focus on girl droids is, in part, due to how one of the main characters, Iko, presents as female/feminine, but the implications are wider. For example, the makeover paradigm dominating contemporary Western culture overwhelmingly applies to women and girls, and androids offer its 'fantas[y] of rearranging, transforming, and correcting, limitless improvement and change' on the body by doing away with the fleshy material body, which always resists that fantasy, especially its goal of 'defying [...] the historicity, the mortality, and indeed, the very materiality of the body' (Bordo 1993, 245). The android offers this fantasy in its ideal form. The android body comprises parts that can be 'special order[ed]', with 'replacement piece[s]' that can keep pace with every fleeting trend – for a price (Meyer 2014, 529). As such, and much like the Lunar glamour, the android offers an avenue for interrogating the specular economy upon which the heroic romance depends. Although the android's break from the fleshy material body offers a different context for considering both the fantasy and its repercussions, while also commenting on what it means to be human.

While the examples of androids are many (including humanoid androids that look more like humans than humans do, Iko, who functions much like Cinderella's mice, offers the most sustained investigation of what it means to be a girl not least owing to the two graphic novels focusing on her (Meyer 2017; 2018). In this discussion, however, I focus on representations in the four core novels. When first introduced, Iko looks more like a robot than a human: 'a bulbous head', wheels and 'pronged hand[s]' (193 and 11). In other words, there is very little chance anyone would identify her as a girl, but they would identify her as an android, a machine. However, Iko identifies as a girl, and she is consistently coded as female and feminine, despite her mechanical existence. Iko's pronoun is she, as is also the case for other androids coded as female. She also presents as heterosexual when fawning over Prince Kai (this world's Prince Charming): '"Prince Kai! Check my fan, I think I'm overheating"' (2012, 14), and Iko is interested in fashion, trends, and love stories – all of which are typically associated with young girls. Angela Insenga even goes as far as suggesting that Iko 'possesses attributes' of not just a girl but a 'stereotypical adolescent girl', particularly noting how Iko's 'metallic voice squeak[s]' when she meets Prince Kai (2018, 61). Identifying Iko as not just a girl but an adolescent girl is particularly powerful given how female adolescence is tied to the emergence of secondary sex characteristics; as a machine, Iko lacks the biology necessary for such emergence and, yet, she's still a girl.

Iko's being a girl when she is an android depends on something more than appearance, something more than biology. In her phenomenological account of girlhood, Iris Marion Young argues that 'femininity' is 'not a mysterious quality or essence that all women have by virtue of their being biologically female' (2005, 144). Instead, Young argues that femininity or being a girl 'is, rather, a set of structures and conditions that delimit the typical situation of being a woman in a particular society, as well as the typical way in which this situation is lived by the women themselves' (144). In the previous chapter, Alanna was able to slip into the heroic romance because she lacked the 'mysterious essence or quality' women are meant to have (because you can't have that without the right anatomy and girls don't have anything until puberty). Like Alanna, Iko does not have some 'mysterious quality or essence' (2005). Unlike Alanna (for whom becoming a girl should have been inevitable), Iko also has no biology; she will never develop, at least 'naturally', those secondary sex characteristics that were integral to Alanna's disruption. Instead, Iko solely comports herself (or is constructed as doing so) in such a way as to signify girlhood, even when her body does not meet the appearance-based standards of the category. Iko is also not limited to this one body, and the bodies she inhabits offer a powerful interrogation of the mind/body split as they continue pushing the boundaries of what it means to be a girl.

Across the series, Iko exists in and through several bodies: the bulbous body, The Rampion (a spaceship) and, finally, as an escort-droid body first associated with Darla. (Darla takes over running The Rampion.) Importantly, Iko's final body isn't final at all – it is one of those customizable android bodies. These moves are made possible by Iko's 'personality chip', which is also responsible for her desire (if androids – like prizes – can have desires) to be human or to at least have a humanoid body. In this way, Iko's body and self, figured as the personality chip, do not align. The breakdown between her self and her appearance offers an avenue for further exploring the effects of hegemonic norms, standards and assumptions, especially as this construction appears to initially reinforce the mind/body split underpinning liberal humanism.

Iko's mind, self or soul is represented by that personality chip, and it can be detached from her 'body' and re-installed in other bodies. For Insenga, this is another instance of Meyer effectively resubscribing to patriarchal norms and standards, as Didicher argued Cinder's 'almost untouched' 'reproductive system' did (Meyer 2012, 116; Didicher 2020, 54). Insenga specifically argues, 'by retaining Iko's mind/body dichotomy, Meyer undercuts the entire concept of material embodiment' she otherwise offers (2018, 62). Material embodiment is an important concept in material feminism and it argues that 'although bodies are mediated by discourse, they are solely constructed by discourse' and that bodies have a kind of agency or presence that we cannot discount (Trites 2018, xvi). Citing Katherine Hayles (1999), Insenga further argues that to be a materialist reading, Iko's personality would have to 'change, [be] shaped by the new environment' (1999). Iko's mind or sense of self would need to change with each new body. I don't actually disagree with the principle of Insenga's argument. For example, the female-hero model insists on material embodiment for the very reasons Insenga deems it necessary: including the body within what it means to be a hero disrupts structure of opposition underpinning the hero story. However, there is a correlation between Iko's personality chip (or mind) and her bodies. Not least because Iko's existence depends on both her material body and her personality chip, and it requires that the two be connected.

Owing to this connection, Iko's personality shifts across each change of body, and it correlates to the kind of body she inhabits even as it changes that body – and the latter is just as important as the former. First, Iko cannot exist without being connected to a body. For example, between her personality chip being removed from the bulbous body in *Cinder* (2012, 282) and its reinstallation in The Rampion in *Scarlet* (Meyer 2013, 154), Iko is not embedded or connected to a body. For 260 pages split across two novels, Iko's personality chip exists in Cinder's calf (remember, pockets but built into the body). According to the world's timeline, she ceases to exist for two weeks (246). During this time, Iko does not exist as a being with any kind of agency or even semblance of being. She ceases to exist in any active way, though she does live on in memory. As Cinder prepares to go to the ball (as I discuss below), she tries 'not to think of Iko, who should have been at her side' (instead of in the compartment in her calf). The memory, Iko's presence, impinges on the present even though Iko is absent. In one sense, this disrupts the linear teleological imperative of the hero story, much as Alanna did in the previous chapter, but it also demonstrates the necessity of a relationship between the mind and body: Iko's existence depends on her connection – on her literally being connected– to bodies; as such, Iko offers a powerful counter to the 'illusory concept of ontological self-sufficiency' underpinning the heroic romance (Moran 2018, 260). Relationality, kinship and ethical responsibility are integral to reframing what it means to be a girl, and they are central to the inclusive model of selfhood female-heroes put forward.

Here, Iko cannot exist without connection, without both herself (self) and a body, and those connections change her, even as she changes the bodies she inhabits. When 'waking up' as/in the Rampion, Iko declares that she 'can't see you [Cinder]' and that she 'feel[s] funny' (Meyer 2013, 155), both of which are a result of her changed shape and the way she engages the world around her owing to that shape/body. Spaceships don't have eyes (or even approximations of eyes), and they are presumably (much) larger than Iko's round, bulbous form. The changes to Iko's body have a direct impact on her sense of self, echoing the cries of too many (especially) adolescent girls, Iko whines, 'I'm enormous' and complains of having 'humungous' feet (landing gear) (156). Iko's sense of self has, dramatically, changed. However, Iko also affects the bodies she inhabits. The ship's heating system becomes a tool for signalling that Iko is blushing, and 'the way Iko's fan used to spin extra fast when she was processing information' becomes a 'rumbl[ing] beneath Cinder's, feet soft as a kitten's purr' (246). The ship changes Iko and Iko changes the ship, if only temporarily. Still, in both cases the boundary between self and other blurs with implications for adolescent girlhood, not least because Iko desires (if androids can) a humanoid, female, and feminine body, which she gets when her personality chip is installed into Darla, an escort droid with 'perfect symmetry and ridiculously lush eyebrows' (2014, 355).

Iko's desire for a humanoid, female body, and her installation into the body of an escort droid appears to recapitulate the 'wrong body discourse' prevalent in transgender YA. This discourse sees 'self-identity put into conflict with and ultimately trump[ing] the body' (Putzi 2017, 423). The 'wrongness' is resolved through a 'teleological trajectory [...] toward the achievement of one's true self, which necessitates that a character be able to pass successfully as the gender of their choice' (426–7). Iko's identification as a girl while existing in bodies that are, quite literally, the antithesis of girlhood seems to recapitulate this discourse (one that also maps onto that mind/body split), especially once Iko receives the escort droid body. The point of trans YA stories operating within this discourse is to re-align identity and the body, reinforcing the one-to-one relationship between self and appearance. Iko achieving the escort-droid body appears to fall in line with this discourse, especially when that body is one of 'perfect proportions, peachy skin, and royalty-approved posture' (Meyer 2014, 84). However, what Iko really demonstrates is that there is no 'right' body.

Darla's body, like the bodies of many escort-droids, has the necessary markers of beauty and femininity to make her a girl, a hero's prize. Her body is premade with those markers. As Cinderella is the 'maid predestined to be his bride', this escort droid is 'pre made' to be a prize. However, and as Cinderella showed, the escort droid must also work to keep up appearances. In this case, she must upgrade and customize her appearance: 'I [Iko] checked the manufacturer's catalogue and I can upgrade to forty different eye colors! I kind of like the metallic gold ones, but we'll see. Trends are so fleeting, you know' (Meyer 2014, 387). Not only does this speak to the consumerism pervading contemporary Western culture (Iko won't be able to purchase those 'metallic gold ones' without money) but it also highlights the superficiality of appearance and the problems inherent in relegating femininity to a bodily property because even as a non-humanoid android, indeed, even as a spaceship, Iko remains a girl, a reality that many are denied.

Dismantling 'fixed' perfection

Ritual rebirth, the point at which the hero dies to his old self so that he may be 'clothed [...] in the mantle of his vocation', is the fulcrum upon which the heroic romance depends (Campbell [1968] 1973, 15). To become a hero, the would-be-hero undergoes a symbolic or ritual death-rebirth. This part of his journey signifies the radical break between his past self and the hero he becomes. As I've mentioned, it's usually difficult, dangerous and disgusting and often symbolized by entering a cave or whale's belly. The hero's prize also undergoes the ritual of symbolic death and rebirth, although hers sparkles. In the garden of her family home, Cinderella is bathed in sparkles and emerges as an 'eligible maiden' (Geronimi, Jackson, and Luske 1950). The locations of both journeys (cave or belly and garden) are symbolically important: the hero's attempts to recreate his first birth by reappropriating it, and the prize's garden symbolizing femininity and fertility. It is also adjacent to her familial home, thus tying those things to the family structure (of which the hero is the head). The garden becomes an important site of ritual transference (moving Cinderella from her father's home to the ball and then the castle).

To become a cyborg, Cinder is not bathed in sparkles, nor is her transformation instantaneous; she spends eight years 'in a tank, sleeping and dreaming and growing' as doctors operate to repair the injuries she received during the fire Levana orchestrated (Meyer 2013, 32). The time and the shift from sparkle to extensive and dramatic reconstructive, life-saving surgery are vital. First, the transformation into a cyborg, including the attempt on her life that made it necessary, disrupts 'normal' linear development, a disruption the eight years compounds. Second, the body produced through this extended rebirth is not the fit and able body both required and produced by the makeover paradigm. It is not only fragmented and scarred and thus seemingly unfit for neoliberal selfhood but it also engages technology in a way that has ramifications for both subjectivity and femininity. In short, Cinder is not 'clothed [...] in the mantle of h[er] vocation' as the hero's (bride) prize during her symbolic death-rebirth (Campbell [1949] 1968, 15). Instead, she is transformed into a human-machine hybrid whose 'bodily awkwardness' (Didicher 2020, 53), or hybridity, offers a platform for reframing the marriage plot purpose of the ball and, thus, the goal of 'successful' adolescent girlhood.

In *Scarlet* (book two of The Lunar Chronicles), Cinder discovers the 'secret chamber' in which her transformation, her symbolic death-rebirth, into a cyborg occurred (Meyer 2013, 318). The secret chamber is half 'operating room', half 'workshop', and this hybrid space produces Cinder's cyborg, her human-machine self (Meyer 2013), and it demonstrates how Cinder occupies a position between the poles of human/machine and woman/man. The 'workshop' half is responsible for her cybernetic technology. While the 'operating room' technically contributes to saving her life, it also speaks to the kind of space in which cosmetic surgery, the pinnacle of makeover activities, takes place. Indeed, in contemporary Western culture, potential prizes do not have fairy godmothers who can magically transform them into prizes. Instead, they can undertake a myriad of mundane makeover practices: new wardrobe, bikini season diet, new hairstyle and – at the pinnacle – cosmetic surgery, where '"difference" is made over into sameness', as Anne Balsamo argues (1996, 58).

Cosmetic surgery actualizes those fantasies 'of rearranging, transforming, and correcting, limitless improvement and change' on the body for people who don't have magical fairy godmothers or aren't androids (Bordo 1993, 245), and as Anne Balsamo describes, images play a key role as a means of 'discipline[ing] the unruly female body' (1996, 56). Of this image, Balsamo suggests:

> it is not so much the inner or essential woman that is visualized; her interior story has no truth of its own. Both her surface and her interiority are flattened and dispersed. Cosmetic surgeons use technological imagining devices to reconstruct the female body as a signifier of ideal feminine beauty.
>
> (1996, 57–8)

I am specifically concerned with the flattening and dispersion that occurs with this image: with how the body's curves and contours, not to mention this interior story, are refused. Within this image, the body also has no meaning; it merely signifies this ideal. As I've discussed, the selfie plays the same disciplining role, but with a twist: through photo editing software, the adolescent girl uses 'technological imagining devices to reconstruct' herself. This image also erases the self that came before; it does away with history and depth.

In the room mentioned above – in which Cinder discovers her origin story as a cyborg – she also finds an image of herself prior to that transformation. She finds a record of a girl she was before, the girl who needed life-saving surgery.

> She was wrapped in bandages from her neck to the stump of her left thing. Her right arm and shoulder were uncovered, showing the skin that was gouged bloody red in spots, bright pink and glossy in others. She had no hair and the burn marks continued up her neck and across her cheek. The left side of her face was swollen and disfigured, only the slit of her eye could be seen, and a line of stitches ran along her earlobe before cutting across to her lips.
>
> (2013, 324)

This image is important for several reasons. One, it makes visible a body of difference, one that does not resemble Cinderella's or the many other images of perfection bombarding girls and women in contemporary Western culture. More importantly, it provides Cinder with a history, which hegemonic discourse refuses women and children.

This image tells the story of her existence prior to her symbolic death-rebirth. Aside from dream fragments or nightmares, Cinder does not remember the fire set to kill her or the surgery that saved her. Aside from some 'scar tissue around her thigh and wrist, where the prostheses had been attached' (2012, 82.), Cinder's body bears 'no scar, no sign of these wounds' (2012). As such, this image is an important means of granting Cinder a history. Symbolic death-rebirth marks a radical break between what was and what is (ideally a rational autonomous being unaffected by embodiment or a shiny, sparkly prize). In this sense, the image is important for disrupting that break. Yes, Cinder may bear little signs of that 'before' now, but it dramatically impacted her now, even if she can't see the injuries. The person she was before still exists; she just looks different. The scar tissue is particularly important.

Scars are central both to how the dominant narrative (hegemonic discourse) assimilates difference into its frame, as I discussed through Cinder, and to how difference might, instead, reshape that frame. For one, scars offer a history. They are a kind of writing of the body's history on its surface. The absence of scars – the story of the body – makes 'sameness' even more pervasive. Crucially, I am not calling for intentional, self-inflicted harming in this interest with scars. Yet, as self-harm, specifically self-mutilation, is an issue faced by many within contemporary Western culture, this reading does not take those scars lightly (Miskec and McGee 2007). Here, I am concerned with scars as a record and with how making scars visible even if only in narration offers a re-mapping of the contours of the body, particularly when scars serve as evidence of where and how the body has been pieced together.

For the remainder of this section, I want to consider how the tension between human and machine, or the irony of Cinder's body, offers a platform to reframe the marriage-plot purpose of the ball, specifically how it offers an opportunity to incorporate Cinder's 'bodily awkwardness', or hybridity, into the story instead of erasing it (Didicher 2020, 53). This intervention is possible because of the change to Cinder's ritual rebirth – both the tank in which she spent eight years 'sleeping and dreaming and growing' (M. Meyer 2013, 32) and the second rebirth that occurred in the secret chamber, a rebirth that provided Cinder with history, depth and complexity.

In many versions of the 'Persecuted Heroine' tale, Cinderella attends the ball (or church) to find 'true love' (Bacchilega 1993; Jones 1993; Uther 2004). In The Lunar Chronicles, Cinder attends the ball to warn Prince Kai, soon-to-be ruler of the Commonwealth, of imminent danger: Levana plans to force Kai to marry her, announcing their engagement at the ball. From there, she'll take over the Commonwealth and use it as a staging ground 'to wage war on the rest of Earth' (Bacchilega 1993; Jones 1993; Uther 2004). The only way Cinder can warn the Prince – comms (text messages) are being monitored – is to crash the ball. To do so, Cinder borrows her now-deceased step-sister Peony's ballgown. (Iko managed to save it when all of Peony's other possessions were destroyed after she contracts letumosis and dies.)

In many ways, the dress Cinder wears to the ball is the dress that Lady Tremaine, Anastasia and Drizella destroy, while simultaneously destroying Cinderella's agency in the Disney films (1950 or 2015). It is also not the gown Fairy Godmother created, and it feels 'like poison ivy sliding over Cinder's skin' (Meyer 2012, 324). She feels like 'a fake', 'an imposter' in it (Meyer 2012). While she may feel this way, wearing this ballgown allows Cinder to entry into the hero story, as the prize. It is, in effect, a disguise, much like Alanna's cross-dressing in the previous chapter. Cinder's disguise, or her entry into the heroic romance as an approximation of his prize, includes three key elements: wearing the 'silk dress' (2012, 324), re-attaching the 'rusted' foot she removed at the novel's opening (2012) and replacing the heavy-work gloves she usually wears with 'silk' ones, as I discuss in the following section (2012). Together, these three actions make Cinder's appearance appropriate enough to access the ball.

First, re-attaching the foot, even if it is 'too-small' (3), makes her body whole, or as whole as it can be. Flanagan notes that the removal of this foot is a representation of Cinder freeing herself from 'a patriarchal symbol of feminine subornation' (2014, 63), one made even richer given *Cinder*'s setting in a futuristic reimagining China, where footbinding was once practised. It is important to note that despite the novel's Asian setting and a range of nominal ethnicities The Lunar Chronicles largely operates through what Green-Barteet, et al. identify as a 'colorblind ideology' (2017, 2). That is, a strategy whereby novels or series 'purport to be racially progressive' in that they 'include characters who are described in ways that suggest they are racialized, but the texts do not directly address race, racism, or racialized difference' (2). Cinder re-attaching this foot is not, however, a moment of resubscribing to viewpoints condoning footbinding. Instead, it is a radical act that allows her to enter the ball. Moreover, it becomes an avenue for disrupting symbols of femininity from within the system – Cinder loses this foot (not some fragile glass slipper) fleeing the ball.

The silk dress, gloves and, if not glass-slippers, high heels are markers of the hyper fantasy femininity necessary for girls and women to take part in the hero story. Cinder usually wears 'comfortable and utilitarian' clothes, as Meyer describes on her website. These clothes, including 'cargo pants' (2012, 14), are appropriate to Cinder's work as a mechanic. For example, she can store a 'wrench' in one of the pockets (97). Silk dresses, most dresses, rarely include such useful things as pockets. The dress and gloves contrast those clothes and her cyborg body continually threatens to break through: 'The silk gloves felt too fine, too delicate, too flimsy, and she worried she might snag them on some poorly placed screw' (2012, 325). While she might be able to wear the ballgown marking sparkly, fantasy femininity for a time, her cyborg body refuses the flattening and erasure that it represents.

Finally, there is also no pumpkin-turned-coach or mice-turned-horses in this trip to the ball. As a mechanic who fixes things, Cinder needs no 'fixer'. The fairy godmother's power to effect change is hers. As such, Cinder drives herself to the ball, in a car that she scavenged and repaired (Meyer 2012, 325–8). In this way, Cinder's attending the ball is an ironic coupling of agency (there is no fairy godmother, and she drives herself) and self-policing (adherence to norms by wearing a dress). Going to the ball offers the possibility of escape from – while at the same time remaining tied to – traditional norms. Indeed, it takes what happens at and after the ball to bring about the kinds of personal and political changes female-heroes, owing to their liminal perspective, can realize.

Seeing through the superficial

These readings – of the Lunar glamour, the way Cinder's being-cyborg complicates gendered expectations and the material changes Iko experiences as she moves between bodies – have been concerned with superficial changes to the body, that is to say, with changes that occur at the level of the body's surface to affect perceptions of the body, as is also the case with the selfie. Iko appears as a robot, spaceship and escort-droid, a disfigured Lunar appears able-bodied, a Lunar man appears as a woman and all gifted Lunars appear, when using their glamour, more 'beautiful' (2012, 172). These changes do not physically alter the body, excluding Iko's moves between bodies, suggesting that these changes are purely superficial. As I asked when considering Levana's glamour, how superficial are 'superficial' changes, especially when the illusion is so pervasive that it is all that is seen and thus known?

To further dismantle 'fixed perfection' (and make sure it sticks), mythopoeic YA also models how these expanded versions of girlhood might come about outside their pages. They model the shifts in perspective needed to bring about change, giving readers tools to make those changes. In *Maiden USA: Girl Icons Come of Age*, Kathleen Sweeney advocates for increasing girls' media literacy. For Sweeney, media literacy gives girls the tools to decode the messages presented by media culture by placing them behind the camera rather than in front of it. Doing so helps, as Sweeney argues, girls 'see' how the images in magazines and on television and film are created. It disrupts the concealed constructedness. In one sense, this echoes my earlier reading of the Lunar glamour; the glamour illustrates the images people need to see through, even as it shows how deeply those images can and do affect how we live and be in the world and how we understand it.

In The Lunar Chronicles, Cinder is preoccupied with hiding her cybernetic parts – because they are not human and not feminine: 'She covered her steel hand first, and though her right palm began to sweat immediately inside the thick material, she felt more comfortable with the gloves on, hiding the plating of her left hand' (2012, 5). While the narration is telling, these 'thick' gloves, one of which is 'hiding the plating of her left hand', directly contrast with the 'silk gloves' Cinder later wears to attend the ball (324). Where those 'felt too fine, too delicate, too flimsy' (324), the 'thick' gloves cause Cinder's 'right palm' to 'sweat' (5). In this way, while the hiding – or revealing – of Cinder's cybernetic parts is obviously at stake with these pairs of gloves, the gloves also speak to what it means to be (human) female within this world. The 'silk gloves', gifted to Cinder by Prince Kai and ostensibly for her to wear at the ball (324), mark (human) femininity within this world. Not only are the gloves 'pure silk and shining sliver-white' as well as 'the finest pair' Cinder 'could have imagined', but they are also 'fit for a princess' (299), a certain kind of heteronormative femininity as I discussed in relation to Disney's Cinderella. The silk gloves mark femininity; the 'thick' gloves hide 'plate metal'.

Gloves may seem like an unimportant or less meaningful intervention into myths of adolescent girlhood than other deconstructions available in mythopoeic YA. After putting on 'a pale pink shift, pink wool stockings, and a fine wool gown', Kel, the female-hero in Pierce's Tortall Universe, sees herself as possibly 'the girl she would have been had she not tried for her shield' (2001, 261). However, she quickly – and somewhat bemusedly – speculates, 'maybe I'm the same whatever I wear, she thought. It's just easier to fight in breeches' (261). This example offers a, perhaps, more obvious intervention in appearance-based expectations, at least in as much as adolescent girls do not usually wear thick gloves for work or to hide their cybernetic parts, nor do they wear silk ones to mark femininity, at least not these days (white, elbow-length silk gloves were once a marker of femininity). However, hands and gloves speak to connection and relation in a way that feet and glass slippers do not, and they foreshadow an interest in touch that I return to in the next chapter and Conclusion.

The 'plate metal' is integral. Not only is it not feminine but it is also that which is not human: 'Then the prince reached for her hand – her cybernetic hand. Cinder tensed, terrified that he would feel the hard metal, even through the gloves [...]. She mentally urged the robotic limb to go soft, to be pliant, to be human' (Meyer 2012, 163). In other words, Cinder is not only not feminine – at least, not the heteronormative feminine marked by the silk gloves. Thus, while there are two kinds of hiding occurring here – the covering with a glove and the mental urging of softness, pliability and humanness, both speak to a preoccupation with keeping the cybernetic body, a body that disrupts expectations of feminine appearance, hidden. In this way, the narration also situates itself within popular and media culture discourses. Cinder could be any adolescent girl hiding braces, a prosthesis or any other 'thing' deemed inappropriate to the appropriate – thin, fit, whole – appearance.

While Cinder is initially ashamed of her cybernetic parts, she 'progresses' to new understandings throughout her journey.

> Cinder peeled off her work gloves and shoved them into her back pocket. There was still a tinge of panic at the action – her brain reminding her, out of habit, that she wasn't supposed to remove the gloves in front of anyone, especially Kai – but she ignored it. Kai didn't blink at the unveiling of her cyborg hand, like he didn't even notice it anymore.
>
> (2015b, 92)

This self-reflexive engagement with Cinder's preoccupation ('out of habit') with hiding the cybernetic parts allows the text to comment on its initial alignment. In so doing, it also offers a comment on that earlier preoccupation while also demonstrating how Cinder's view has changed, '[s]he knew she was thinking about it less and less. Sometimes she was even surprised upon seeing a flash of metal in the corner of her eye when she went to pick something up. It was strange. She'd always been aware of it before, mortified that someone might see' (92). While problematically still giving weight to Kai's not 'notic[ing]' her hand anymore, the narration makes it clear that not being 'mortified' upon the 'unveiling of her cyborg hand' is an accomplishment of Cinder's because she 'knew she was thinking about it less and less' (2015b).

Interestingly, within the transition, the gloves become not that which hides her body but, instead, her 'work gloves' – they are given a purpose. They are helpful to her work as a mechanic. While gloves do not feature in contemporary discourses of girlhood, Cinder's shift in perspective is integral. It models precisely the kinds of changes in perspective girls could make outside of the texts if exposed to images, like these, within the texts. Moreover, gloves could be glasses, a brace or a uniform, things adolescent girls do more frequently engage. These sorts of narrations – the reflexive engagements with issues of popular and media culture that show alternatives – are crucial for demonstrating, for modelling, how such shifts in perspective can, and do, occur.

The importance of this kind of reframing work is reiterated by how frequently the text demonstrates this change in perspective. Here,

> Putting them [heavy gloves] on had dredged up a number of memories. There had been a time when she wore gloves everywhere, when she'd been so ashamed of being cyborg she refused to let her prostheses show. She couldn't recall when that had changed, but now the glove felt like a lie.
>
> (2015, 167)

Speaking to issues of disability and difference, Cinder is no longer 'ashamed' not just of 'being cyborg' but also of 'let[ting] her prostheses show'. The prostheses are a part of her body's 'truth', and they can be included within Cinder's body image (her sense of self), and in so being, they create a new 'true skin' or 'body image' (Grosz 1994, 39; Meyer 2015b, 96). They demonstrate how 'truth' changes; it is not stagnant. Thus, the transition to the 'glove [feeling] like a lie' is crucial to this modelling of how differences can be made acceptable and normal through these narrations.

Owing to the Lunar Glamour, clothing isn't the only way the body might be obscured or re-presented in this world. As such, I want to turn to one final example – Cinder being able to create and see through a glamour – as one more instance of the text systematically offering a way out of the trap of appearance. Cinder's cybernetic makeup not only allows her to 'netlink', to access the universe's internet system from within her head, but her brain's cybernetic parts can also see through the Lunar glamour. While Cinder is not the only being who can see through these illusions (shells also can), the narration of Cinder 'seeing through', first, her own glamour and, then, Levana's is particularly provocative. Not only does it mirror the task adolescent girls face in contemporary Western culture when they, too, are bombarded with conflicting images but it also demonstrates the power of occupying the spaces between oppositions.

Cinder can see through the glamour because of her liminal, human-machine status. She is able to disrupt the specular economy at work through the Lunar glamour even as she has the power to use it. As Michael Joseph writes, 'doubled beings are granted wisdom by force of their unique perspective, but they are unpredictable and dangerous' (2011, 140). For example,

Her cyborg hand began to morph in her vision. Little wrinkles appeared in her knuckles. Tendons stretched beneath her skin. The edges softened. Warmed. Turned to flesh.

She was looking at two hands, two human hands. Small and dainty with perfectly sculpted fingers and delicate, rounded nails. She flexed the fingers of her left hand, forming a fist, then stretched them out again.

An almost giddy laugh fell out of her. She was doing it. She was using her glamour.

(2013, 196)

This is the power of the glamour and of the makeover: with it Cinder can see small and dainty perfection. The glamour gives her the possibility of a whole fleshy body (at least appearing as such). This glamour also models the same manipulation that girls outside of the texts do through photo-editing software. The glamour is Cinder's selfie.

Yet, Cinder's cybernetic parts will not let her fall prey to the deception; they see through the glamour: 'And then – too soon – an orange light flickered in the corner of her vision, her brain warning her that what she was seeing was a lie. That this was not real, would never be real' (2013, 196). The glamour is an illusion; the selfie is an illusion, and with this netscreen embedded in her eye, Cinder has the ability to not only see through the lie but also see 'lie' and 'truth' simultaneously: 'She shut her eyes, sure she was imagining things, then opened them again. The diagram realigned. Lines pinpointing the exact angles of Levana's face. Coordinates showing the placement of her eyes, the length of her nose, the width of her brow. A perfect illustration overlaid the perfect woman – and they were not the same' (2012, 361). The simultaneity of this seeing is key, for in seeing both the 'illustration' and the 'illusion', the text calls attention their disjointedness – not the superiority of one over the other. Moreover, these 'lines', 'angles' and 'coordinates' speak to the mapping, and re-mapping, with which this book is concerned. Cinder's cybernetic parts effectively allow for the re-mapping of the contours of Levana's body in narration and, crucially, her own.

Importantly, this seeing that Cinder models also narrates the complexity of seeing faced by the adolescent girl in popular and media culture, as a narration of Cinder seeing through Levana's glamour in the Chronicles' final text demonstrates. Here, rather than seeing both at the same time, Cinder 'let the cyborg side win' (448), and the process of letting this 'cyborg side win' begins with a battle between Cinder's 'cyborg eyes' and 'her own brain': 'It wasn't an easy task. Her cybernetic eyes were in conflict with her own brain and the queen's manipulation, and her mind couldn't figure out what it was seeing. The result was a stream of confused data, blurred colors, fragmented lines trying to piece together what was real and what was illusion' (435). This 'stream of confused data, blurred colors, fragmented lines' and the difficulty 'trying to piece together what was real and what was illusion' perfectly describes the position of the adolescent female girl in popular and media culture, given the bombardment of images, often edited, that she faces. However, the text also offers a way out of this confusion.

> She stopped fighting the onslaught of data being pieced together by her brain-machine interface. The glamour was a biological construct. Using a person's natural bioelectricty to create tiny electric pulses in the brain, to change what they saw and thought and felt and did. But the cyborg part of Cinder's brain couldn't be influenced by bioelectricity. It was all machine, all data and programming and math and logic. When faced with a Lunar glamour or when a Lunar tried to manipulate her, the two parts of her brain went to war, trying to figure out which side should be dominant.
> This time, she let the cyborg side win.
>
> (2015b, 447–8)

This is a way out of the trap of appearance engendered by the visuality of popular and media culture. Cinder demonstrates the possibility of seeing through the superficial. Thus, while Cinder's 'brain-machine' interface is not (yet) available, the seeing Cinder models is, through narrations like these and the media literacy Sweeney calls for, which I can't help but understand as a kind of brain-machine joining.

'A girl full of wires'

Mirrors play a critical role in constructing subjectivity, both the mirrors in which we check our appearances and those offered by the images of media and social media. Mirrors can also be problematic. The mirrors provided by social and popular media – filtered selfies and 'photoshopped' celebrities – offer a very particular way of living and being a body, one that actual mirrors (as in reflective surfaces) police through reflecting achievement or failure. These mirrors – images and reflective surfaces – perpetuate a superficiality of self that traps girls and women within, not just their body but its appearance. As Cinder demonstrates,

> A mirror filled the wall. Her own face stared wild-eyed back at her. Her ponytail was a mess: dull, tangled, in need of a wash. Her skin was too pale, almost translucent, as if the voltage had drained her of more than energy.

> They'd taken her gloves and her boots and rolled her pant legs up.
> She was not looking at a girl in the mirror. She was looking at a machine.
>
> (2012, 78)

This image in the mirror, as well as the seeing of it, is complicated. Cinder 'sees' both 'her own face', 'her ponytail' and 'her skin', and also a 'machine'. This seeing provocatively offers a body of difference, but it also offers that difference in binary terms: 'girl'/'machine', because this is still (merely) a reflection. But, how might these texts reconfigure this mechanism of hegemonic discourses of self? Are there other kinds of mirrors?

In The Lunar Chronicles, mirrors are posited as having an 'uncanny way of telling the truth', at least in terms of the mirror's capacity to expose the Lunar glamour. While the queen's glamour is called an 'endless lie' because she continually presents it (Meyer 2012, 351), 'just as she cannot trick the netscreens, neither can she trick a mirror' (172). While this is technically because mirrors and netscreens are not 'living creatures' and therefore have no bioelectricity for manipulation (Lunars also dislike androids), it is also because, within this world, the glamour remains a superficial alteration of the perception of appearance. The glamour is just a trick. It is not real, and it is in this way the text insists that we look below the surface. However, as Cinder has demonstrated, looking below the surface is still not enough. Instead, we need a new map, a new way of conceiving the body in its fleshy, material, lump and bumpy existence.

Scars are central to this re-mapping, although I do not want to offer scars as the only possible means of re-mapping the body; instead, scars hold a particular interest because of their raised nature and because, in Cinder's case, they demonstrate a kind of interdependency, a relationship between her fleshy, physical body and her cybernetic body parts, like a hologram of Cinder depicts:

> It was as if someone had chopped her down the middle dividing her front half from her back half [...]. Her heart, her brain, her intestines, her muscles, her blue veins. Her control panel, her synthetic hand and leg, wires that trailed from the base of her skull all the way down her spine and out to her prosthetic limbs. The scar tissue where flesh met metal. A small dark square in her wrist – her ID chip.
>
> (2012, 82)

While this medical image demonstrates a keen neoliberal sense of self-awareness in its fracturing of Cinder's body – 'chopping her down the middle' – and its cataloguing of her body parts – 'heart', 'brain', 'intestines' and so on – it also does something different: this image makes 'scar tissue' visible.

Not only have 'flesh' and 'metal' met but the flesh and metal are held together as one within this image. They are held together by the 'scar tissue' linking the parts, a joining that is antithetical to the ideals of contemporary Western culture. There is unity in this fragmentation. This holographic image of Cinder directly contests the flat medical image of cosmetic surgery and the selfie and the many other images – magazine covers and advertisements – proliferating superficiality. This medical image is different, and it refuses flatness in two ways: it not only makes visible the scars, thus refusing flatness within the image, but it is also a hologram; it is three-dimensional, thus refusing the flatness of the image itself. In this way, this image is not the medical image with which Balsamo engages; it is, rather, something else. It is an image that makes visible fragmentation to expose unity ('scar tissue') in that fragmentation and to contest flatness.

Thus, while Cinder's cyborgian state visually disrupts what it means to be human – through the incorporation of mechanical, inorganic parts onto the surface of the body – the text makes it quite clear that this disruption goes much deeper, and it is an insistence that relies on futuristic medical technology – technology that operates like magic. For example,

> Cinder opened her eyes. The net screen on the wall had changed, no longer showing her life stats. Her ID number was still at the top, headlining a holographic diagram,
> Of a girl.
> A girl full of wires.
>
> (2012, 82)

The netscreen, previously devoid of anything save Cinder's 'name and ID number' (78), now displays an image of Cinder, but it is an image with a difference. Where the mirrored reflection showed Cinder's surface, this image exposes her insides while maintaining the external form through the holographic diagram and offering the contours of that external. This hologram is also a mirror, but it is three-dimensional. The hologram has the potential to (re)create life: 'it was a girl, life-size, her different layers flickering and folding into one another' (2014, 302) – explicitly, this is not a flat image ('life-size'), just as it is not a dispersion of parts (Balsamo 1996), or, even, a separating of the inside and outside ('layers flickering and folding'). This image is a Möbius strip; it occupies the space between surface, and depth, making space for 'hybridity' or 'irony' (Haraway 1991, 149; Merrylees

2018, 76). Moreover, this is no longer an instance of 'looking at a girl in the mirror' and seeing, instead, 'machine' (2012, 78); rather, it is looking and seeing both simultaneously. In so being, it is quite like the three-dimensional nature of scars and that 'magical' map of Owlshollow. This is about a topographical approach to the body that takes depth into account.

The visual, multi-dimensional appeal of this image is not the only way it contests hegemonic discourses. There is also a layering of meaning, a history, held within the image, one that speaks to my concern with discourse in the following chapter. 'But those things she had known. Those things she had expected. She had not known about the metal vertebrae along her spine, or the four metal ribs, or the synthetic tissue around her heart, or the metal splints along the bones in her right leg' (2012, 82). This is not the making known of the body to others – at least initially; the first narration of the hologram is Cinder's viewing of it, and in this way, it is a making known of the body to the self. Cinder discovers that which 'she had not known' about her body, and this reading of the self, in all its depth and complexity, is pivotal. This is, in other words, not the medical image that, as Balsamo argues, aids in the 'assembly-line beauty' by which '"difference"' is made over into sameness' (1996, 58). This image is not concerned with such aesthetics. It is, rather, illustrating the whole of Cinder's body. It is about re-mapping that body, and, by extension, other bodies. However, to fully counter the dominance of the visual, depth must also be taken into account.

Finally, in her reading of Cinder as a posthuman fairytale, Angela Insenga suggests that The Lunar Chronicles 'requir[es] readers to turn from surface to subtext, from the slipper to the foot that wears it' (2018, 56). As this chapter details, The Lunar Chronicles does ask readers to consider bodies – a vital task in reframing the myths of adolescent girlhood. However, I argue that rather than asking us to turn from one to the other (an inversion), The Lunar Chronicles asks readers to hold both surface and subtext – and perhaps something deeper – in simultaneity, as the cover of Cinder demonstrates. Featuring an apparently human lower leg and foot, with metal 'bones', in a (red) glass slipper, this cover image, or portal into the world of the story, establishes the kind of intervention at work in the imaginary world. First, there is a layering of meaning within the image. While the glass slipper is an obvious homage to Cinderella's, the shoe's colouring evokes, perhaps, images of Little Red Riding Hood or Snow White, whose 'lips are red as the rose' (Hand et al. 1937) – both heroines, as Scarlet and Winter, become part of the narrative fabric of this world in subsequent books. The gentle nod to their presence speaks to the ways in which The Lunar Chronicles pushes back against the heroic romance's isolating individuality. The metal bones, visible through a sort of x-ray technique, do seem to suggest a turn from the surface (slipper) but not just to the foot wearing it (subtext); the image calls for a consideration of something even deeper than the subtext, or foot wearing the slipper. Moreover, the ambivalence of this image (multiple fairytale heroines and human-mechanical leg) does not just ask readers to consider depth; it asks them to consider both, together.

5

Engendering a new myth: Daine is 'of the people'

Daine is the daughter of a mortal mother (Sara) and a lesser god (Weiryn, God of the Hunt), and she is, or will be, the Wildmage, an epithet she earns 'for her ability to communicate with animals, heal them, and shapeshift' (Pierce 2000, 268); however, at her journey's start, Daine thinks she is an orphan and a bastard. Owing to this, she is also unaware of her powerful magical legacy, believing her relationship with animals to be merely a 'knack' (1992, 15). In short, Daine, the female-hero of Tamora Pierce's Immortals quartet, is an 'Other', and she is so on several levels. In her village, Daine's lack of a father places her in a position of alterity; the 'folk' at home 'scorn' Daine, 'talk about her' and call her a 'bastard' – an identity that she recognizes even if derisively (23 and 90). Compounding this alterity, Daine is also from a 'poor mountain village' in Galla, a country north of Tortall (11). The Tortall universe includes a north–south divide mapping onto the real-world cultural, economic and social disparities. At the same time, the geographic isolation of her mountain community echoes real-world conditions in much of, for example, the United States' Appalachia region (where I am from). Daine's social and cultural situation is at odds with her being a demigoddess with a magical ability aptly described as 'wild' and 'real' (65).

In complex and sometimes conflicting ways, Daine's quartet is about negotiating what it means to be human-animal, especially as the capacity to shape-shift sits at the core of both Daine's magical ability and her 'self'. In so being, Daine's 'narrative thread' engages the heroic romance's positioning of women as 'more biological, more corporeal, and more natural than men' in ways that neither Alanna's nor Cinder's do (Grosz 1994, 14). Although the relational model of self she offers builds on Alanna's disruption of the hero's story's linear, teleological trajectory and Cinder's breaking the representational economy upon which it depends. Indeed, Daine 'may look like a human', but she is not, at least not wholly (1992, 70). Daine is both human and 'of the People' – 'the folk of claw and fur, wing and scale' (1992). In this world, (capitalized) People are animals, while humans are (lowercase) people. The capitalization distinguishes animal People from human people while simultaneously creating an ambiguity that serves to push the boundaries between People (animals) and people (humans), an ambiguity that Daine embodies; she is both, neither one nor the other but both – and, sometimes, in quite complicated ways, especially when she shape-shifts into multiple animals forms at once.

In earlier publications, I used shape-shifting to describe Daine's ability simply because Pierce uses it. However, I now use it for far more complex reasons, and in contention with *metamorphosis*, the most commonly employed term for describing fantastic transformations of humans into animals, especially in studies of children's literature and YA (Lassén-Seger 2006; Waller 2009; Yarova and Kokkola 2015; Viswanath 2019). For one, metamorphs are overwhelmingly teenage boys, as Jo Coward first noted and Lassén-Seger confirmed (Coward 1999, 135; Lassén-Seger 2006, 45). Daine is female and identifies as a girl, usually a human girl. Moreover, and as Clute and Grant note, metamorphosis tends to imply 'radical, unique and permanent' changes, while shape-shifting is marked by 'repeatabil[ity] and reversibil[ity]' (1997b). Daine can partially and wholly shift into animal forms, and when in an animal form, she can partially and wholly change back into Daine-the-human, depending on want or need. Tellingly, Lassén-Seger uses shape-shifting 'with some reservations' and only to describe 'changes of shape that are voluntary, self-induced, multiple, and reversible' in *Adventures into Otherness* (2006, 22). Lassén-Seger's most sustained discussion of shape-shifting occurs in her analysis of Owl's transformations in Patrice Kindl's *Owl in Love*. Lassén-Seger describes these shape-changes as a 'playful outsider's perspective on adolescence and the process of maturation' (Lassén-Seger 2006, 47). Specifically, she views Owl's transformations as disrupting the linearity of the 'Western goal-orientated quest myth' and, importantly, doing so in a way that is not an inversion of that heroic norm (Lassén-Seger 2006). Like Owl's, Daine's shape-shifting does not simply invert heroic norms and standards; it offers 'mutation, variation, and becoming' (Seaman 2007, 247).

Building on Chapters 3 and 4, language – expanding who gets to speak, what it means to speak and what is spoken about – is central to this chapter. Daine's ability to communicate with and act as a 'bridge between' humans and animals (as well as immortals) is not an escape from language, nor is it a return to the real. It is also another reason why I refer to her ability as shape-shifting and not metamorphosis. Metamorphosis, particularly into animal forms, is usually understood to represent both an escape from the restrictions of language and culture and a 'loss of language and, by implication, of reason'

(Viswanath 2019, 117; see, also, Clarke and Lutts 1998; Weil 2012). Coward argues that the 'ideology behind the metamorph' presupposes a boy turning into an animal and (ideally) back to human again (1999, 125). Coward further argues that metamorphosis is part of the boy's 'rite of passage' into adulthood (1999). Metamorphosing into an animal is an instance of ritual death and rebirth in which the novice becomes what he is not to conquer it. Language is intimately bound up in this rebirth – because it is assumed that animals do not have language. As Bruce Clarke argues, '[p]hysical transformation into nonhuman kinds' is an act of 'refusing to identify with a communal body or with the given norms of a system' (1995, 55). Specifically, 'the metamorph attempts to escape the possession of language itself' (1995). While Clarke's argument might hold for some male metamorphs, adolescent girls do not have the privilege of 'refusing to identify' with a 'communal body' or 'the given norms' of the system: you cannot refuse that which you are not, that from which you are radically excluded and that for which you are the escape.[1]

In contemporary Western culture, the categories of human and animal are generally considered distinct and form an oppositional pair (human/animal). In Daine, they exist together and become a powerful avenue for undoing opposition. Daine is both, though she appears to be human most often. Daine's narrative thread is deeply concerned with expanding the boundaries of what it means to be a being – animal, human, immortal – who is valued and valuable within her world and, by extension, ours. Through the power granted by her liminal perspective, it is also concerned with undoing assumptions, especially honing in on women, animals, magic, power, language, divinity and the real. It is also about an interrogation of the structural inequalities barring folks from power, personal and political. It is also fundamentally about destabilizing the superiority and dominance embedded in mainstream Western ideologies (the heroic romance, phallogocentric discourse). Daine's coming into her power, both in the Foucauldian sense and her wild magic (which is a manifestation of that other power), represents a new structure, a way of recognising plurality and change. It forms through connection, makes space for kinship, and is underpinned by possibility and a sense of ethical responsibility. Explicitly, as the child of a mortal mother and divine father connected to animals and as a teenage girl with the power to shape-shift, Daine renegotiates the opposition central to the heroic romance. In so doing, she offers a model of self 'impregnated by otherness', 'scored by relationality into uniqueness' and 'with the potential to generat[e]' new selves 'from within the embodied self' (Battersby 1998, 7 and 18).

Daine is a demigoddess

Daine is arguably the most 'god'-touched of all the female-heroes I consider; she is, after all, the daughter of a mortal woman who becomes a goddess and a god, albeit a lesser one. Being 'god'-touched, a 'symbol of the elite' or 'the chosen-one' is one of the central markers of the archetypal hero. The latter is an ever-present trope in mainstream YA. Harry Potter is, perhaps, one of the most iconic examples, but as I discussed in Chapter 1, Katniss Everdeen and Bella Swan are also in their role as 'exceptional heroines' (Wilkins 2019, 19). The hero's status as god-touched (or any displacements of god, like science or beauty) is about maintaining order and control. It sets him (or her) above and apart from that which he is not to reaffirm and maintain the 'natural' superiority of white, middle-class, cisgendered and heterosexual, 'fit' young men (and some women). However, while Daine might be the most god-touched of my female-heroes, her narrative thread, or hero's journey, uses her privileged position to dismantle hierarchal structures. Throughout her quartet, this social and cultural work occurs in several ways – giving voice to the voiceless, overturning a tyrannical king, saving the People (animals), people (humans) and immortals from a plot to overthrow the king and destroy the land. Here, though, I want to focus on how Daine's status as a demigoddess opens a space to expand what it means to be a god and who gets to be one.

From Mithros (a Great God appearing as a Black man) through to mosquitoes (animal gods), there are many gods in the Tortall universe, and their interests do not always align; power is multiple and diffuse in this world. While the Great Gods are nominally the most powerful, the minor gods (such as Weiryn and the Green Lady) and animal gods more actively participate in Daine's story, an inclusion that expands what it means to be a god. Indeed, several animal gods feature throughout Daine's quartet – Badger, Old White and Night Black ('the first wolf and his mate'), and Queenclaw (goddess of house cats), to name a few (Pierce 1996, 109). (Queenclaw is as impressive and impertinent as the goddess of house cats should be, at one point ordering Daine to 'pet me' because, according to Queenclaw, Daine wasn't doing anything useful (54).) While these gods feature the most, I want to start by taking a closer look at Daine's father, Weiryn, and the implications of his godhood and her mixed heritage (mortal mother and divine father) before briefly considering three encounters – Daine meeting her mother as a goddess, basking in the sun with a skink god and meeting Broad Foot, the male god of the duckmoles – that occur when Daine (and Numair) inadvertently visit the Realms of the Gods. While there are many scenes of interest, these three offer insights into Daine's being-hero and contribute to an expansion and democratization of godhood.

Weiryn "'is rooted in the forest and rock, kin to all that walks or swims or flies'", as Tait, a northern huntsman, tells Daine in Wolf-Speaker (book two of her quartet) (1993, 232). He also tells her that Weiryn has "'antlers like a deer'", making him a human-animal hybrid, albeit a divine one (1993). Lydia Kokkola notes the stag's 'long, but ambivalent' representation in traditional (Western) stories (2013, 146). As Sax Boria notes, the stag is generally a 'symbol of male sexuality' with male transformations into the stag form 'understood as being possessed by sexual desire' (1990, 127). Sexual desire and loss of language generally go hand-in-hand. Still, as I mentioned above and will discuss in more detail below, Daine's shape-shifting (which is a direct result of her parentage) is not a loss of language. As I will show, Pierce also situates him within a particularly domestic space, which seems at odds with a god of the hunt.[2] Weiryn's human-animal nature and Daine's mixed heritage (mortal mother and divine father) also raise the possibility that Daine is ethnically ambiguous,[3] even as she is undoubtedly specifically ambiguous; that is, Daine is not a taxonomical species (at least according to current systems).

As I discussed in the Introduction, the hero 'is white', and his whiteness is one of the most challenging heroic markers to disrupt, and it is intimately bound up in the hero's class and mastery; his being 'god'-touched (Hourihan 1997, 58). Admittedly, Daine is probably white in her human form. For one, she describes herself as 'pink', and while pink is not expressly white, it is code for white. Female-heroes of colour are still greatly needed, as are disabled, queer, trans and neurodiverse female-heroes (especially ones in which those alterities intersect). I cannot offer a new myth of adolescent girlhood – or even stumbling steps towards one – if it only makes space for white, middle-class, affluent, cisgender and heterosexual, 'fit' young women. To undo this myth, undoing the structure 'A/not-A' is vital, for it hides so many alterities and dominances. Thus, to ignore Daine's ambiguities and the potential implications of Daine's being would be to participate in the form of racism known as 'colour-blindness' (a term that is also ableist), even as Daine's narrative does employ it. As Melanie Ramdarshan Bold describes, colour blindness 'has whiteness as "the default setting"' (2019, 102). Ramdarshan Bold further argues that the concurrent narratives of progressivism (of places and institutions being 'beyond race') work to maintain 'the structural barriers to those who are not the "default" affluent, white, middle-class male' (2019).

Daine – and all the female-heroes I've discussed – do not address race and ethnicity overtly, which is a failing. Nevertheless, while Daine is probably white in her human form, she is also not 'just' human or even 'just' People (animal), and, here, the novel's playful descriptions of animals as People come to the fore. Daine may be 'pink', but the narrative is very concerned not only with making a space for people and People of all kinds but also in demonstrating that Daine is, as is the case for adolescent girls outside of this story, more than those things mainstream culture uses to profile people. Incidentally, some immortals use 'pink pig' as an insult against humans (against Daine at least twice). From the immortal's perspective, the insult dehumanizes the person it is used against. In other words, it is complicated; Daine engages that ambiguous space between 'is' and 'not' in complex and nuanced ways. In the remainder, I want to show how Daine's quartet uses her familial relationship – Weiryn is her 'da' (1996, 30) – with a god and a now-goddess to dismantle assumptions around power and authority. I do so because if you change what the group holds to be divine or holy, even just perceptions of it, the structures, rituals and expectations in service to that divine also shift.

After Daine's mum, Sarra, died in the mortal realms, Weiryn 'petitioned the Great Gods to allow [her] to live with him' (1996, 39). The Great Gods allowed it, so Sarra became the Green Lady, a minor goddess who watches over 'village gardens and childbearing' because 'the Great Mother Goddess can't be everywhere' (32). Significantly, the text also notes that Sarra 'liked such things already' and that her transformation into a goddess would not have been possible without that predilection. During Daine's visit, Sarra responds to two supplications as the Green Lady, helping Isa with a 'breach birth' and listening to Lori Hillwalker (41 and 54). Amusingly, these activities cause Sarra to neglect 'the stew' she is making for dinner (55). With some impertinence, Queenclaw insists that Daine 'better do something with it' (1996). While a seemingly insignificant and mainly domestic moment in Daine's story, the episode speaks to how the Immortals quartet undoes the power-through-dominance embedded in the archetypal hero story: Daine's mother cares for two women, helping one deliver a baby. In attending to her goddess duties, she neglects the dinner. (Like the Great Mother) Sarra cannot be everywhere; she sometimes needs help. This goddess, at least, is kind, caring and open to help – to letting someone else check on the stew.

Not long after waking in the divine realms, Daine goes for a walk to clear her head. Briefly, Daine's parents pull her and Numair (friend, mentor and ultimately husband) from the mortal realms because Daine 'was in danger of [her] life, against a foe [she] could not fight' (1996, 32). Daine's parents are able to pull them into the divine realms because their encounter with chaos happens on midsummer's day: when the boundary between the mortal and divine realms is thinnest. Because of this thinness – the erosion of the boundary-ness of this boundary – Weiryn and Sarra can 'pluck' Daine and Numair from otherwise inevitable assimilation by the chaos-skinners. The journey is hard on both her and Numair: 'Every inch of her throbbed. Hands gripped her; she fought' (1996, 26). In many ways, this trip to the Divine Realms is a period of ritual rebirth; when a pair of dragons take Daine and Numair back to the mortal realms, they are 'reborn'. As such, this book narrates the liminal period or that which is structurally impossible (i.e. cannot be described because it is the space between). Daine and Numair have stepped out of 'the structural realm', the mortal one and into a limbo (a liminal space) between their mortal world and chaos (Turner 1967, 110). They have entered the realm of 'pure possibility whence novel configurations of ideas and relations may arise' (Turner 1967). In this case, a reconfiguring of godhood that makes space for ambiguity, uncertainty and change, as two encounters, with a skink god and Broad Foot, god of the duckmoles, make clear.

On this walk, she almost falls prey to a 'Chaos vent' (1996, 45), a pathway into chaos further demonstrating the porosity of boundaries (the divine realms stand between the mortal realms and chaos). A skink saves Daine by biting her ankle, breaking the vent's hold on her mind and body. Girl and skink then spend several paragraphs together in which the skink allays some of Daine's fears and sits with her for a while. They '"bask"' in the sun because, as the skink says, '"the sun will do you good"' (47). Daine listens even as she does not quite believe 'sunning would help'. Fittingly, it does, and 'the rock warmed her and banished the fear caused by the chaos vent'. In being open to the skink's advice, Daine recovers from her fright and gets to witness 'the sunbirds dazzling flight', a spectacular occurrence that only happens in the divine realms. In other words, the relationship she enters with the skink both supports and nourishes her.

Nearing the end of this exchange, Daine asks the skink, '"Why are you being so nice?"' further commenting that she would '"have thought a god would be more, well, aloof"' ([1996] 1998, 49). In response, the narrator suggests, 'the skink couldn't smile, but Daine heard amusement in her voice' ([1996] 1998). The gentle disruption of 'aloofness' both in the skink's 'being so nice' and noted 'amusement' is worth noting, as is the skink's response: '"When you were a little girl, you once saved a nest of young skinks from two-leggers who wished to torture them. For my children, I thank you – and I hope to see you again"' ([1996] 1998). This response contributes to Daine's being-hero; she looks out for the vulnerable, whether they are human or People (animals). It also furthers the disruption of divinity that I'm interested in – at least in as much as skink gods say 'thank you'.

The final encounter occurs when Daine meets Broad Foot, an animal (and a god) she has never encountered in the human realms; 'at first she thought that someone had played a very bad joke on a young beaver' – the animal 'sported a duck's bill' and a beaver-shaped tail but 'covered with hair' ([1996] 1998, 36). In the exchange that follows, Daine asks Broad Foot who and what he is before asking if she can pick him up. She discovers 'springy and thick fur' and 'webbed feet with heavy claws', which contribute to her knowledge and understanding of Broad Foot's existence as a duckmole (platypus). In this passage, sight is not enough to determine who or what Broadfoot is, as is also the case for Daine. Her appearance, her 'look', belies the complexity of her existence as a demigoddess and her status as both human and 'of the People', as I consider in the following section. Here, the touch Daine employs to know better and understand Broadfoot becomes an increasingly important part of her narrative, one that I discuss throughout this chapter and in the book's conclusion. In all cases, I am especially interested in touch's capacity to convey more than sight and to collapse the distance between distinct entities (Grosz 1994, 98–9).

In the final part of this exchange, Daine asks Broadfoot, "'What on earth do you eat?'" ([1996] 1998, 36). Broadfoot's answer contributes to his status as a god and ensures that touch does not supplant sight as a means of perceiving or knowing the world. As with sight, touch is not enough for Daine to understand Broadfoot. She must also speak with him and listen to him.

> My people eat shrimps, insects, snails – frogs and small fish if we can get any. I usually eat the same things as my people, though gods are more venturesome. Sarra cooks the best fish stew in the Divine Realms. I spend warm seasons here, just for that.
> 'You come here for Ma's cooking?'
> His eyes twinkled. 'That's right'.
>
> (37)

Daine learns both what duckmoles eat and what this god eats. In one sense, the gods are set apart from their mortal 'People' in at least as much as they are 'more venturesome'. However, the nature of this 'venturesome' – he visits for the 'fish stew' that is a part of 'Ma's cooking' – further pushes back against aloofness, dignity and superiority while also reaffirming that Sarra makes good stew, even with help again show how the inclusion of what Alison Waller would call 'ordinary things and everyday actions' are vital tools for disrupting the superiority and dominance, and isolating individuality usually implicit in godhood and heroic requirements of selfhood (2020, 1).

On looking inside herself (and what Daine found there)

Perhaps unsurprisingly, there are very few mirrors in Daine's story. The specular economy upon which the heroic romance depends requires an imaginary other than the subject ('I') apprehends in a mirror. This image 'provides the child with an anticipatory image of its own body as a Gestalt [a totalized image of the self]', and that image 'both is and is not' the child (Grosz 1994, 39 and 42). Within the heroic romance (which is a manifestation of patriarchy), girls and women have no mirror; they are the mirror. For Alanna in Chapter 3, cross-dressing allowed her to borrow her brother's signification, making it possible for her to see the 'boy in the mirror' that was both her and not her ([1983] 1997, 9). Opposition was upheld (even if inverted) until Alanna started incorporating her masculine and feminine selves (her abilities to kill and heal; destroy and make) – until the distance between self and other began to collapse. Although I would argue those purple eyes, neither hers nor his but theirs, at least foreshadowed her deconstruction. As a cybernetic Cinderella, Cinder broke the mirror in the previous chapter. As the hero's prize, Cinderella is the mirror, the inverted image of himself that he internalizes to complete himself. Cinder's body resisted the shiny, sparkly flatness required of mirrors and in so doing disrupted the specular economy underpinning the hero story. For Daine, there is no mirror.

Daine initially rejects even the possibility of being 'of the People' because she does not look the part: '"Impossible", the girl said flatly. "Look at me. I'm pink, my fur's patchy, I walk on two legs. I'm human, human all over"' (70). Mirroring the expected position of adolescent girls in contemporary Western culture – where appearance plays a particularly heightened role in a girl's sense of self and the self she is perceived to be – Daine's sense of self is tied to her appearance. She is 'pink' (flesh) with 'patchy fur' (hair) and 'two legs', giving her the appearance of a human, making her human – or so she believes at her journey's start. Daine's sense of self is here predicated on her being able to 'see' herself in others, but because her identity emanates from 'inside' and because the most accurate representation of it requires movement, as I discuss below, a mirror (flat, shiny, sparkly) is incapable of representing Daine. Here, I want to take a closer look at the complex web of connection linking her 'self' to other humans, animals and organic matter that Daine finds when she looks inside herself, as this web is integral to the relational model of selfhood female-heroes offer.

Daine's being 'of the People', despite appearing human, is made available through the narration of the pony Cloud's ability to see inside Daine because he is also People. In this passage, Tahoi, a dog, has just shown Daine an image of Onua and Numair meditating, and in this image, 'a shimmering, pearly light gleamed around each of them'. The trio – human, pony and dog – then discuss the meaning of the magic (alongside Tahoi's desire to play; Daine sends him to fetch a stick). Within the discussion, Daine asks Cloud, "'Do I have the light inside?'" ([1992] 1997, 70). As one of the People, Cloud can see the 'light' that Daine cannot (yet) see. Sagely, Cloud responds, 'On the outside, the pony insisted. Not inside. Inside you're People' ([1992] 1997). (Cloud's response is an instance of mind-speech, thus it does not receive speech marks.) This inside that Cloud is narrated as seeing is, in fact, a seeing of either the Gift – the magic some humans have – or, in Daine's case, her being 'of the People', which is signified as copper fire. While this plays into a difference between the Gift and wild magic (that I discuss in the following section), it also grants access to the depth of Daine's identity, even as it insists that neither surface nor depth can fully account for or represent Daine's being.

For Daine, there is no external model for her being; she is the first of her kind, and a flat mirror is incapable of representing the hybridity and ambiguity integral to Daine's being 'of the People' – both because it emanates from 'inside' her and because the most accurate representation of it requires movement. Daine's internal hybridity is symbolized by a 'wellspring of copper fire' surrounding 'a white core' ([1992] 1997, 181), and it is actualized through the many shape-changes she makes (several of which I discuss throughout the rest of this chapter). This combined unit (white core surrounded by copper fire) is the conceptual centre of Daine's self, or what Roberta Trites might call her 'locus of power' (2000a, 85). As Daine's wild magic – a type of power – emanates from this core, the phrase is particularly apt. To access this core and to begin unpacking the depths of her self and figuring out how surface (human) and depth ('of the People') relate, Daine must look inside. That is, instead of looking in a mirror to form her sense of self, Daine to find not the 'other', but, rather, a complex web of connection linking her 'self' to other humans, animals and organic matter.

Before turning to Daine's journey inside and the web of relation she finds there, it is necessary to address the anxiety around the loss of self that is deeply embedded in Western rationality and Daine's narrative in its relationship to that discourse. The heroic romance models the path towards unique, individual, rational, autonomous self-sufficiency that is not troubled by embodiment. As I discussed in the Preface and Chapter 1, it achieves that goal (as much as it can) through violent hierarchy and radical alterity; the archetypal overcomes that which he is not. To work, the story requires a radical break between hero and not-hero. The space between them is a void but not a neutral one. The space between, for example, the hero and the monster is chaos; it is that which could engulf, assimilate and destroy. To undermine this view and offer an alternative, it is crucial to address both the 'challenges and promise' of relation, as Mary Jeanette Moran notes (2018, 260). Daine's quartet is preoccupied with chaos and loss of self, even as it depicts Daine's sense of self as formed and forming through relation. Indeed, Uusoea, the Queen of Chaos, works through mortal agents to take over the human realms in the final book of Daine's quartet (Pierce 1996). However, even here, at her journey's start, the threat is real and must be addressed.

Daine is terrified of losing herself 'to the herd', to the nearest group of People, and while People refers to the animals with whom she has a bond, the ambiguity of 'people' is worth bearing in mind. In short, Daine is afraid of assimilation, or as Moran describes, 'a destructive kind of communal identity that subsumes individual difference' (2018, 260). Daine fears assimilation because she did lose herself, to a local wolf pack, before the start of her story (disrupting linearity, the narrative is included as a flashback) (Pierce 1992, 175–8). Moreover, as she progresses in her training with Numair, she nearly loses herself again, this time to a herd of horses (147–8). In both cases, Cloud, a horse Daine considers family, comes to her rescue while admonishing Daine to learn to hold on to herself because she 'won't always be here to wake you up' (148). Daine's hero's journey resolves this problem in two ways: one, through teaching Daine how to control her wild magic. (Yes, I recognize the irony of that statement, and you should too.) I begin laying the foundation for that process below and explore it more fully in the following section. Here, I want to focus on the other method, the 'magical barrier' Numair places between Daine's copper (People) and white (human) fires.

Daine's core, her internal self, comprises two (not one as it should be) 'fires'. These fires symbolize her human and People selves, and – together – they form the core of Daine's self. Before the barrier, the white fire 'bled into the copper as the wild magic bled tendrils into it' (Pierce 1992, 181). Without being able to maintain a sense of 'inner silence' [1992] 1997, 146), calmness or, what Mary Jeanette Moran would call, 'balance', Daine loses not only her grip on her self but any self (2018). In this way, while seeming to reaffirm some sense of 'essential' self that aligns with 'mind' or 'I', the passage is deeply concerned with acknowledging the fear of loss of self that pervades Western culture so that it can deconstruct the concept.

Daine's 'white fire' (her human self) could be read as her 'essential self', a core of being that allows growth while also centring and organizing her. In this reading, the copper fire represents the 'real' or other. It is that which the hero works to overcome. To break it down further, the opposition between white fire/copper fire maps onto self/other, human/animal, mind/

body, discourse/materiality, epistemology/ontology and rationality/myth. In securing the white fire, the text seems to reaffirm humanist principles (i.e. all that the archetypal hero represents). However – and as the remainder of this chapter demonstrates – even with this magical border between her two parts, Daine's self is (in)formed by both. In other words, Numair may be able to build a wall between the copper and white fire, but they both, plus the barrier, exist within her; they cannot be separated. It is also worth noting that the barrier is a hybrid: a physical, material form (glass) and language (runes). Daine's conceptual centre is formed and forming through hybridity, and learning to access her 'inside' is a critical part of her heroic romance and the relational model of selfhood she, like all female-heroes, offers.

> The first time she does this, with Numair's help, Daine sees a web of connections.
> All that was green by day grew from emerald threads now. Awed, she reached down and plucked a blade of grass. The needle of green fire that formed its spine flared, and went dark.
> She gasped, remorseful. 'I didn't mean to – '
> 'Hush,' Numair said quietly. 'Look at the earth.'
> A pale bronze mist lay on the piles of dead matter under the trees. When she let the blade of grass fall, its spine turned the same dim bronze as it touched the ground.
> (Pierce ([1992] 1997, 132–3))

The way this passage makes the inside 'fire' (or life force) of the world – human, animal, vegetation, organic matter – visible is profound, especially the web of connection it illustrates, a web that is vital to Daine's overall intervention in the hero paradigm, which encodes 'superiority, dominance, and success' (Hourihan 1997, 1).

This passage does so by, first, demonstrating what happens when dominance is enacted, Daine 'plucked a blade of grass' and '[t]he needle of green fire that formed its spine flared, and went dark' (Pierce 1992, 132). The blade of grass died. However, the passage does not stop there. Daine's remorse is apparent, 'she gasped, remorseful' (Pierce 1992). The narrative then shows how that blade of grass re-joins the system or the whole; once of 'green fire', the blade of grass is now made of the 'same dim bronze' as 'the ground' (Pierce 1992). It is worth bearing in mind that the change, from green to bronze, occurs as the blade 'touched the ground' (Pierce 1992). For now, this narrative – or counter-narrative – offers a disruption to the heroic romance's logic of superiority,[4] but it is not an oppositional response or alternative to the hero story. Instead, it works from within the story, if only on a micro-level, to dismantle and disrupt the story's structure of dominance and enact change.

After focusing on the wider world, represented by the blade of grass that 'returns to the Goddess', Daine looks at herself; more specifically, she looks at 'her hands' (Pierce 1992, 133). Looking outward before turning inward is a subtle deprioritizing of the self, even as Daine's self is precisely what is under focus in this exercise. It also sets the stage for an ambivalent outward-inward looking, a way of perceiving the world and self that includes both surface and depth (one that I began to call for in the previous chapter). As was the case in the last chapter, hands are again important. Indeed, Cinder's shifting attitude towards her hands, particularly her cybernetic one, laid a foundation for Daine's.

> They were laced through with strands of reddish light, almost as if her veins had the power to glow. Intertwined with the red were strands of copper fire. She looked at the owl, at the vole, and at her hands – all the same shade of copper.
>
> Half twisting, she managed to see part of Numair. He too was laced with red fire. In addition a white, pearly glow flickered over his skin like a veil.
>
> (133)

When Daine looks at her hands, she sees how she is connected to others – she, the owl and the vole share copper fire while she and Numair share the red fire. She also sees how she is different – the owl and vole do not share the red fire, and Numair does not have the cooper. There is distinctiveness in this narration but also commonality. Daine's going inside grants her access to that and more, particularly to 'wild magic', one of the several magics in the Tortall universe and one that gives her a 'knack' with animals.

Animals: Daine has a knack

Daine's liminal being, her existence between the god/mortal and human/animal binaries, grants her a magical power; her power derives from her and is shaped by her hybridity. Specifically, being Weiryn and Sarra's daughter, not to exclude her unique self, gives Daine 'wild magic'. This magic manifests in the mortal world as 'a bond with animals' ([1992] 1997, 116). Briefly, this bond allows Daine to mind-speak with, mind-share (or 'ride along' with), heal and shape-change into animals ([1993] 1999, 146). Daine's wild magic is part of the complex system of magic at work in the Tortall universe, much of which is beyond the scope of this section. For example, the intricacies of divine and immortal magic, the magic of dragons, and the Sight, an ability manifesting differently in different individuals. For example, Alanna's husband George can 'tell when he was being lied to' and their daughter Aly can 'see immediately whether [...] someone had magic or godhood' (among other things) (T's Choice?). For this section and what Daine's magic means for her being-hero, there are two broad kinds of magic within this world: the Gift and wild magic – and Daine's magic disrupts assumptions about both.

First, the Gift is an 'all purpose' magical skill, and it is the recognized and sanctioned magic within this world (Pierce 2003, 48); it is an institution, and it is institutionalized (taught in schools). As much as any magic can be understood, ordinary and legitimate, the Gift is thus, particularly because it is discursively structured. Gifted individuals are taught in 'schools', and after the first book of Alanna's quartet, training for knighthood includes magical instruction for those who are Gifted. There are also hierarchies within the Gift. Hedgewitches, for example, are individuals 'with basic Gifts, taught by other hedgewitches, never hoping to be more than village healer-mid-wives'; they are usually women ([1992] 1997, 65). While anything is theoretically possible through the Gift, there are fundamental aspects of the Gift that everyone with the ability possesses – Daine suggests that she does not have the Gift because she cannot magically 'start a fire, and Gifted babies manage that' ([1992] 1997, 15, emphasis original). Aside from a few abilities that seem to precede language, like starting a fire, the Gift is linguistically structured and derives at least some of its power from language.

Wild magic is the other, and sometimes othering, magic within this world, and it most frequently appears as a bond with animals; it is a magic that has very little to do with language. While all magic is at least somewhat 'wild, spectacular, idiosyncratic, and surprising', wild magic is more so (Bennett 2001, 58). It is both unknown and already known; 'it's in everything', according to Numair (Pierce 1992, 246), and many within the world dismiss it – the Carthakis, a neighbouring (sometimes hostile) country, 'think it old wives' tales' (272). Wild magic is both wild, 'thus the name' and uncontrollable, 'unpredictable' (207). It is 'real power', and Daine is 'brimming with it' (65). Numair has 'never seen a human with so much' (Pierce 1992). Daine's magic is constituted not only as power, which can also be read as natural, but it is also 'real power' – Numair 'felt it when [he] was a bird, half-crazy and dying' (Pierce 1992, emphasis mine).[5] In an article examining how 'the wolf is mobilized' in Jack London's fiction, especially *White Fang*, and criticism of that fiction, Sue Walsh argues that 'the "Wild" [...] is both the locus of ultimate knowledge, and indefinite, interminable and unfathomable' (2013, 71). It is also, as she continues, 'written as not needing to be interpreted because its meaning is transparent and immediate'

(2013, emphasis original). Wild magic is potentially more 'real' or natural than the Gift but also possibly more obvious; it can be felt and so it does not need teaching, training or recognition, a belief Daine disrupts, through not without difficulty.

The Gift's privileged position – at the expense of wild magic – has a profound impact on Daine's sense of self, one that intertwines with those alterities I discussed in the introduction. On one level, Daine's mother 'had the Gift for birthing, healing', '[p]rotection' and '[s]he was best with plants' (Pierce 1992, 111). In fact, '[a]ll the girls in her family was [*sic*] healers' (Pierce 1992). Sarra wanted her daughter would follow in her footsteps: 'Didn't Ma test and test me? Don't you think I'd've grabbed magic, if I had it, just to please Ma?' (115). Daine does not have the magic, even in its hedgewitch form, that her mother wanted her to have and that is, at least, part of her heritage. However, Daine does have magic, and she has the ability to heal her animal friends by using her skill to look inside them, 'deep, but into your patient instead of yourself' (184). Daine's wild magic just does not look like the Gift, the dominant magic, and so people do not recognize or believe in it, and this ignorance contributes to Daine's alterity within her community. At worst, it causes the Snowsdale villagers to utterly turn on Daine after she took revenge against the bandits killing her family. At the best, it presents her ability as 'mere knack' (Bengson 2020, 215).[6]

Knacks are intuitive abilities. They are often seen as clever or resourceful, but they are not skills. Julia Annas describes a knack as 'an ability to manipulate the world which is not at a sufficiently rational level to be judged epistemically' (2001, 48). As she further explains, knacks are 'inarticulate and practical' (2001). Skills, on the other hand, require a person to, as Annas further describes, '"give an account" of what he does, which involves being able to explain why he is doing what he is doing. Such a person understands what he is doing, unlike the person who can pick up a knack in a purely unintellectual way, without understanding what it is he is doing and why' (2011, 20). John Bengson argues that skills also require a 'certain systematicity and generality' (Demmerling and Schroder 2021, 177). Daine, perhaps, explains it best: when asked if she as the Gift because of the ways animals respond to her, she answers, 'Oh, please. I've a knack with animals but no Gift. Ma [...] tried to teach me but I never learned' (Pierce 1992, 15). Daine cannot explain – indeed, she does not yet know the full extent of – her power, so it is a knack. However, Daine's 'knack with animals' is a powerful magical legacy that manifests in the human realms as 'wild magic', as I have discussed. As such, it disrupts what it is to have a 'knack' with profound epistemological (how we know what we know) implications that, in turn, call for a reconceiving of the wild.

The first step in this undoing is a questioning of the authority, legitimacy and power of names. Quite early on, Miri, a friend of Daine's, points out that having or not having magic "'depends on what you mean [...] the sea's full of magic, but we can't use it like the Gift. It isn't the same'" (Pierce 1992, 96). Magic is still magic irrespective of how 'we' (humans) can use it, a point a conversation between Daine and Cloud develops. Having just been told she possesses wild magic, Daine vocally asks Cloud, "'You ever hear of "wild magic"? They say I have it'" (69). Cloud responds using mindspeech: 'You have something, and you know it. Who cares what name it has? Or did you really think the wild creatures visit because they like humans?' (Pierce 1992). (It is worth remembering that Cloud's speech does not get quote marks as it is not spoken out loud, paving the way for a new kind of speaking.) Here, Cloud offers a kind of practicality that is in opposition to Daine's worry over the name of this wild magic, and it is a practicality that speaks to something outside of language; it defies the 'naming' that is always associated with institutions and the legitimate, as such it also relates to that moment of writing that initiated Alanna's cross-dressing. It also demonstrates, as all my readings have, the necessity of taking materiality and discourse into account when conceiving the adolescent girl, even if we can only talk about materiality in discursive terms.

Pushing back against the idea that wild magic is natural and obvious and that it cannot – because it is a knack associated with animals – involve learning, Daine must be taught how to use her 'knack' that is really magic. The teaching she receives from Numair and the badger god disrupts common assumptions about both wild magic and the Gift, while Daine's learning, as the remainder of this chapter explores, disrupts what it means to be human. Importantly, Numair's instruction includes mediation, book learning and practice; things wild magic should not require, and while each are important, I want to focus on books for a moment, particularly 'a book on mammalian anatomy' that Numair gifts Daine on the first day of their work together (Pierce 1992, 140).

The topic of the book is important, but the fact that it is a book, that Numair gifts to Daine, is too. As Daine makes clear, "'Mine!' she gasped. "No! It's – it's too valuable. The likes of me don't keep such things!" Her fingers shook, she wanted it so much, but peasant girls didn't own books' ([1992] 1997, 141). Daine's wild magic, particularly its framing as 'knack', speaks to real-world concepts such as 'raw talent' and 'meritocracy', the idea that with talent and enough effort a person may 'rise to the top' (become Cinderella or the archetypal hero). Here, meritocracy's elision of class comes particularly to the fore.[7] The topic of the book, 'mammalian anatomy' – and its use in Daine's magic – disrupts conceptions of the wild with implications for epistemological assumptions. That is, while Daine's magic is not linguistically structured in the same way as the Gift, it can use those structures; the book on anatomy teaches Daine not only the 'insides' of her animal friends – '"muscles, veins, organs, and so on"' – but also gives her the words she did not know: '""Mammalian" refers to mammals. You know what they are; you just don't know the fancy term"' (140). Numair has the skill to teach Daine, at least partially, because he knows the words.[8] Importantly, this book learning works in conjunction with practical application.

Daine uses this knowledge of mammalian anatomy to heal her animal friends. Healing and healing magic are particularly important and not only because Sarra wanted her daughter to share in her family's magical legacy. For Daine, healing becomes a bridge, a place of connection not just between her and the animal she is healing but also between her human self and a lineage running through her mother and her father's connection to the People (animals). Before learning to use her knack as a skill, Daine's 'healing was done with stinging liquids, needles, thread and splints, not magic', as Brokefang a wolf with who she shares a particular bond notes ([1993] 1999, 7). Daine's ability to help animals prior to discovering her inner potential took, Brokefang implies, time and it 'stung'. After learning to access her wild magic, Daine can heal without stinging and much more quickly. In other words, while Daine can manipulate the world – or, at least, her own and other's bodies (and bodies are a kind of world) – and initially cannot give an account of her actions, this is not a mere 'knack', despite the text's claims. Instead, as I have shown and will continue to show, Daine's wild magic is considered a 'knack' because hegemonic patriarchal discourse cannot account for her skill; it does not have the capacity to do so.

Speaking the unspeakable

Daine's being 'of the People' and her ability to transform into animal forms offer a platform for expanding who gets to speak and what it means to speak ([1992] 1997, 70). It does because, at least in part, Daine is not escaping herself in her transformations. She is, instead, transforming into different aspects of herself. Through this, the text is able to offer an undoing of the privileged assumption that (human) language, including speech and writing, are the only or superior forms of representation, signification and communication. Language is also, as Maria Nikolajeva explains, a 'vehicle of power' (2010, 17). She further argues that 'whoever possesses this power can also suppress and govern other *people*' (2010, emphasis mine). While Chapter 3's concern with Alanna's cross-dressing and subject formation began exploring this issue (especially in that Alanna's father and brother could write and she could not), Daine's narrative expands the reading to include People (animals).

Daine's narrative is conscious of this power and addresses it on several levels, especially in recognizing that animals have thoughts and feelings of their own. Daine's mind-speech, all her interactions with animals, does not assume an 'empty' animal mind and goes to great lengths to make space for and includes animal thoughts, feelings and perceptions within the narration. In so doing, it expands the boundaries of speech and embeds an ethic of care within that expansion. This work occurs in four key ways: the representation of mind-speech in narration, the inclusion of animal speech within that representation, translation work and finally instances of new sign-systems that can be understood by both humans and animals. That is, while Daine can 'speak' with animals, this invisible and silent speech is represented in narration, which is a form of translation but Daine also translates for others. In so doing, Daine uses her liminal perspective to level the communication field.

Even before Daine knows that she has wild magic, she has an ability to understand animals to a degree most humans do not. For example, not long after meeting Numair, he encounters Daine greeting a woodchuck: 'The girl lay on the ground her eyes on level with the chuck's. The animal stood on his hind legs, chattering to her' ([1992] 1997, 66). Approaching, Numair observes, '"He seemed to have a lot to say"' to which Daine responds, very nonchalantly, '"Oh, it's the usual spring talk. Freshening up the burrow, getting nice-smelling leaves. I told him where to find some wild mint"' ([1992] 1997). There are several things at play in this passage. On some level, Daine has had a conversation with the woodchuck, and it seems to be such an ordinary occurrence, not least because 'it's the usual spring talk', but not everyone has this ability (that Daine still believes is a knack). On another level, equality is also being modelled in this exchange. Daine is lying 'on the ground' and 'her eyes' are 'level with the chuck's' ([1992] 1997). She meets the chuck where he is and listens to him.

This conversation with the woodchuck also introduces an opportune moment to think about sex, specifically the common association of 'female metamorphosis' as expressing 'deviant sexual desire' or monstrosity, a representation that intensifies with lycanthropy (transformation into wolf forms) is involved (Viswanath 2019, 115). The argument echoes my discussion of 'the horror of the blood' in Chapter 3. In effect, because Daine shape-shifts and because she can transform into the form of a wolf the assumption is that this shifting is both tied to her sexuality and an expression of its deviance. As I discuss below, Daine has a particular affinity with wolves, and her first full-body transformation is into the form of a wolf. However, Daine's shape-shifting, and her coming into her power, is not tied to menstruation or the moon. In fact, Daine's period is never mentioned even though including menstruation is something Pierce excels at. Daine's narrative is, yet again, doing something different, pushing the boundaries that much further.

Despite the absence of menstruation, sex and procreation are deeply embedded in Daine's narrative, even as the narration goes to considerable lengths to signal Daine's lack of interest in the topic (even as it makes it an ordinary part of her world). For example, 'two plops ahead: a pair of mating frogs. She had no interest in that', immediately followed by 'ducks nesting' (Pierce 1992, 34). These encounters prompt Daine to muse 'didn't people think of anything else' (Pierce 1992). While she is referring to frogs and ducks here, it is worth remembering that People are animals within this world but, without capitalization, she could be referring to animals or humans. Moreover, in the first novel alone: Daine serves as midwife for breech 'twin lambs' (74), witnesses a sea lion gives birth to a 'pup' while '[a]nother pup, already born, suckled at his mother's teat' (181) and awakes 'to a stable cat giving birth near her ear' (221). Alanna and Queen Thayet's children also follow Daine around 'like ducklings' (225), and she meets a pregnant dragon – saves her unborn kit and becomes the dragonet's, Skysong's, adoptive mother.

The dragon also offers another instance of speaking the unspeakable, this time incorporating touch or connection. Mages working for raiders attacking Daine and her friends accidentally pull the dragon from the divine realms as she was flying home to give birth. The magic they used and the trip between realms killed the unborn kit. In fury and rage, the dragon begins to attack Daine and her friends, incorrectly thinking they were responsible. Daine tries to communicate with the dragon, but the dragon is in such a rage she cannot hear Daine. In a moment of inspiration, 'Daine jumped to her feet and raised her hands', exclaiming 'I think I have the knack of it now' (Pierce 1992, 260). It is ironic that the ability to communicate with animals that Daine has developed through her work with Numair becomes, again, a knack. It does so, at least in part, because the communication involves more than verbally speaking; Daine has to touch the dragon to ensure communication, 'Putting her hands on that scarlet breast, she called, – *Listen, wing-sister*! –' (Pierce 1992, emphasis original). In addressing the dragon, Daine speaks to a 'divine' being, and so the speech is represented using the written form of divine speech (italicized). Through this touch Daine and the dragon form a bond that makes communication possible; it also creates an avenue through which Daine can heal the mother and unborn child albeit without knowing that is what she's doing, though she does understand the results: 'Daine felt the dragon's hide ripple. It was like a convulsion – or a contraction! Ma's daughter realized' (262). Not only is this not about deviant sexuality or desire but it also models connectivity that is integral to dismantling oppositions and bringing about change.

As Daine's skill develops, the kinds of conversations and the potential for speaking, and for what counts as speech, also expand. For example, in novels, speech is usually indicated by quotation, or speech, marks. In what appears to be a fairly standard example of dialogue in narration, Daine responds to a question posed by Numair stating, '"She says I'm feeling sorry for myself. I don't think she understands"' (Pierce [1993] 1999, 6). As a reader, I recognize this as speech because it is offset by quotations. However, Daine's speech is a translation of mind speech occurring between Daine and Cloud, a horse: 'Strong teeth gripped her elbow hard. Daine looked around into the bright eyes of her pony, Cloud. If I have to bite you to stop you feeling sorry for yourself, I will, the mare informed her. You are being silly' ([1993] 1999). The mare, Cloud, is clearly represented as speaking, to Daine, in this exchange, but Numair cannot hear it. Readers, however, are privy to it, and so, being the assumption around who gets to speak and how speaking occurs, at least within the narration, is disrupted. In the first, Cloud, a horse, is represented as having access to human language, at least in her ability to communicate with Daine. Second, this speech is not contained by – it is not restricted by – speech marks, and so it becomes a liminal speaking, a speaking of the unspeakable.

The 'mind speech' is at once outside of hegemonic discourse (which requires speech marks, the symbol indicating speech) and, yet, within a discourse (the narrative of the text). It both is and is not speaking. Importantly, the text is especially concerned with establishing the normalcy, or at least regularity, of such 'mind speech'; Numair is 'used to these silent exchanges', and, by extension, so should be the reader (Pierce [1993] 1999, 6). In this way, the narration offers an expanded sense of 'speaking'. Not only does Daine's wild magic, and thus her shape-shifting, grant her access to an additional language. This language in conventional terms ought not to exist for its alignment with 'non-signification' (Waller 2009, 47), but it is rendered as speech within the text, crucially without the symbolic marker of speech. This is, in other words, one more way in which Daine's narrative is preoccupied with making visible that which is invisible and speaking that which is unspeakable.

Finally, there is a consensus within critical theory that engages the animal that, as Kari Weil (2012) suggests, animals are 'being[s] that resist our flawed system of language' (2012, 12). Animals are posited as outside of representation (the Symbolic), much like woman (who is body). Daine's quartet disrupts this assumption by giving language to animals, by not assuming an 'empty' animal mind, by speaking the unspeakable, and by expanding who gets to speak and what counts as speaking. Haraway argues that while 'nature may be speechless, without language', it also 'highly articulate' (2004, 106). As she further argues, '[d]iscourse is only one process of articulation', and '[i]n obsolete English, to articulate is to signify. It is to put things together, scary things, risky things, contingent things'. Daine's being 'of the people' is such a putting together of things, and the subsequent articulations have the power to re-shape the world, especially as they undo the privileged assumption that human language, including speech and writing, is the superior or only form of communication, representation, signification.

Not only does Daine's being 'of the People' insist that animals have language (it's just different from human language), but her being also systematically works to deconstruct the differences between languages, especially disrupting the privileged position of human speech. Translation and translation adjacent work are central to this process: Numair's teaching Daine how to use her wild magic, Cloud and Miri suggesting things might have other names (indeed, that names might not even matter), and the text's (re)presentation of mind-speech in narration are kinds of translation. Daine's translation of People into human and human into People is another example, for instance, when Daine tells Numair that Cloud 'says I'm feeling sorry for myself' (1992, 66). In another exchange, Daine translates human into a language Quickmunch, a marmoset, understands: '"Nod", Daine told the marmot, and Quickmunch nodded stiffly. This means something to him? she asked. "It means yes", the girl said. It means we understand human speech' (1994, 176). As the exchange progresses, Quickmunch does rather a lot of nodding, learning as she goes. The scene ends when Quickmunch 'turned her back to Numair and flipped her tail up, then faced him again' (1994). Un-prompted by Daine, Quickmunch added her own statement to the conversation before declaring to Daine, 'I like this way of talking' (1994).

Importantly, to translate, one must listen, and Daine's first lesson, even before she knows has wild magic, is about listening,: 'If you look hard and long, you can find us. If you listen hard and long, you can hear any of us, call any of us, that you want' (1992, 24). This listening forms the basis of a powerful narrative of empathetic listening that is central to the relational model of self Daine models and has world-changing implications for Daine because it leads to shape-shifting.

Learning to shape-shift

At the end of her quartet and when she is at the height of her powers, Daine can transform into multiple birds, at once: '[t]here was no one bird that she drew on, but many, as Daine shaped angled wings to give her speed, a ripping beak and talons to match for combat, a starling's talent for quick midair dodges. She stayed as large as she dared' (Pierce [1996] 1998). Daine is, here, quite literally 'of the People' (animals within this world) – all the People, or, at least, all the birds she draws upon. Her shape-shifting is, in this transformation, very much about expressing multiplicity. Not only does it further blur the distinction between human and animal, a blurring that Daine embodies, but it also blurs the differences between different kinds of birds: this is an amalgamation of 'no one bird' as well as of no particular bird. Apart from the starling, narration does not name the birds whose appearance and abilities Daine adopts – with the one it does identify, Daine does not take on its appearance but, rather, an attribute: the bird's 'talent'. In terms of the bodily transformations, the birds remain un-named; Daine is 'no one bird'.[9] However, before Daine reaches this place of being able to move between bodies, she has to learn how and the account of that learning offers an opportunity to develop the empathetic listening I mentioned above and the 'ethical responsibility' underpinning the model of selfhood Daine offers as a female-hero (Moran 2018, 260).

Building on the first lesson in listening, the badger (god) tells Daine that she 'can learn to enter the mind of a mortal animal' and that in so doing she will be able to use their eyes, ears and noses as she would her own (Pierce 1993, 20). To do so, Daine must 'make [her] mind like that of the animal [she] wish[es] to join' (Pierce 1993). She must think like that animal does, until [they] become one (Pierce 1993). The first time Daine attempts this symbiotic joining, it does not work.

> The girl closed her eyes. Breathing slowly, she reached deep inside to find the pool of copper light that was her wild magic. Calling a thread of fire from that pool, she reached for Cloud, thinking to bind their minds with it.
>
> Cloud whinnied, breaking the girl's concentration. That hurt, the mare snapped.
>
> ([1993] 1999, 23)

The pool of copper fire is, in other passages, surrounding a 'white core' of fire that is Daine's human self ([1992] 1997, 181). The copper fire is the part of her that is animal (70). Most humans only have white fire while most animals only have copper. Daine, however, has both, and her hybridity allows her to relate to both people and People. Daine's first, 'second, third and fourth attempt[s]' also fail. They do so because Daine is acting from a place of dominance, but the text offers a solution: listening.

To join with Cloud, Daine 'finally asks "How can I do it without paining you?"' ([1993] 1999, 24). In this moment, she opens herself up (or is represented as doing so) to the presence of the other, in this case, Cloud, who suggests, 'Without the fire [...] You don't need it to talk to us, or to listen. Why should you need it now?'. Things change after this conversation. Daine's next attempt, with Brokefang, the leader of the Long Lake Pack, goes much better: 'She closed her eyes, took a breath, let it out. Sounds pressed on her. Numair's snore, short Snout's moan as he dreamed of rabbits the pups chewing, Battle washing a paw. She concentrated on Brokefang until she heard fleas moving in his pelt. He yawned inside her ears' ([1993] 1999, 42). This time, Daine listens, and this is not just a physical hearing through her ears, which 'she closed her eyes signals'. This listening is part of Daine's meditative practice, and it involves opening her consciousness, the core of her very self, up to others.

In listening in this way and in focusing on Brokefang, she moves closer and closer to him, until she can see things from his point of view.

> She listened for his thoughts and found them: the odour of the blood from his kill, the drip of water from the trees overhead, the joy of being one with the Pack. Brokefang sighed.
> Daine was sleepy; her belly over-full and rumbling as it broke the elk-meat down.
> ([1993] 1999, 42)

The change from Brokefang and Daine (independence) to Daine within Brokefang (interdependence) is subtle, but it occurs after Brokefang's sigh, from that point he and Daine are sharing a single consciousness, his. For Daine, this is a powerful moment of recognizing the other within herself. As she continues to develop this skill, through sharing the minds of the wolves Battle and Russet as well as a marmoset, bat, squirrel and eagle, she learns more and more about the People (who happen to be animals) with whom she shares a bond. In this way, Daine and her magic are about demonstrating, indeed embodying, relation not opposition, as the resulting implications for Daine's body make clear.

As a direct result of Daine's speaking and listening to the People, she learns to shape-shift, learning that pushes the boundaries of what it means to be human. In the first instance of sustained, albeit partial, bodily transformation, Daine's ears become those of a bat, after she joins with the mind of Wisewing, a member of the 'Song Hollow Colony of bats' (Pierce 1993, 144). After leaving Wisewing's mind, Daine 'ears were tired and sore, the muscles round them cramped from use' (151). When she reaches up to 'rub them', she 'touche[s] a long flap of leathery skin that flicked to and fro, catching each quiver of sound in the air' (Pierce 1993). These are not Daine's ears, and, yet, because they are on her body, they are somehow her ears. The surface of the body is here a place of amalgamation. Its liminality is made explicit. Furthermore, while the change itself disrupts the visual certainty of the body, the narration of the touch also disrupts, in offering an alternative way of perceiving the body, one that I return to in 'Towards and New Myth'. Here, I want to return, briefly, to the mind/body split issue that Iko raised in the previous chapter.

Like Iko, Daine's shape-shifting would seem to reaffirm some unchanged and unchanging core of self given Daine remains Daine even when looking the least like herself – or, at least, what Western consensus reality would consider her 'self'. For Daine, the notion of an unchanging core is too rigid, as a later transformation makes clear: 'She looked at her hands and feet. They were still human but a fine grey fuzz covered them and the tips of her nails were black claws' ([1993] 1999, 213). Daine's body is constructed as unstable – change is introduced onto its surface. Furthermore, this narration establishes what that change is by defining what does not change: the 'human' that somehow exists before, and yet also after, change has occurred. The narration of bodily transformation, in other words, establishes an opposition between changed and not change, while, simultaneously, questioning it. For, by remaining 'human', despite being 'covered' and despite 'black claws' – despite change – the 'hands and feet' in their 'not changed' states appeal to a stable core, a core of 'human' that has somehow not changed during this transformation, much like Iko's personality chip apparently does not change in Marissa Meyer's Lunar Chronicles. However, the narration of Daine's shape-shifting establishes this binary opposition between changed and not changed only to immediately question it; in so being, this shape-shifting is explicitly about showing how an unchanging core is impossible to maintain.

The shape changes that Daine makes influence and modify both the body and the core, as 'they were still human but' demonstrates – 'but' calls any stability of the body or otherwise into question (Pierce 1993, 213, my emphasis). 'But' introduces the possibility that neither complete change nor complete non-change has occurred, thus calling the stability of both into question. The act of change produces the results of that act as existing on, or as, a continuum, effectively uniting the oppositions. In other words, while the hands and feet are claimed to be 'still human', 'a fine grey fuzz' and 'black claws' are not human, and while these things are now connected to the hands and feet (to that which is 'human'), they are not human and potentially jeopardize the humanness of what they touch. The stability of human is worried, just as the lingering human worries the completeness of change because this is not about change/not changed, for all that the narration terms it as such; this is about Daine's embodying multiplicity, change and becoming.

Finally, this narration of fantastic bodily change is a modelling of the very real (as in physical) changes associated with the adolescent girl: while the adolescent girl might not develop 'black claws' or grow 'a fine grey fuzz' (Pierce 1993, 213), she does (typically) begin growing underarm and pubic hair at the onset of puberty, while also in the West often experimenting with nail polish and other body modification techniques. Moreover, while Daine's 'human' appears to be expressed on the body – much like femininity – it also begins implementing a deeper sense of self. Here, the allusion appears in how the change only covers her hands and feet. The 'fuzz' is covering a body-cum-self that has been, perhaps, obscured rather than utterly changed, a reading that the specific location of this change – on the outer extremities – reinforces. It is about layering change onto the (unchanged) body, thus the body is the site of continuum, of possibility. In other words, Daine's body is still body, whether it is human-shaped or animal-shaped.

'No one bird'

Even before she began shape-shifting, Daine was 'no one bird' – she is 'of the People' regardless of the shape of her body, thus the shape-shifting (merely) makes visible or external that internal being. While adolescent girls are not usually 'of the People' – despite how patriarchal ideology aligns them – many of them do have the capacity to conceive a child. Pregnancy and adolescence, despite the cultural distaste for teenage pregnancy, are rather intimately related, and not just because adolescence is yoked to the biological changes of puberty (when menstruation begins). They are both liminal states. In fact, Gennep devotes just as much attention to 'Pregnancy and Childbirth' (1960, 41–9) as he does to adolescence. Regarding pregnancy, he states, 'it has been established that at the onset of pregnancy a woman is placed in a state of isolation, either because she is considered impure and dangerous or because her very pregnancy places her physiologically and socially in an abnormal condition' (41). This 'abnormal' condition is the same abnormality associated with adolescence, manifested in different terms. Both the adolescent and the pregnant woman are between: the adolescent is between the oppositional pairs adult/child and the pregnancy woman between the pair self/other. She, like the adolescent, is neither one (self) nor the other (Other); she is both.

During the time span covered by *Lady Knight* (2002), the fourth book of the Protector of the Small quartet, Daine becomes pregnant. Tortall is at war with Scanra, a country to the north, and Daine is the front line of defence, flying reconnaissance missions as various birds. By this time, she and Numair are married, but she is still using contraceptives – particularly an anti-fertility charm.[10] However, owing to 'all the shape-changes she made', Daine lost it (Len 2007a). Pierce explained this 'why' in interviews. She goes on to say that, Daine 'doesn't remember where or when she lost it. She only realized something was a little off in September, when she couldn't lace up her breeches. She went to a healer, who gave her the news that she was pregnant. Numair was over the moon' (Len 2007b).[11] There are several things going on in this passage: issues of how pregnancy is known as well as a securing of the joy for this pregnancy, a joy for the child it will bear. While this last has little to do with the bodily instability with which I am concerned, it does speak to the wider issue of making available narrations of difference within these texts; in that, this background provides a story, a narrative of not just acceptance but happiness, both of which are often lacking in most realistic YA featuring stories of pregnant teenage girls.

While not a part of any specific quartet, these interviews are integral to the development of, generally, the imaginary world of Tortall and, specifically, Daine's pregnancy. In this case, these paratextual materials not only situate Daine's pregnancy but also explain why Daine has to shape-shift below the waist every time her unborn child does: 'she changed shape so many times in her first three months that the baby got used to it, and has continued to shape-shift ever since' (Lennard 2007). This makes explicit a relationship between mother and child that is crucial; the pregnant woman is not one self in one body, and the relationship forged here extends beyond pregnancy and into motherhood. For example:

> 'Your aunt is having a baby shape-shifter within the month,' replied her mother. [...] 'If she doesn't change below the waist whenever the child does, it might kick its way out of her womb.' Alanna shuddered. '[...] it made me queasy to see her go from bear to donkey to fish every now and then, while her upper half remains the same.'
>
> (Pierce 2003, 17)

Daine's having to shape-shift each time her unborn child does establish a tension between the outside appearance (where shape-shifting is available) and the inside womb (where the unborn child is shape-shifting). While pregnancies typically require some sort of 'shape-change' – as Aly's 'slight swell' indicated ([2004] 2005, 441) – Daine's shape-shifting to match the baby takes that change to an entirely different level: it makes explicit the shape(s) of the child; Daine's form shifts to match the unborn child. It is about 'accomodat[ing] the baby's changes (infant to horse to rabbit to bird to fawn to cub to [...] you name it)', as Pierces states (Len 2007a). In this way, the narration of Daine's pregnancy makes explicit not only a connection between mother and child but also Battersby's (1998) argument that the mother is no longer one – the mother is two (or more). It also makes visible the mundane, or ordinary, accommodations of any pregnancy.

The origin story is especially also necessary because this pregnancy produces a child formed in and shaped by multiplicity. Owing to this, the appearance of Daine's child – that is to say, the child's self – is not fixed; the continual shape-shifting indicates as much. Moreover, Daine, and readers, does not know what, or who, this child is: 'No one could even magically tell the child's sex while it was in the womb. It had shifted both sex and shape constantly, pummelling poor Daine with everything from elephant feet to ostrich claws' (Pierce 2003, 130). Before the child is born, the child's self, identity and shape are not fixed. Moreover, they are directly tied to the mother: the child is part of the mother and the mother part of the child, again expanding a sense of self, as where does one begin and the other end? While this is the case for any pregnancy – the relationship between mother and child is one of interdependency and relation, as opposed to opposition – this fantastical pregnancy can demonstrate that relationship in ways that are impossible to mundane pregnancies (that is, 'normal' or non-fantastical pregnancies). In this way, where woman confuses boundaries – specifically, the boundary of self/other underpinning Western philosophy, as Battersby (1998) argues (see, also, Irigaray [1974] 1985) – the pregnant woman makes this confusion explicit and the pregnancies in these fantasy texts offer a further, heightened example of that confusion. In short, not only is Daine 'no one bird' but neither is her daughter.

Daine's child continues to shape-shift after birth and does so until, the Green Lady (Daine's mum) issues a divine grandmotherly command instructing the child to 'choose a shape and a sex and stick to it, right now' (2003, 246). However, this is not a command delimiting the child's potential nor is it without the empathetic listening that was so paramount to Daine's quartet. For example, Sarra 'listened for a moment, then shook her head. "Five years at least. Learn the limits of one body. Then, if you're good, you may try others. Now *choose*." A moment later she held a human baby girl in her hands' (ibid., emphasis original). Of note, while choose is italicized for emphasis, within the logic of this world, italics also represent the gods speaking (the Badger's speaking whether out loud or via the mind was italicized to represent the divine nature of that speaking). Here, it adds weight to the choice both telling the child she must but also that she gets to choose. Importantly, this choice – and choosing 'human baby girl' – does not limit the potentialities of self. Yes, the child chooses this shape and, presumably, 'stick[s] to it', but the possibility of 'whatever shape' remains. In so doing, Daine's shape-shifting and the legacy of it in her child disrupt the assumption that we are who appear to be, that humans and animals are distinct (and oppositional) categories, and that there can be a radical break between self and other. Daine clearly shows that there cannot be and offers a way, touch or connection, to conceive selfhood through relations instead of oppositions.

6

Being-Hero: Relational, embodied, procreative selfhood

Myths are powerful. They shape how we know and understand the world and how we live in it. For too long, the dominant myth has privileged one story and one way of engaging the world, at the expense of, I would argue, everyone – even the hero it purports to value. To disrupt and dismantle this myth, I've focused on female-heroes: girls who are pushing the boundaries of what it means to be hero, girl and even human. They undertake this work by radically and dynamically occupying the space in-between. In so doing, they are able to offer a model of selfhood recognizing plurality and change, forming through connection and making space for kinship informed by an ethos of ethical responsibility. They also offer a pattern or map of how to achieve such a model, as Chapter 3's separation from heroic romance, Chapter 4's intervention in initiation (or symbolic death and rebirth) and Chapter 5's 'return' demonstrated.

In this reflexive 'conclusion' and as a means of drawing together the chapter threads, I want to keep the female-hero's radical occupation of the middle ground in mind, as I take a closer look at, first, how these female heroes disrupt linearity by allowing repetition and making spaces for plurality (this reading draws on Alanna's disruption of the heroic romance in Chapter 3); second, how they break the hold of visuality by including touch as a powerful means of perceiving the world and connecting with others in it, work that I began in Chapters 4 and 5; and third, by offering an image, The Pack, of relational and inclusive selfhood.

Disrupting linearity

The heroic romance is male, and it encodes and naturalizes a linear, teleological, goal- or quest-driven narrative, at the expense of other patterns and people. It excludes girls and women by tying them to the biological, fleshy, material body, and to the cyclical patterns of reproduction. In Chapter 2, I explored how Alanna's female-hero's journey inserted cyclicality and ambiguity into the linearity of the hero's journey, thereby disrupting it from within its frame. As part of building up the relational model of selfhood female-heroes offer, I want to focus on repetition as a disruption of linearity. I am interested in these repetitions because in developmental theories of adolescence, cyclicality is what makes the girl unsuitable for hegemonic models of development because cyclicality is posited as the antithesis to linear development. It is where, in Waller's reading, the adolescent girl 'slips back into [...] "woman's time"' (2009, 35), and in my larger concern, it is where one of the most profound silences occurs: we do not talk about that which makes us uncomfortable, and not talking about, for example, menstruation increases shame and exclusion (the girl's from the hero story because the blood is abject).

Disguised as a boy whilst training to become a knight – and, crucially, without a mother – menarche, for Alanna, is a horrifying occurrence because she is both alone in its occurrence and unknowing of its meaning; as I demonstrated, it is this combination of isolation and ignorance that contrived to produce the horror of the blood and how that horror was neutralised by talking about the blood. The conversation between Mistress Cooper and Alanna also introduces repetition, cyclicality, nature, and future children into the hero's story.

> 'You poor child', she chuckled. 'Did no one ever tell you of a woman's monthly cycle? The fertility cycle?'
>
> Alanna stared. Maude had mentioned something, once –
>
> 'That's what this is? It's *normal*?'
>
> The woman nodded. 'It happens to us all. We can't bear children until it begins.'
>
> 'How long do I have to put up with this?' Alanna gritted.
>
> 'Until you are too old to bear children. It's as normal as the full moon is, and it happens just as often. You may as well get used to it.
>
> (Pierce 1983 [1987], 136–7, emphasis original)

Here, I want to focus on the repetitions. The one implied by cycle ('woman's monthly cycle'), offered by Maude's having 'mentioned something, once' (this telling a repetition of that original mentioning), the one imbedded in 'it happens to us all', how it repeats like the 'full moon', and – most importantly – 'the children'.

First, menstruation is constructed in terms of plurality. Not only does the conversation itself insist upon a notion of community (at least two beings are required to converse), but it also reiterates the importance of relation through insisting that this bleeding happens to 'us all', the women of the 'women's monthly cycle'. This is not to say that all women experience this bleeding in the same way; it is, rather, that this blood, the physical material thing, offers connection, if discursive constructions will only take it up. Typically, they do not, as Alan illustrates. Faced with this bodily function – this aspect of being-female – Alan cannot apprehend the meaning of the bleeding. Alan is the ideal of hegemonic models of self: the individual, the hero. Yet, for him, the bleeding has no meaning. Thus, for Alanna to come into her full-self, to become a warrior-maiden, menstruation must be acknowledged. Not because it makes her a woman (or because its absence would've allowed her to remain Alan but because menstruation is a facet of her being female). The being-female – and being so with another woman – must be acknowledged.

Moreover, this monthly cycle – itself a repetition – has the potential to produce (other) children, at least until it ends. In relating the 'it' to 'bear[ing] children', narration not only relates the cycle to something outside of itself – another kind of making normal through linking – but it also produces a repetition that problematizes the linearity of dominant conceptions of development. In other words, Alanna is narrated as being a 'child', though one transitioning into 'womanhood', and this cycle constructs her as now being able to bear other children, to perpetuate the cycle and to produce multiplicity of self. This perpetuation of the 'child' through the 'bear[ing]' of other 'children' constructs the cycle as at once ending and never ending. While Alanna may one day be 'too old', the narration of the cycle – in terms of 'tell', of story – constructs that cycle as never ceasing. In so doing, the narration offers cycles (repeats monthly) within cycles (the bearing of children), modelling a kind of spiral of identity in the process. This is about, as Irigaray suggests, 'frustrate[ing] the opposition through the economy of repetition' ([1974] 1985, 77). Repetition is not linear, which problematizes traditional developmental models that are based on linear development through time, and it speaks to a kind of interdependency that contributes to the relational model of existence with which I am concerned. Repetition refuses autonomy, since without links between occurrences there would be no repetition.

Alanna and Thom, as twins, offer a heightened example of repetition. Hunt (1986) suggests that twins offer unique possibilities for identity formation through the mechanism of 'identity exchange' (109). One way this kind of exchange may occur is through the notion of a 'counterpart', and of this Hunt suggests,

> here we may point out that the idea of counterparts calls up not only facile masquerades but deeper ambiguities – for example, the notion that

both counterparts really have their existence within a single individual. In this essentially Jungian interpretation, the counterparts become the self and the shadow.

(1986, 112)

As I have demonstrated, this is the relationship between the twins Alanna and Thom. From the outset, they are constructed as not merely two distinct parts of one whole but as a whole split in two parts. After the cross-dressing, Alanna 'looks enough like Thom to fool anyone but Coram' (1983, 9) and she – not Thom – possesses the skills coded as masculine within this world: 'quicker [...] rarely tired [...] [and has] a feel for the fighting arts' (15). While I discussed above how this allows Alanna to not only construct her 'own gender niche' (Flanagan 2008, 104) and to serve as a 'third', it also posits her self in relation to, or in dialogue with, Thom's (Garber 1992, 11). They, in other words, complement one another, while in appearance, they repeat one another: despite being brother and sister, Alanna and Thom are identical, once Alanna cross-dresses.

Of this doubleness, McCallum notes, 'a primary effect of the double is to destabilize notions of the subject as unified, or coherent, or as existing outside of a relation to an other' (1999, 75; see, also, C. C. Hunt 1986; Waller 2009). This is the aim of these Conclusions: to demonstrate how the self – that is multiple and fragmented – might exist in relation to other selves, in this case, through repetitions of, or related to, that body. However, as I have demonstrated, the goal of hegemonic YA is to enact the unification of the fragmented self. Hegemonic YA hails the adolescent outside of the text through the adolescent inside the text to assist the 'real' adolescent in their journey towards a unique and individual self, foreclosing relationship or interdependency in the process. Thus, the double must be 'resolved'; the liberal humanist ethic underscoring these texts requires resolution. McCallum specifically notes that in 'gothic novels closure is usually achieved through the death of the double' (76). On the surface, this would appear to be the case with Alanna and Thom, as Thom does die at the end of 'The Song of the Lioness' quartet, concomitant to Alanna finally coming fully into her powers and her sense of self. However, these are mythopoeic YA fantasy texts, and as such, they complicate matters.

Mythopoeic YA's capacity to continue narrative threads beyond the boundaries of a single text or grouping of texts is one of its key features, one contributing greatly to the strength of its impact. Here, Alanna's three children thwart any easy resolution of Alanna's self as singular or individual – refigured as her eldest son (Thom), Alanna not only gives birth to her dead brother/other half (Thom) but the twins Alan and Alianne represent the boy she became and the female-hero she became. Aly is a trickster, a liminal figure often responsible for disrupting cultural norms and standards, for creating new myths (see Hyde 1998). Through having children, these 'other' parts of Alanna's identity are actualized. The multiple aspects of Alanna are offered through her children, another kind of repetition and further disruption to the linear, teleological impetus of the hero story.

Breaking visuality

The economy of opposition dominating hegemonic discourse relies on visuality – or the paradigmatic way in which the visual has become not only the dominant means of perceiving this world but of also being a self in it. This visuality has led to a representational economy of self-through-appearance that produces not only a pervasive superficiality – you are who you appear to be – but it does so through furthering opposition itself: viewing may occur at a distance, leaving a space, a potential opposition, between the viewer and the viewed. Touch refuses this distance. This call for touch – as an additional means of perceiving the body – utilizes Grosz's in *Volatile Bodies* (1998). Specifically, her argument that the touch's 'contiguous access to an abiding object; the surface of the toucher and the touched must partially coincide', while also 'grant[ing] the subject access to the texture' and, potentially, 'to the depth – of objects, depending on their composition' (1998, 98–9). In this way, touch offers more access to the contours of the body than does vision, and it does so through connections between individuals or between individuals and other things (be they animal or mechanical), a reading that Daine and Cinder's relationships with animals and machines (respectively) narrates particularly well.

In Daine's shape-shifting, touch is explicitly engaged in order to make the changed body available: 'Daine explored with her hands [...] Her top and bottom incisors were long and extremely sharp, sharp enough to cut her skin' ([1994] 1999, 177). Touch allows her to grasp, as it were, just how sharp her teeth are and it allows for the texture of her furred nose to be made known, to both her and to the reader. Within the narration, Daine discovers the body's changed shape through this touch, but it is also through the narration of the touch that this change is conveyed to the reader. A narration of seeing the changes to Daine's body would not offer the same kinds of details (textures, changed contours) to which even a narrated touch can appeal. Yet, even here, there is a tension between touch (Daine's 'explor[ing] with her hands') and sight, as Daine immediately asks her companions if they 'can all see this?' (177), thus reiterating conventional reliance on the visual. Yet, while acknowledging that tension, the passage does offer touch as an alternative. After all, the narration only confirms that what was touched can be seen: "'Of course,' Maura replied scornfully' (178). The touch made the change known; the seeing merely confirmed it. Moreover, the touch grants access to the characteristics of these changes, characteristics that sight would only be able to approximate.

There is no mirror for these kinds of changes. They are outside of signification (discourse, the hero story), so a new system – touch – is needed. Crucially, because of that tension between seeing and touching, this narration of touch does not aim to replace sight; it works to supplement sight, often through the garnering of additional information about, for example, a body. It is a powerful narrative of perceiving the changes to one's own body, but touch can also be employed in relation to other bodies: 'Daine felt the dragon's hide ripple. It was like a convulsion – or a contraction! Ma's daughter realized' ([1992] 1997, 262). Here, the touch not only grants knowledge but it also begins to offer an access to depth, to the internal, while also foreshadowing a kind of touch that (much like a medical scan) makes the internal available. For this reason, I now turn to Cinder and how, through the iteration of a touch, the extent of Cinder's 'cybernetic makeup' is made known (2012, 81). This development of touch, and this turn to the mechanical, is important for two reasons: first, in popular and media culture, adolescent girls are no longer strictly fleshy (as in animal) creatures; they are integrated with and reliant on technology – how often does an adolescent girl appear without a mobile phone in her hand? – and second, the re-envisioning of the medical scan, through this frame of touch, speaks back to the hologram as an alternative, to the flat and superficial image of popular and media culture.

Having been volunteered for 'plague research' (2012, 66) by her legal guardian, Lingh Adri, Cinder's body undergoes, ostensibly, a medical scan; however, given her cyborg state, it involved 'the click of prongs' (80) as an android connected to 'the panel in the back of her head' (81) as opposed to the external scan typical of such imaging. This connection, or 'plugging in' (195), is a kind of touch. In fact, I consider it a development of the touch that I read in relation to Daine, one that is made specifically possible because of Cinder's cybernetic body (fleshy bodies do not have control panels or sockets). It is a development that grants access not just to the surface of the touched and toucher but also to the internal: from this connection, Cinder's cybernetic makeup is made known – something as internal as the composition of her heart, 'primarily silicon, mixed with bio tissue', is made known (117). For both Daine and Cinder, the touch not only reveals multiplicity but it also holds the internal in simultaneity with the external (Daine's shape-shifting occurs because of that internal being 'of the People'

(Pierce [1992] 1997, 70)), and in so doing it becomes a powerful way of perceiving the body (and its changes).

Yet, prior to the scan's (forced) connection, Cinder uses this kind of connection to join with an android in need of repair, and the narration of that connection is quite telling in relation to the potential risk of this kind of touch.

> The only way to determine what was wrong and if a reboot was necessary was to check the android's internal diagnostics, and that required plugging in. Cinder hated plugging in. Connecting her own wiring with a foreign object had always felt hazardous, like if she wasn't careful, her own software could be overridden.
>
> (2012, 195)

While lending a certain weight to the previous reading and, perhaps, also speaking to what Balsamo (1996) refers to as the invasiveness of medical imaging – 'plugging in' reads as a euphemism for rape – this narration suggests a possibility, or at least fear, of losing the self through this kind of touch, and it is an uneasiness that Daine's narration also discusses, though in a slightly different way, as I considered in Chapter 5.

Both Daine's shape-shifting and Cinder's cybernetic bodies continue engaging this issue of loss of self through several passages that narrate just how such other things become incorporated into the body image – the body, according to Grosz (1994), 'insofar as it is imagined and represented for the subject by the image of others [including its own reflection in a mirror]' (39). While returning to an image is questionable (since doing so revisits Lacan's imaginary and the images that bombard social and media culture), the body image offered by these texts is an image with a difference: it is an imagined image, a fiction. In popular and media culture, body image is problematic not only because of the particular fiction – perfection – required by the images (mirrors) of that space – airbrushed models and digitally edited selfies, for example – but also because of the sheer preponderance of those images. However, images are not always contentious, and Grosz's understanding of body image is useful here because of how it allows 'the peculiar, nonorganic connections formed in hysteria and in such phenomena as the phantom limb' (40) to be included within one's conception of oneself. It is relevant to both Daine and Cinder, but it is the narration of Cinder's removing a 'too-small foot' (2012, 3) from her body that I find most provocative. This narration of Cinder's removing and replacing her cybernetic foot establishes a difference between the (inorganic) 'too-small foot' that has not grown and her (organic) body that has grown, '[t]he screw through Cinder's ankle had rusted, the engraved cross marks worn to a mangled circle. [...] By the time it was extracted far enough for her to wrench free with her prosthetic steel hand, the hairline threads had been stripped clean' (3). The foot has become useless because it is too small; as an inorganic thing, it has not grown with the body, and has thus become unfit for its purpose. Yet, it has not deteriorated in the same way as the screw. The screw is failing. It is 'rusted' and 'stripped clean'.

However, despite this tension, the foot is still a part of her, and as such, it is constructed as different from other inorganic things. It is this difference that makes the inclusion of some things into the body image (that is to say, one's sense of self) possible, [t]ossing the screwdriver onto the table, Cinder gripped her heel and yanked the foot from its socket. A spark singed her fingertips and she jerked away, leaving the foot to dangle from a tangle of red and yellow wires' (3). The foot, as well as Cinder's cybernetic hand, is quite different from the (rusted) screw and the screwdriver that is tossed onto the table, and this difference hinges upon how one group of things has become incorporated into her body image, while the other has not. It is a reading evidenced by the change from the possessive pronoun in 'her heel' to the definite article in 'the foot'. While attached to the body – via those red and yellow wires – the cybernetic foot is hers, but once removal begins, the possession diminishes. Thus, it is a connection that depends on those wires; it depends on another kind of touch, in that the wires link.

While it could be argued that the foot becomes part of the body because it is human in shape (although – since it is plate metal – it is, for me, humanoid, not human) and the screw does not become part of the body because it does not appear human, the connective function, the touch, of those wires makes incorporation possible. Cinder's removal of the 'too-small foot' (3) precipitates the connection of a 'replacement foot' (12). This connection begins, 'She propped her ankle on the opposite knee and began connecting the color-coordinated wires' (15), and is followed by '[s]he tightened the last screw and stretched out her leg, rolling her ankle forward, back, wiggling the toes. It was a little stiff, and the nerve sensors would need a few days to harmonize with the updated wiring' (15). The screws merely hold the foot in place, whereas the wires – through 'harmoniz[ing]' with 'the nerve sensors' (15) – make connection possible.

Thus, where this process of removing the 'too-small foot' (3) (and replacing it with a 'brand-new steel-plated foot' (11)) not only insists upon the juxtaposition between the human, fleshy body and this body's mechanical body parts, it also illustrates different kinds of connection made possible by Cinder's being cyborg: that which is only connected, that which is incorporated into the body image (the hand and foot) and that which threatens ('plugging in' (195)). This acknowledgement of what I consider to be a fear of the loss of self is integral to this reading: by acknowledging a potential flaw, these narrations do not seek to replace sight with touch as the means for perceiving the body; doing so would risk merely replacing one dominant means with another. Rather, they show touch and sight working together to develop, most particularly, Daine's and Cinder's perception of their own (changed) bodies. Thus, touch becomes a provocative means of expanding the self's perception of itself, while also demonstrating how it might be connected to other bodies.

Modelling relation: The pack

According to the opening pages of *Wild Magic*, Daine has always had a 'knack with animals, but no gift' (Pierce 1992, 15), at least not in the traditional, Tortallan sense. This 'knack' not only sets her apart from other humans but also lays a foundation upon which her ability to shape-shift, that is, to transform into the shapes of animals, eventually evolves. As I have argued, it is a foundation that establishes oppositions (Gift/wild magic, outside/inside and human/animal) to question them. In other words, where the text establishes a (binary) difference between humans and animals, Daine's shape-shifting – through an expanding of what it means to be Gifted, a blurring of inside/outside and a countering of individuality – holds together those opposing identities. Daine is 'of the People' (1992, 70), and this is imperative because it is through the relationships that Daine develops with animals that her shape-shifting offers a relational model of being that counters the individuality of popular and media culture.

In a provocative narration, Onau, Daine's friend and employer, makes this relationship clear.

> 'We share this world, Diane. We can't hold apart from each other – humans and animals are meant to be partners. Aren't we, Tahoi?' The dog wagged his tail. He knows. He saved my life, when my husband left me to die. I've saved his life since. He can't cook or sing, and I can't chase rabbits, but we're partners all the same.
>
> (Pierce 1992, 266–7)

When she shape-shifts, Daine literally embodies this bond humans and animals already share because 'we share this world'. The relational model of self as demonstrated here considers the interdependency between not just generations – this is a conversation between Daine and 'the older woman', also an issue at play in the conversations between Alanna and Mistress

Cooper as well as Kel and her maid – but also humans and animals; this narration is striking in its espousing not just relationship but a relationship between a woman and her dog (see, also, Haraway 2003).[1]

This notion of companionship is one that Daine's quartet offers in many forms: Daine is 'Hoof-sister', or 'hoof-kin', with horses ([1994] 1999, 308); she is 'night-sister' to an owl (1992, 134), as she is 'wing-sister' to a dragon (260). These relationships suggest kinship, an important web of relations, often between blood relatives but also including those who have entered a family group through marriage.[2] In Daine's case, her wild magic links her to these animals, producing a relationship of kin. Metaphorically, her magic is the blood of a 'blood relation', speaking back to my concern with menstruation as the blood of life in Chapter 4 and the 'blood' both literately and metaphorically shared between Alanna and her children as well as Daine and hers.

Poignantly, Daine is also 'Pack-sister' ([1994] 1999, 28), and this 'Pack' is linked to a sense of community and collectivity that not only problematizes the binary opposition between human and animal but also demonstrates a sense of cooperation and camaraderie that is absent in the individualism required by neoliberal narratives of choice – and it does so without a loss of self. Moreover, this metaphor of 'the Pack' is not restricted to Pierce's Immortals quartet, as The Books of Pellinor also include a notion of 'the Pack', and both these quartets use this image of 'the Pack' to establish a metaphorical framework for a relational model of self. In other words, while adolescent girls may not be able to experience 'the Pack' in the same way Daine and Maerad (Croggon's female-hero) do through their literal transformations into wolves, 'the Pack' does have the potential to serve as a powerful metaphor of interdependency and community that is absent from the discourses of, especially, adolescent development in contemporary Western culture.

While Daine ultimately learns to transform into any animal (including multiple animals at once) and to incorporate animal parts within and on her human self as well as human parts into her animal self, she shares a particular bond with wolves; Brokefang, the Pack leader of the Long Lake wolves, regards her as Pack, despite her looking quite human ([1994] 1999, 3). Daine's inclusion within the Pack, despite a visible difference between her and a typical Pack member, is crucial. It is a key difference between mythopoeic YA fantasy representations of the Pack and hegemonic offerings, which are often incredibly appearance-driven. For Daine, appearance does not matter because 'The Pack' means kinship, support and relation: '"You're my pack, aren't you? I'll do my best. I can't promise they'll listen to me, but I'll try" ([1994] 1999, 14)', and 'It's so lonely outside the pack' (1992, 161). While Maerad's ability differs from Daine's, the idea of 'Pack' offered by her 'being wolf' is like that constructed by Daine's texts: Maerad 'can share our kill and drink our water, he said. We will give her the protection of the pack' (Croggon 2005, 435). Here, the pack is about 'shar[ing]' and 'protection'. For Daine, this community is demonstrated in a need for companionship: 'he's a good pack leader for you. Brokefang went on. Humans are like wolves. We all need a pack' ([1994] 1999, 93). Brokefang's statement not only demonstrates an importance of the Pack but also establishes a further similarity between humans and wolves, at least concerning this need for a Pack – humans are like wolves in this need.

Daine and Maerad find care, companionship and unity in 'the Pack', just as Alanna and Kel find support and understanding in their conversations with other women. These are relational models of self, and they are crucial for undoing the dominance of binary oppositions. As repetition and connection demonstrate, relationship frustrates economies of opposition by occupying the space between oppositions, and as this final reading of 'the Pack' demonstrates, the relational model of self that is available in these texts also refuses the competition and isolating individuality implicit in hegemonic narratives of self (narratives underscored by the system of binary oppositions). Moreover, as mainstream offerings of 'the Pack' demonstrate, the power of the dominant to recuperate, to stabilize, that which threatens its systems is strong. Thus, these texts also demonstrate how challenges to this narrative must come from the periphery. Peripheries are edges, boundaries between that which we are and that which we are not. When mythopoeic YA began, YA was not the cultural powerhouse it is today, a status this is still, arguably, ignored and devalued by the mainstream dominant perspective. Still, this gives mythopoeic YA a unique position to comment on the mainstream by drawing on its liminal status.

Finally and beyond the 'packs' formed between mothers and daughters, Pierce offers a human model of the 'pack' in her Circle Universe books, in the partnership wrought between the four ambient mages Sandry (thread mage), Tris (weather mage), Briar (plant mage) and Daja (smith mage). Ambient magic is somewhat akin to Daine's wildmagic and many parallels between the two can be drawn. While all the texts of this universe are preoccupied, in some way, with the children's relationship, *The Magic in the Weaving* is crucial for it sets them upon a particularly bonded path, one that runs counter to hegemonic narratives of individualism.[3] Trapped underground by an earthquake and at risk from subsequent tremors, Sandry weaves the children's magics together to make them stronger: '*Fibres by themselves are weak – so are we. Spin them together, and they become strong. I think the spindle will bring our powers together and strengthen us*' (1997, 203). The metaphor of spinning and weaving is beautiful, as it speaks to how we are 'stronger together' and not when in competition.

Appendices

Appendix I: Tamora Pierce's Tortall Universe and Marissa Meyer's Lunar Chronicles

The Tortall Universe

The Song of the Lioness
1983 *Alanna: The First Adventure*
1984 *In the Hand of the Goddess*
1986 *The Woman Who Rides Like a Man*
1988 *Lioness Rampant*

Immortals
1992 *Wild Magic*
1994 *Wolf-Speaker*
1995 *Emperor Mage*
1996 *The Realms of the Gods*

Protector of the Small
1999 *First Test*
2000 *Page*
2001 *Squire*
2002 *Lady Knight*

Daughter of the Lioness
2003 *Trickster's Choice*
2004 *Trickster's Queen*

Beka Cooper: A Tortall Legend
2006 *Terrier*
2009 *Bloodhound*
2011 *Mastiff*

The Numair Chronicles (ongoing)
2018 *Tempests and Slaughter*

The Numair Chronicles
2011 *Tortall and Other Lands*
2017 *Tortall: A Spy's Guide*

The Lunar Chronicles

2012 *Cinder*
2013 *Scarlet*
2014 *Cress*
2015 *Fairest*
2015 *Winter*

2016 *Stars Above: A Lunar Chronicles Collection*
2017 *Wires and Nerve*
2018 *Wires and Nerve: Gone Rogue*

Notes

Preface

1 Rank's text was originally published in German as *Der Mythus von der Geburt des Helden* (1909).
2 Campbell's hero is also older than the figure of concern in the work of Rank and Hall, though this does not necessarily make this iteration of the hero any less 'adolescent' in approach to and engagement with the world. As adolescence is an 'interstructural situation' (adolescence describes the stage between the relatively stable 'states' of child and adult), and the hero story concerns the (successful) navigation of such a situation (Turner 1967, 234), the hero, of whatever age, is always 'adolescent' in outlook and engagement with the world (Hourihan 1997a, 74). Part of the work of female-heroes is undoing the negative associations (juvenile, immature) mainstream culture has with the concept 'adolescent', offering instead a way of being steeped in flexibility and responsiveness with the potential to collapse dominant and dominating binaries.

Chapter 1

1 Currently, Snow White, Cinderella, Aurora, Ariel, Belle, Jasmine, Pocahontas, Mulan, Tiana, Rapunzel, Merida and Moana.
2 The Tale Type index uses recurring sets of motifs, or plots, to group tales, and it has layers. At the broadest, Cinderella is a 'tale of magic', as are all the tales identified within the 300–749 range. Drilling further down, hers is further classified by its 'magical helper', placing it within the 500–518 section of tales. Cinderella's specific number, 510a, refers to tales sharing the plot I describe the text. Finally, there is a 510b, and it is very similar to the 'a' version, except that in it, the king tries to marry his daughter. Versions of the guide are available in many places on the internet. 'Unpacking World Folk-Literature', curated and compiled by Shawn Urban, is a handy one.
3 It is also in the names of characters, as a change to Lady Tremaine's name demonstrates. In *Cinderella* (1950), the character is named; she is Lady Tremaine. However, in the live-action film, she becomes Stepmother. As a 'real' person who is played by Cate Blanchett, the character risks becoming too real. In folktales, names also tend to match a character's role or function: Prince Charming, Grand Duke, Coachman.

4   It is worth noting that Parsons borrows 'positions to occupy' from Valerie Walkerdine (1984), and while it is Parsons' use with which I am most interested, Walkerdine is concerned with the psychoanalytical implications of such positions in terms of the young girl's insertion into romantic heterosexuality, which is also relevant.
5   Jaq and Gus' storyline is a hero story, with Jaq serving in the role of hero and Gus, in complicated and sometimes conflicting ways, standing in for the heroic romance's view of women.
6   The strategies behind this move are complex. I'd highly recommend Gerda Learner's *The Creation of Patriarchy* for a more in-depth look at how patriarchy uses procreation to exclude women and the strategies it employs to achieve its goal.
7   Kenneth Kidd and Derritt Mason's edited collection *Queer as Camp: Essays on Summer, Style, and Sexuality* offers an excellent, recent exploration of 'queer' and 'camp', especially focusing on camp as space outside of dominant, normative time and place (2019).
8   *Princess Cultures: Mediating Girls' Imaginations and Identities*, edited by Miriam Forman-Brunell, offers a more in-depth reading of princess culture and its complex impact on what it means to be a girl than I can explain here (2014).
9   For a reading of the tween girl, this little sister of the adolescent girl, see Melanie Kennedy's *Tweenhood: Femininity and Celebrity in Tween Popular Culture* (2018).
10 Tinkerbell, from the film *Peter Pan* (Luske, Geronimi and Jackson 1953), briefly featured in the franchise.
11 I use 'of colour' with much trepidation and as the 'best' option from a pool of problematic terms.
12 At her time of writing, Orenstein notes some 26,000 Disney Princess items available, a number that has astronomically grown (especially considering the unlicensed merchandise flooding the market). See Orenstein (2011, 14).
13 Girl power versus girl saving has been the dominant discourse constructing adolescent girlhood since the mid-1990s. 'Reviving Ophelia', the moniker of 'girl saving', comes from the trendy book *Reviving Ophelia: Saving the Selves of Adolescent Girls* by Mary Pipher. Tapping into parents' fears, Pipher's text both defines and establishes the 'girl poisoning culture' in which the adolescent girl of the 1990s existed (1994, 267).
14 Despite existing in the poorest district of Panem, the fictional world in which her story takes place. Indeed, in a narrative arc that should include issues of class and attendant issues around maintaining a certain standard of appearance – beauty work is not cheap – Katniss is remarkably nourished, arguably because she can hunt, but also exceptionally well groomed.
15 For discussions of the absence of menstruation in YA, see, for example, Cummins (2008), Sayantani (2010), Burns (2013), Jensen (2014) and Kennon (2015).

16 Carrie has been much analysed for its navigation of the feminine and feminist and its handling of menstruation. See Moseley (2002), Clover (1993) and Creed (1993).
17 While I address issues of shape-shifting, often termed metamorphosis, in Chapter 5, *Ginger Snaps* alludes to a werewolf motif that is strongly present in terms of both animal studies, which my reading of shape-shifting engages, as well as the perceived horror of a girl's transition into woman, in which hair and body hair do play a role. For discussions of werewolves, see, for example, McMahon (2012), Coudray (2006), Douglas (1994), Otten (1986).

Chapter 2

1 Robin McKinley, Anne McCaffrey, Patricia Wrede, Diane Duane and Mercedes Lackey also play a key role, but Pierce's influence is the most profound. Perry offers an in-depth reading of McKinley and her work (2010).
2 Jodi McAlister's investigations of new adult fiction, a field intimately related to YA, informs this chapter's methodology (2018; 2021). McAlister employs a 'snapshot' approach to show how 'genres are not stable categories, but are endlessly evolving and shifting signifiers' (2018, 4). McAlister's work is underpinned by Fletcher, Driscoll and Wilkin's theory of 'genre worlds', a conceiving of genre through 'the collective activity that goes into the creation and circulation of genre texts' (2018, 998). Specifically, and as Wilkins, Driscoll, Fletcher states, 'the multiple dimensionality of popular genres: as bodies of texts, collections of social formations that gather around and produce those texts, and sets of industrial practices' (2018, 1–2).
3 A full reading of imaginary world theory and mythopoeic YA is outside the scope of this chapter. For detailed studies of imaginary worlds and world-building, see Mark Wolf's *Building Imaginary Worlds* (2012), Colin B. Harvey's *Fantastic Transmedia – Narrative, Play and Memory across Science Fiction and Fantasy Storyworlds* (2015), and Wolf's edited collection, *Revisiting Imaginary Worlds: A Subcreation Studies Anthology* (2016). I cite all of these throughout this chapter.
4 Deleuze and Guattari's concept of the 'rhizome' is useful for conceptualizing these networks of connection. They describe the rhizome in *A Thousand Plateaus* as a nonlinear network that 'connects any point to any other point' (Deleuze and Guattari 1987, 21). Where these networks of connection differ is how they include linearity (a group of books will progress in a linear fashion) but through subsequent groups, fanfiction and art, maps, and an array of other avenues, they also include nonlinear connection. In this sense, could refer to these networks of connection as a hybrid.
5 Maps help us to 'see' that which is not readily or easily conceived because of size, location and temporal restraints. They help us find our way – through, and to, places.

6   There are 8,000 instances of fanfiction on FanFiction.net concerning The Song of the Lioness quartet alone. See also AO3, which includes (at time of writing) 2,067 fanfics related to Tortall ('Tortall – Tamora Pierce – Works | Archive of Our Own' n.d.).

7   Many thanks to Kae Marie for allowing me to mention her tattoo.

8   Crucially, this is not to establish the physical geography, or body, as more 'real' or 'true' than their maps, each has a truth.

9   This point is underpinned by Rudine Sims Bishop's foundational 'Windows, Mirrors, and Sliding Glass Doors' (1990), and I recognize not all readers will find themselves in the worlds of mythopoeic YA or see themselves reflected in the currently available mirrors, female-heroes, offered therein. However, I hope that this chapter and the book can go some ways towards dismantling the structure of opposition at the root of so much alterity, personal and political. For further reading, I highly recommend Stephanie Toliver's recent 'On Mirrors, Windows, and Telescopes' (2021) and 'Imagining New Hopescapes: Expanding Black Girls' Windows and Mirrors' (2018b).

10 For example, I first encountered Tortall through The Immortals quartet, which comes after The Song of the Lioness, according to both Tortall's timeline and the books' publication order. This is just one of the ways in which mythopoeic YA frustrates the linearity embedded into hero stories.

11 Robin McKinley's *The Blue Sword* and *The Hero and the Crown* share a similar cross-dressing motif. While Angharad Crew (the female-hero of this text) may not cross-dress to the same extent as Alanna, Angharad does insist on being called Harry, implying a masculine identity and both acts are interventions in the fields of myth and fantasy at their time. Inserting female-heroes into a field structurally requiring male heroes is not easy. By taking on masculine identities, Alanna and Angharad – two girls – become heroes, expanding the archetype, to a degree.

12 I specifically draw field from Pierre Bourdieu's work, *The Field of Cultural Production*, which is a useful starting point (1993).

13 This issue, and Trites' subsequent monograph, *Disturbing the Universe: Power and Repression in Adolescent Literature* (2000a), played pivotal roles in establishing YA as a field related to, but different from, children's literature.

14 For a reading of these shifts, albeit from a distinctly US perspective, see Cart (2001; 2016a; 2016b).

15 According to Cart, YA's interest in the 10- to 14-year-old was a 'youthening' of the field from the 'traditional 16–17' year-old protagonist to a prepubescent one (hence menarche in mythopoeic YA, a shift he positions as starting in the 1970s (2016b, 3).

16 Maerad is sixteen when she experiences menarche. Sold into slavery after the sack of her home, Maerad is malnourished, which gives rise to her amenorrhoea.

17 The phenomenon of 'crossover' fiction, that is books with a multigenerational appeal, is interesting here. See, for example, Beckett (2011; 2017) and Falconer (2010).

18 In an article for *The Bookseller* reporting on the Bologna Children's Book Fair (the largest industry event dedicated to children's publishing), Benedicte Page notes a dramatic rise in publisher's interest in 'pre-teen' reads (2010); this interest is one of the earliest marker of MG emergence.
19 New Adult, or NA, almost arose to fill this void, but for a variety of reasons was unsuccessful, not least because the label is dreadful. Pattee (2017) discusses NA's emergence, while McAlister (2018) traces its trajectory and eventual assumption by the romance genre.
20 As with any shift, there are earlier forerunners (as that fracturing of YA and MG in 2010 suggests), but 2012 seems to mark a concerted turn in the kinds of YA, not just mythopoeic YA, being published. The field would welcome research tracing mythopoeic YA's threads before the early 1980s.
21 My reading of mirrors, of course, draws on Lacan (2001), but I'm indebted to Karen Coats *Looking Glasses and Neverlands* for helping me make sense of things. For this particular point, see the section on 'Lacan and the Subject of Children's Literature' (Coats 2004, 4–6). Specifically, 'the child looking into a mirror sees an idealized image of his potential. This image, in its specular completeness, is at odds with how he *experiences* his body' and the completeness it offers becomes his goal (6). The problem: wholeness of this fashion can never be achieved, and so in seeing this ideal image, the hero enters into a system (language, representation) that requires he forever seek wholeness. His prize is one of the objects he uses to approximate wholeness.
22 Christine Geraghty's definition of a soap opera offers another way of conceiving of these worlds. As Geraghty argues soap operas are often created to appear 'as if life has been going on without us' and are set across many series that are distinct in themselves but contribute to the whole of the opera (1990). However, mythopoeic YA does not share the soap operas serial nature. Pattee makes the case that within YA the 'soap opera' is akin to the early publisher's format series (2010): The Hardy Boys, Nancy Drew, Sweet Valley High.
23 The inclusion of journal entries from characters appearing in novels published earlier but occurring after Beka's blur its temporal boundaries.

Chapter 3

1 In *The Rhetoric of Character*, Maria Nikolajeva argues, 'Children's fiction is "pregendered" in the sense that in the majority of children's novels, protagonists are gender-neutral-that is, more or less interchangeable, in terms of gender' (2002, 44). Alanna and Thom both are and are not interchangeable, even as children. Alanna's cross-dressing takes advantage of this premise to destabilize gender norms and standards and assumptions about children's gender.

2. Flanagan notes that 'this introduction frames Alanna's decision to cross-dress as a response to her dissatisfaction with traditional femininity and desire to escape it by assuming a masculine identity as a royal page' (2008, 68).
3. Using language to bring worlds and beings into being has been the ideal form of creation since the development of monotheism in the book of Genesis, and it is the purview of men (Lerner 1986, 198; Weigle 1989).
4. Narratives of birth control – of the girls actively choosing to protect themselves from unwanted pregnancies – are central to Pierce's world. In *Squire*, Kel seeks out a 'midwife-healer' to purchase a charm against pregnancy, 'as declaration that she could decide some things for herself' (2001, 301). In one respect, this is another means of demonstrating positive embodiment. Choosing this 'thing for herself' – choosing not to get pregnant while still having sex – is an act of agency, a choice Pierce's Beka Cooper series develops. Corinne Matthews offers an excellent reading of not only another mythopoeic YA world in which periods and related issues are discussed but how Matthews ties those issues to consent and community makes it particularly relevant (2019).
5. There are actually a few ritual rebirths within Alanna's narrative. For example, she enters the Chamber of the Ordeal at the end of *In the Hand of the Goddess* to officially become a Knight of the Realm of Tortall (Pierce 1984, 188–207). In *Lioness Rampant*, Alanna enters Chitral's cave to do battle for the Dominion jewel, her final rebirth and the one that sees her return home as Alan-na (Pierce 1988, 125–32). They are all vital to producing the ultimately ambiguously gendered self she becomes. I am interested in these initial makeovers because of their tie to Cinderella's ritual rebirth and for the ways in which they initiate gender performances/identities.

Chapter 4

1. A full exploration of posthuman is outside of this book's scope. Moreover, several examinations that probably, almost certainly, do a better job of explaining the topic than I could already exist. Victoria Flanagan's chapter on 'Posthumanism in Young Adult Fiction' in *Technology and Identity in Young Adult Fiction* (2014), like Tarr and White's collection, does a brilliant job of outlining issues within posthumanism and linking them to YA. The 'Introduction' includes a discussion of the changing approaches to technology within YA. More widely, see Hayles (1999), Vint (2007), Toffoletti (2007).
2. Jennifer Mitchell also engages posthumanism when reading Cinder as queer, specifically as a 'sustained resistance to fixity' to 'expand previous conversations about metaphors for queerness' (2014, 53).
3. Kai proposes to Cinder at the end of 'Something Old, Something New' (2016a), which is included in Winter (Meyer 2015b) as an epilogue. It is also included in Stars Above: A Lunar Chronicles Collection (2016).

4   Most articles that discuss Cinder mention her status as property. Alexandra Lykissas offers a particularly insightful analysis in her 'Cyborg-erella: Marissa Meyer's Cinder as a New Type of Other' (2020, 209–11). Miranda Green-Barteet and Meghan Gilbert-Hickey, on the other hand, use Meyer's prioritizing of Cinder's cyborg-ness at the expense of any nuanced discussion about 'race, racism or racialized difference' (2017, 2). For them, 'Cinder's cyborg identity is a concrete, visual marker of her otherness' but her status as presumably white person and a Lunar is 'invisible in the face of her mechanical subtext' (2017, 13). They are right to point out the novel's failings.
5   Melanie Kennedy's landmark study of tweenhood as a forerunner of adolescence includes an excellent analysis of 'authenticity' and how it relates to femininity and especially tween burgeoning femininity (2018).
6   Susan Squier's *Babies in Bottles: Twentieth-Century Visions of Reproductive Technology* offers an excellent analysis of the issues surrounding reproductive technologies and the 'ideological constructions' behind 'achieving human control over reproduction' (1994, 23).
7   Gill's markers of this postfeminist sensibility are 'the notion that femininity is a bodily property; the shift from objectification to subjectification; the emphasis upon self-surveillance, monitoring and discipline; a focus upon individualism, choice and empowerment; the dominance of a makeover paradigm; a resurgence in ideas of natural sexual difference; a marked sexualization of culture; and an emphasis upon consumerism and the commodification of difference' (2007, 149).
8   For a social history of glamour in the West, see Dyhouse (2010).

Chapter 5

1   A note on speech marks. There are several kinds of speaking within this world, and the texts employ several strategies to represent those 'speakings', especially the ones that do not involve vocalizations. There are a few instances where these rules do not hold but for the most part:

- Dialogue between beings who can speak in human languages is represented through speech marks but only when it is spoken out loud;
- Dialogue taking the form of 'mind-speech' (it is re-presented on the page but is not spoken aloud) does not receive speech marks;
- In the mortal realms, divine speaking is represented using italics. When that speaking is voiced, it is marked by opening and closing em dashes.

There are a few other forms of speaking within this world, but the above are the most pertinent to this chapter.

2   Sax further argues that 'the hunt of the stag', a particular – but also the chief – hunt, 'has usually functioned as a ritualistic taming of the forest'

(1990, 121). My question, what kind of taming happens when the god charged with overseeing the hunt (that is, with establishing, the shape tenor and tone) is both that which hunts and is hunted?

3   This is not a project exploring issues of race and ethnicity. However, I am interested in adolescent girls, and there are adolescent girls of colour. I also recognize and acknowledge the heightened disparity girls of colour face, though I can never fully understand that lived experience. As such, I would direct readers to several people doing that vital work disrupting power imbalances. Concerning the representation of girls of colour in speculative YA fiction, Ebony Elizabeth Thomas (2019) and Stephanie Toliver (2018a; 2018b; 2019; 2019b; 2019a) both work on representations of Black girlhood; Cristina Rhodes (Forthcoming) and Marilisa Jiménez García (2018) consider Latnix representations. *Race in Young Adult Speculative Fiction*, edited by Meghan Gilbert-Hickey and Miranda A. Green-Barteet, explores the depictions of young people of colour in YA speculative fiction (2021). Beyond both my interests (adolescent girlhood and speculative fiction) but considering the representations of young people of colour in children's literature and YA, Mandy Suhr-Systma (2018) works on Indigenous representations, and *Growing up Asian American in Young Adult Fiction*, edited by Ymitri Mathison, explores representations of Asian Americans (2017).

4   The concept of counter-narratives emerged from critical race theory in the late 1980s and early 1990s through, especially, the work of Richard Delgado (Delgado 1989; 1984; 2013; Delgado and Stefancic 2013). These narratives are not about replacing the dominant narrative; instead, they are concerned with creating a space in which marginalized groups might be heard and understood (Ladson-Billings 1998). As Ramdarshan Bold argues, citing Anderson (2006) and Bhaba (2013), '[c]ounter-narratives are particularly useful for challenging essentialist identities created through "imagined communities"' (Bold 2019, 5).

5   As a black robe mage (highest rank), Numair can shape-change into a hawk form, but as Daine notes, his form is a reproduction of the hawk, not the real thing (as hers is): 'Anyone less familiar with hawks might have taken this bird for one: she [Daine] could not. He was too big, and hawks were not solid black. His colour was dull, like velvet – there was no gloss to his feathers at all. He wasn't wrong as those Stormwings were wrong, but he was not right, either' (Pierce 1992, 35). Even here, Daine has a knowledge of animals that largely goes unrecognized within her world – because she is a working-class, bastard, girl and the skill is with animals.

6   Alanna's learning to fight with a sword offers a similar commentary on knack/skill but from the perspective of not having a knack so needing to develop the skill. Insightfully, once she has learnt the skill, it presents like a knack: 'Alanna attacked, feeling divorced from her arm as she moved through pass after pass. […] She never took the time to think about what she was doing. Instead, her muscles remembered the patterns of endless drills' (Pierce 1983, 175). The difference, Alanna has worked to develop this ability. She has developed a skill.

7   Jo Littler's *Against Meritocracy: Culture, Power and Myths of Mobility* offers an excellent deconstruction of the ideology. It exceptionally illuminates how meritocracy 'endorses a competitive, linear, hierarchical system' (3), 'assumes that talent and logic are innate' (4), 'ignores the fact that climbing the ladder is simply much harder for some people than others' (5), promotes an 'uncritical valorisation of particular forms of status' and knowledge (6) and 'functions as an ideological myth to obscure and extend economic and social inequalities' (7). The contemporary myth of meritocracy is the archetypal hero story, at least since Campbell's reconfiguring of it in the middle of the twentieth century.
8   I am playfully drawing on Chapter 2 – '"I don't know the words": Institutional Discourses in Adolescent Literature' – of Trites's Disturbing the Universe in this phrasing (2000b). The chapter is highly relevant here, in my concern with Daine's wild magic but also to the themes connected to her throughout her quartet and within the wider Universe.
9   For readers in, at least, the UK this is particularly poignant, as human girls are often colloquially referred to as 'birds', evidencing one further example of how these texts might hail a reader outside of the text.
10 Corinne Matthews discusses magical methods of contraception, including Pierce's influence on how contraception is represented in YA fantasy, in 'Contraception, Consent, and Community in Kristin Cashore's Graceling Trilogy' (2019).
11 Sadly, the original discussion has been archived. However, Pierce's comments have been collected by 'Len' on Words of Tamora Pierce, which is the source I reference.

Chapter 6

1   Amy Holdsworth and Karen Lury explore the relation and interdependency between generations in 'Growing up and Growing Old with Television: Peripheral Viewers and the Centrality of Care' (2016).
2   For a cultural materialist approach to kinship patterns, Cultural Anthropology offers a useful starting point (Harris and Johnson 2006). Cultural materialism, in its concern with the material, physical aspects of culture, speaks quite strongly to my concern with the body.
3   Outside of present scope, this series also speaks to the diversity that is still often missing in YA and children's literature. The children are a 'crew', but they are different: in terms of class (Sandry is a noble, Tris a merchant, Briar an orphan and pickpocket and Daja a Trader), race (Daja is Black), sex (Sandry, Tris and Daja are female, and Briar is male) and even sexual orientation (Daja is gay). Here, their differences make them stronger.

Bibliography

Aasi, Rummanah. 2012. 'Song of the Lioness Quartet by Tamora Pierce'. 11 December 2012. http://booksinthespotlight.blogspot.com/2012/12/song-of-lioness-quartet-by-tamora-pierce.html.

Aisenberg, Nadya. 1994. *Ordinary Heroines: Transforming the Male Myth.* New York: Continuum.

ALA. 2012. 'Edwards Award'. Text. *Young Adult Library Services Association (YALSA)*, 27 February 2012. https://www.ala.org/yalsa/edwards-award.

Alaimo, Stacy, and Susan J. Hekman, eds. 2008. *Material Feminisms.* Bloomington, IN: Indiana University Press.

Alexander, Lloyd. 1971. 'High Fantasy and Heroic Romance'. *The Horn Book Magazine*, December 1971.

Al-Sadi, Amina, and Lindy West. 2018. *Girls Can Be Heroes, Depending on What Books You Read Growing Up.* http://kuow.org/post/girls-can-be-heroes-depending-what-books-you-read-growing.

Altmann, Anna E. 1992. 'Welding Brass Tits on the Armor: An Examination of the Quest Metaphor in Robin McKinley's The Hero and the Crown'. *Children's Literature in Education* 23 (3): 143–56. https://doi.org/10.1007/BF01131038.

Anderson, Benedict. 2006. *Imagined Communities: Reflections on the Origin and Spread of Nationalism.* Revised edition. London: Verso.

Arnett, Jeffrey. 2014. *Emerging Adulthood: The Winding Road from the Late Teens through the Twenties.* 2nd edition. Oxford: Oxford University Press.

Arnett, Jeffrey Jensen, and Hamilton Cravens. 2006. 'G. Stanley Hall's Adolescence: Brilliance and Nonsense'. *History of Psychology* 9 (3): 186–97. https://doi.org/10.1037/1093-4510.9.3.186.

Averill, Lindsey. 2016. 'Do Fat-Positive Representations Really Exist in YA? Review of Fat-Positive Characters in Young Adult Literature'. *Fat Studies* 5 (1): 14–31. https://doi.org/10.1080/21604851.2015.1062708.

Bacchilega, Cristina. 1993. 'An Introduction to the "Innocent Persecuted Heroine" Fairy Tale'. *Western Folklore* 52 (1): 1–12. https://doi.org/10.2307/1499490.

Bachelard, Gaston. 2014. *The Poetics of Space.* Translated by Maria Jolas. Reprint edition. 1958. New York, NY: Penguin Classics.

Balsamo, Anne. 1996. *Technologies of the Gendered Body.* Durham, NC: Duke University Press.

Bartyzel, Monika. 2013. 'Girls on Film: The Real Problem with the Disney Princess Brand'. *The Week*, 17 May 2013. https://theweek.com/articles/464290/girls-film-real-problem-disney-princess-brand.

Batt, Catherine. 1994. '" Hand for Hand" and "Body for Body": Aspects of Malory's Vocabulary of Identity and Integrity with Regard to Gareth and Lancelot'. *Modern Philology* 91 (3): 269–87.

Battersby, Christine. 1998. *The Phenomenal Woman: Feminist Metaphysics and the Patterns of Identity*. New York: Routledge.
Bayron, Kalynn. 2020. *Cinderella Is Dead*. New York: Bloomsbury Children's Books.
Beckett, Sandra L. 2011. 'Crossover Literature'. In *Keywords for Children's Literature*, 58–61. New York: New York University Press.
Beckett, Sandra L. 2017. 'Crossover Literature'. *Oxford Research Encyclopedia of Literature*, March. https://doi.org/10.1093/acrefore/9780190201098.013.176.
Bengson, John. 2020. 'Practical Understanding: Skill as Grasp of Method'. In *Concepts in Thought, Action, and Emotion*, 215–35. New York: Routledge.
Bennett, Jane. 2001. *The Enchantment of Modern Life: Attachments, Crossings, and Ethics*. Princeton: Princeton University Press.
Berlant, Lauren. 1994. 'America, "Fat," the Fetus'. *Boundary 2* 21 (3): 145. https://doi.org/10.2307/303603.
Bettelheim, Bruno. 1976. *The Uses of Enchantment: The Meaning and Importance of Fairy Tales*. New York: Random House.
Bhabha, Homi K. 1990. *Nation and Narration*. New York: Routledge.
Bishop, Rudine Sims. 1990. 'Mirrors, Windows, and Sliding Glass Doors'. *Perspectives* 6 (3): ix–xi.
'The Books of Pellinor'. 2008. 13 May 2008. https://web.archive.org/web/20080513083635/http://www.alisoncroggon.com:80/fantasy/books.html.
Bordo, Susan. 1993. *Unbearable Weight: Feminism, Western Culture and the Body*. Berkeley: University of California Press.
Bourdieu, Pierre. 1993. *The Field of Cultural Production*. Cambridge: Polity Press.
Branagh, Kenneth. 2015. *Cinderella*. Motion Picture. Walt Disney Studios Motion Pictures.
Broadway, Alice. 2017. *Ink*. Skin Books 1. London: Scholastic.
Brumberg, Joan Jacobs. 1998. *The Body Project: An Intimate History of American Girls*. New York: Random House.
Brunvand, Jan Harold. 1998. *The Study of American Folklore: An Introduction*. 4th edition. New York: W. W. Norton & Company.
Burns, Elizabeth. 2013. 'It's That Time of the Month'. School Library Journal. *A Chair, a Fireplace and a Tea Cozy* (blog). 13 January 2013. http://blogs.slj.com/teacozy/2013/01/13/its-that-time-of-the-month/.
Butler, Judith. 1990. *Gender Trouble*. New York: Routledge.
Campbell, Joseph. 1949. *The Hero with a Thousand Faces*. Bollingen Series, XVII. Princeton: Princeton University Press.
Campbell, Joseph. 1968. *The Hero with a Thousand Faces*. Bollingen Series, XVII. Princeton, NJ: Princeton University Press.
Campbell, Joseph, and Bill Moyers. 1991. *The Power of Myth*. New York: Anchor.
Cantavella, Anna Juan. 2017. 'Between Fiction and Reality: Maps and Cartographic Logic in the Works of Peter Sís'. *Children's Literature in Education* 48 (1): 39–55. https://doi.org/10.1007/s10583-016-9304-4.

Carroll, Jane Suzanne. 2012. *Landscape in Children's Literature*. 1st edition. New York: Routledge.
Cart, Michael. 2001. 'From Insider to Outsider: The Evolution of Young Adult Literature'. *Voices from the Middle* 9 (2): 95–7.
Cart, Michael. 2016a. *Young Adult Literature: From Romance to Realism*. 3rd edition. Chicago: Neal-Schuman Publishers.
Cart, Michael. 2016b. 'Young Adult Literature: The State of a Restless Art'. *SLIS Connecting* 5 (1): Article 7. https://doi.org/10.18785/slis.0501.07.
Cecire, Maria Sachiko. 2019. *Re-Enchanted: The Rise of Children's Fantasy Literature in the Twentieth Century*. Minneapolis: University of Minnesota Press.
Chapman, Brenda, and Mark Andrews. 2012. *Brave*. Walt Disney Studios Motion Pictures.
Chappell, Shelley Bess. 2007. 'Werewolves, Wings, and Other Weird Transformations: Fantastic Metamorphosis in Children's and Young Adult Fantasy Literature'. New South Wales: Macquarie University. http://www.researchonline.mq.edu.au/vital/access/services/Download/mq:314/SOURCE3?view=true.
Chinn, Sarah E. 2009. *Inventing Modern Adolescence: The Children of Immigrants in Turn-of-the-Century America*. New Brunswick, NJ: Rutgers University Press.
Cixous, Hélèn. 1976. 'The Laugh of the Medusa'. *Signs* 1 (4): 875–93.
Clarke, Bruce. 1995. *Allegories of Writing: The Subject of Metamorphosis*. Albany: State University of New York Press.
Clarke, Bruce, and Ralph Lutts, eds. 1998. 'Roosevelt on the Nature Fakirs'. In *The Wild Animal Story*. Philadelphia: Temple University Press.
Clover, Carol J. 1993. *Men, Women, and Chain Saws: Gender in Modern Horror Film*. Princeton, NJ: Princeton University Press.
Clute, John, and John Grant. 1997. 'Epic Fantasy'. In Encyclopedia of Fantasy, Online. http://sf-encyclopedia.uk/fe/fe.php?nm=epic_fantasy.
Clute, John, and John Grant. 1997a. 'Secondary World'. In *Encyclopedia of Fantasy*, Online. http://sf-encyclopedia.uk/fe.php?nm=secondary_world.
Clute, John, and John Grant, eds. 1997b. 'Shape-Shifting'. In *Encyclopedia of Fantasy*, Online. http://sf-encyclopedia.uk/.
Coats, Karen. 2004. *Looking Glasses and Neverlands: Lacan, Desire, and Subjectivity in Children's Literature*. Iowa City: University of Iowa Press.
Collins, Suzanne. 2008. *The Hunger Games*. New York: Scholastic.
Coste, Jill. 2020. 'New Heroines in Old Skins: Fairy Tale Revisions in Young Adult Dystopian Literature'. In *Beyond the Blockbusters: Trends and Themes in Contemporary Young Adult Fiction*, edited by Rebekah Fitzsimmons and Casey Alane Wilson, 95–108. Mississippi: University Press of Mississippi.
Coste, Jill. 2021. 'Enchanting the Masses: Allegorical Diversity in Fairy-Tale Dystopias'. In *Race in Young Adult Speculative Fiction*, edited by Meghan

Gilbert-Hickey and Miranda A. Green-Barteet, 54–71. Children's Literature Association. Jackson: University Press of Mississippi.

Coudray, Chantal Bourgault du. 2006. *The Curse of the Werewolf: Fantasy, Horror and the Beast Within*. London: I.B. Tauris.

Coulthurst, Audrey. 2018. *Inkmistress*. Of Fire and Stars, 5. New York: Balzer + Bray.

Coward, Jo. 1999. 'Masculinity and Animal Metamorphosis in Children's Literature'. In *Something to Crow about: New Perspectives in Literature for Young People*, edited by Susan Clancy and David Gilbey, 135–45. Wagga Wagga, Australia: Centre for Information Studies.

Cox, Carolyn. 2018. 'Tamora Pierce Talks Writing & Reading about Female Warriors'. *The Portalist*, 7 March 2018. https://theportalist.com/tamora-pierce-female-warriors.

Creed, Barbara. 1993. *The Monstrous-Feminine: Film, Feminism, Psychoanalysis*. New York: Routledge.

Croggon, Alison. 2004. *The Gift*. The Books of Pellinor 1. London: Walker.

Croggon, Alison. 2005. *The Riddle*. The Books of Pellinor 2. London: Walker.

Cuddon, John Anthony. 1999. 'Archetype'. In *The Penguin Dictionary of Literary Terms and Literary Theory*, edited by Preston, 4th edition, 53–4. London: Penguin.

Cummins, June. 2008. 'Hermione in the Bathroom: The Gothic, Menarche, and Female Development in the Harry Potter Series'. In *The Gothic in Children's Literature: Haunting the Borders*, edited by Anna Jackson, Karen Coats, and Roderick McGillis, 177–93. New York: Routledge.

De Palma, Brian. 1976. *Carrie*. Motion Picture. United Artists.

Delaney, Janice, Mary Jane Lupton, and Emily Toth. 1976. *The Curse: A Cultural History of Menstruation*. New York: E.P. Dutton and Co.

Deleuze, Gilles, and Felix Guattari. 1987. *A Thousand Plateaus: Capitalism and Schizophrenia*. Translated by Brian Massumi. Minneapolis: University of Minnesota Press.

Delgado, Richard. 1984. 'The Imperial Scholar: Reflections on a Review of Civil Rights Literature'. *University of Pennsylvania Law Review* 132 (3): 561. https://doi.org/10.2307/3311882.

Delgado, Richard. 1989. 'Storytelling for Oppositionists and Others: A Plea for Narrative'. *Michigan Law Review* 8 (87): 2411–41.

Delgado, Richard. 2013. 'Storytelling for Oppositionists and Others: A Plea for Narrative'. In *Critical Race Theory: The Cutting Edge*, edited by Jean Stefancic and Richard Delgado, 3rd edition, 71–80. Philadelphia, PA: Temple University Press.

Delgado, Richard, and Jean Stefancic, eds. 2013. *Critical Race Theory: The Cutting Edge*. 3rd edition. Philadelphia, PA: Temple University Press.

Demmerling, Christoph, and Dirk Schroder, eds. 2021. *Concepts in Thought, Action, and Emotion: New Essays*. Routledge Studies in Contemporary Philosophy. New York, NY: Routledge.

Derrida, Jacques. 1981. *Positions*. Translated by Alan Bass. Chicago: University of Chicago Press.

Dharmadhikari, Deepa. 2009. 'Surviving Fantasy through Post-Colonialism'. *Foundation* 107: 15–20.

Didicher, Nicky. 2020. 'Losing Your Footing: The Transformation of Gender Roles and Gender Ideology in Marissa Meyer's Cinder'. In *Retelling Cinderella: Cultural and Creative Transformations*, edited by Nicola Darwood and Alexis Weedon, 49–66. Cambridge: Cambridge Scholars Publishing.

Diehl, Amanda, and Holly Vaughn. 2014. *The Queen's Readers: A Collection of Essays on the Words and Worlds of Tamora Pierce*. California: CreateSpace Independent Publishing Platform.

Donaghue, Daniel, ed. 2002. *Beowulf: A Verse Translation*. Translated by Seamus Heaney. Norton Critical edition. New York: W. W. Norton & Company.

Doughty, Terri. 2015. 'Putting the Punk in a Steampunk Cinderella: Marissa Meyer's "Lunar Chronicles"'. *Filoteknos* 5: 46–58.

Douglas, Adam. 1994. *The Beast within/a History of the Werewolf*. New York: Avon Books.

Dyhouse, Carol. 2010. *Glamour: Women, History, Feminism*. London: Zed Books.

Ekman, Stefan. 2013. *Here There Be Dragons: Exploring Fantasy Maps and Settings*. Middletown, CT: Wesleyan University Press.

Eliade, Mircea. 1956. *The Sacred and the Profane: The Nature of Religion*. Translated by Willard Trask. San Diego: Harcourt Brace.

Falconer, Rachel. 2010. 'Young Adult Fiction and the Crossover Novel'. In *The Routledge Companion to Children's Literature*, edited by David Rudd, 13. London: Routledge.

Fawcett, John. 2000. *Ginger Snaps*. Motion Picture. Motion International.

Flanagan, Victoria. 2008. *Into the Closet: Cross-Dressing and The Gendered Body in Children's Literature and Film*. Children's Literature and Culture. New York: Routledge.

Flanagan, Victoria. 2014. *Technology and Identity in Young Adult Fiction*. Basingstoke: Palgrave Macmillan. http://www.palgraveconnect.com/doifinder/10.1057/9781137362063.

Fletcher, Lisa, Beth Driscoll, and Kim Wilkins. 2018. 'Genre Worlds and Popular Fiction: The Case of Twenty-First-Century Australian Romance'. *The Journal of Popular Culture* 51 (4): 997–1015. https://doi.org/10.1111/jpcu.12706.

Flood, Alison. 2018. 'Tamora Pierce: "Everybody Thinks Fantasy Is so Safe. Are You Kidding?"' *The Guardian*, 9 October 2018, sec. Books. https://www.

theguardian.com/books/2018/oct/09/tamora-pierce-everybody-thinks-fantasy-is-so-safe-are-you-kidding.

Forman-Brunell, Miriam, ed. 2014. *Princess Cultures: Mediating Girls, Imaginations and Identities*. Mediated Youth. New York: Peter Lang.

Freud, Sigmund. 1933. 'Femininity'. In *New Introductory Lectures on Psychoanalysis*, edited by James Strachey, 139–67. New York: W. W. Norton & Company.

Frye, Northrop. 1957. *Anatomy of Criticism*. Princeton, NJ: Princeton University Press.

Frye, Northrop. 1961. 'Myth, Fiction, and Displacement'. *Daedalus* 90 (3): 587–605.

Frye, Northrop. 1983. *The Great Code: The Bible and Literature*. New York: Harcourt Brace Jovanovich.

Garber, Marjorie. 1992. *Vested Interests: Cross-Dressing and Cultural Anxiety*. New York: Routledge.

García, Marilisa Jiménez. 2018. 'En(Countering) YA: Young Lords, Shadowshapers, and the Longings and Possibilities of Latinx Young Adult Literature'. *Latino Studies* 16 (2): 230–49. https://doi.org/10.1057/s41276-018-0122-2.

Garner, Alexandra. 2020. 'Neomedievalism, Feminism, and the Sword in Tamora Pierce's Song of the Lioness'. *Children's Literature Association Quarterly* 45 (4): 364–82. https://doi.org/10.1353/chq.2020.0044.

Genette, Gerard. 2010. *Paratexts: Thresholds of Interpretation*. Cambridge: Cambridge University Press.

Gennep, Arnold van. 1910. *Les Rites de Passage*. Paris: Emile Nourry.

Gennep, Arnold van. 1960. *The Rites of Passage*. London: Routledge.

Geraghty, Christine. 1990. *Women and Soap Opera: A Study of Prime Time Soaps*. Cambridge: Polity Press.

Geronimi, Clyde. 1959. *Sleeping Beauty*, Film. Buena Vista Pictures. https://en.wikipedia.org/w/index.php?title=Sleeping_Beauty_00281959_film0029&oldid=898961160.

Geronimi, Clyde, Wilfred Jackson, and Hamilton Luske. 1950. *Cinderella*. Motion Picture. RKO Radio Pictures.

Gilbert-Hickey, Meghan, and Miranda A. Green-Barteet, eds. 2021. *Race in Young Adult Speculative Fiction*. Children's Literature Association. Jackson: University Press of Mississippi.

Gill, Rosalind. 2007. 'Postfeminist Media Culture: Elements of a Sensibility'. *European Journal of Cultural Studies* 10 (2): 147–66. https://doi.org/10.1177/1367549407075898.

Gill, Rosalind. 2008. 'Culture and Subjectivity in Neoliberal and Postfeminist Times'. *Subjectivity* 25 (1): 432–45. https://doi.org/10.1057/sub.2008.28.

Gill, Rosalind, and Christina Scharff, eds. 2011. *New Femininities: Postfeminism, Neoliberalism, and Subjectivity*. Houndmills: Palgrave Macmillan.

Gilligan, Carol. 1979. 'Woman's Place in Man's Life Cycle.' *Harvard Educational Review* 49 (4): 431–46.

Gonick, Marnina. 2006. 'Between "Girl Power" and "Reviving Ophelia": Constituting the Neoliberal Girl Subject'. *NWSA Journal* 18 (2): 1–23.
Green-Barteet, Dr Miranda A., Meghan Gilbert-Hickey, Stella Guttman, and Charles Guttman. 2017. 'Black and Brown Boys in Young Adult Dystopias: Racialized Docility in The Hunger Games Trilogy and The Lunar Chronicles'. *Red Feather Journal* 8 (2): 1–22.
Grimm, Jacob, and Wilhelm Grimm. 1812. 'Aschenputtel'. In *Kinder und Hausmärchen Gesammelt durch die Brüder Grimm*, 1, 109–26. Göttingen: Verlad der Dieterichschen Buchhandlung. https://books.google.co.uk/books?id=y9tLAAAAIAAJ&pg=PP9&redir_esc=y#v=onepage&q&f=false.
Grosz, Elizabeth. 1994. *Volatile Bodies: Toward a Corporeal Feminism*. Bloomington: John Wiley & Sons.
Halberstam, Jack (Judith). 1998. *Female Masculinity*. Durham: Duke University Press Books.
Hall, G. Stanley. 1904a. *Adolescence: Its Psychology and Its Relations to Physiology, Anthropology, Sociology, Sex, Crime, Religion and Education*. Vol. 1. 2 vols. New York: Appleton and Co.
Hall, G. Stanley. 1904b. *Adolescence: Its Psychology and Its Relations to Physiology, Anthropology, Sociology, Sex, Crime, Religion and Education*. Vol. 2. 2 vols. New York: Appleton and Co.
Hand, David, Wilfred Jackson, Ben Sharpsteen, Pearce Perce, William Cottrell, and Larry Morey. 1937. *Snow White and the Seven Dwarfs*. Motion Picture. RKO Radio Pictures.
Haraway, Donna. 1991. 'A Cyborg Manifesto: Science, Technology, and Socialist-Feminism in the Late Twentieth Century'. In *Simians, Cyborgs and Women: The Reinvention of Nature*, 149–82. New York: Routledge.
Haraway, Donna. 2003. *The Companion Species Manifesto*. Chicago: University of Chicago Press. http://www.press.uchicago.edu/ucp/books/book/distributed/C/bo3645022.html.
Haraway, Donna. 2004. *The Haraway Reader*. New York: Routledge.
Harley, J. B. 1989. 'Deconstructing the Map'. *Cartographica* 26 (2): 1–20.
Harris, Marvin, and Orna Johnson. 2006. *Cultural Anthropology*. 7th edition. London: Pearson.
Harvey, Colin B. 2015. *Fantastic Transmedia - Narrative, Play and Memory across Science Fiction and Fantasy Storyworlds*. London: Palgrave Macmillan.
Hassler-Forest, Dan. 2017. 'Worlds and Politics'. In *The Routledge Companion to Imaginary Worlds*, edited by Mark J. P. Wolf, 305–13. New York: Routledge.
Hayles, N. Katherine. 1999. *How We Became Posthuman: Virtual Bodies in Cybernetics, Literature, and Informatics*. Chicago: University of Chicago Press.
Head, Patricia. 1996. 'Robert Cormier and the Postmodernist Possibilities of Young Adult Fiction'. *Children's Literature Association Quarterly* 21 (1): 28–33. https://doi.org/10.1353/chq.0.1267.

Heatwole, Alexandra. 2016. 'Disney Girlhood: Princess Generations and Once Upon a Time'. *Studies in the Humanities* 43 (1): 1–19.
Heckerling, Amanda. 1995. *Clueless*. Motion Picture. Paramount Pictures.
Herz, Sarah K., and Donald R. Gallo. 2005. *From Hinton to Hamlet: Building Bridges between Young Adult Literature and the Classics*. 2nd edition. Westport, CT: Greenwood.
HiHo Kids. 2018. 'Kids Meet an Opera Singer'. YouTube. *HiHo Kids* (blog), 30 August 2018. https://www.youtube.com/watch?v=95RLviccrQc.
Hirsch, Marianne. 1989. *The Mother/Daughter Plot: Narrative, Psychoanalysis, Feminism: 532*. Bloomington: Indiana University Press.
Holdsworth, Amy, and Karen Lury. 2016. 'Growing up and Growing Old with Television: Peripheral Viewers and the Centrality of Care'. *Screen* 57 (2): 184–96. https://doi.org/10.1093/screen/hjw019.
Holmes, Linda. 2013. 'What Really Makes Katniss Stand Out? Peeta, Her Movie Girlfriend'. *NPR*, 25 November 2013. https://www.npr.org/2013/11/25/247146164/what-really-makes-katniss-stand-out-peeta-her-movie-girlfriend.
Hourihan, Margery. 1997. *Deconstructing the Hero: Literary Theory and Children's Literature*. London: Routledge.
Hume, Kathryn. 1984. *Fantasy and Mimesis: Response to Reality in Western Literature*. New York: Routledge.
Hunt, Caroline. 2017. 'Theory Rises, Maginot Line Endures'. *Children's Literature Association Quarterly* 42 (2): 205–17. https://doi.org/10.1353/chq.2017.0017.
Hunt, Caroline C. 1986. 'Counterparts: Identity Exchange and the Young Adult Audience'. *Children's Literature Association Quarterly* 11 (3): 109–13. https://doi.org/10.1353/chq.0.0320.
Hunt, Peter. 1987. 'Landscapes and Journeys, Metaphors and Maps: The Distinctive Feature of English Fantasy'. *Children's Literature Association Quarterly* 12 (1): 11–14. https://doi.org/10.1353/chq.0.0498.
Hyde, Lewis. 1998. *Trickster Makes This World: Mischief, Myth and Art*. Edinburgh: Canongate Books.
Insenga, Angela. 2018. 'Once Upon a Cyborg: Cinder as a Posthuman Fairytale'. In *Posthumanism in Young Adult Fiction: Finding Humanity in a Posthuman World*, edited by Anita Tarr and Donna R. White. Mississippi: University Press of Mississippi. https://doi.org/10.2307/j.ctv5jxn92.
Irigaray, Luce. 1974. *Speculum of the Other Woman*. Translated by Gillian C. Gill. Ithaca: Cornell University Press.
Jameson, Professor Fredric. 1991. *Postmodernism, or, the Cultural Logic of Late Capitalism*. Durham: Duke University Press.
Jarvis, Erika. 2015. 'When Did Cinderella Get so Nice'. *Vanity Fair*, 17 March 2015. http://www.vanityfair.com/hollywood/2015/03/cinderella-fairy-tale?
Jenkins, Henry. 2006. *Convergence Culture: Where Old and New Media Collide*. New York: New York UP.

Jensen, Karen. 2014. 'No Not the One in Sentences, Talk about a Different Kind of Period in YA Lit'. *School Library Journal*, 23 October 2014. http://www.teenlibrariantoolbox.com/2014/10/no-not-the-one-in-sentences-talking-about-a-different-kind-of-period-in-ya-lit/.

Jones, Steven Swann. 1993. 'The Innocent Persecuted Heroine Genre: An Analysis of Its Structure and Themes'. *Western Folklore* 52 (1): 13–41.

Joseph, Michael. 2011. 'Liminality'. In *Key Words for Children's Literature*, edited by Philip Nel and Lissa Paul, 138–41. New York: New York University Press.

Kearney, Mary Celeste. 2015. 'Sparkle: Luminosity and Post-Girl Power Media'. *Continuum* 29 (2): 263–73. https://doi.org/10.1080/10304312.2015.1022945.

Kelly. 2015. 'Alanna of Trebond'. *Reading with Dragons* (blog), 17 February 2015. https://readingwithdragons.wordpress.com/kick-butt-heroines/tortall-heroines/alanna-of-trebond/.

Kennedy, Melanie. 2018. *Tweenhood: Femininity and Celebrity in Tween Popular Culture*. London: I.B. Tauris.

Kennon, Patricia. 2015. '"Little Girls Are Even More Perfect When They Bleed": Monstrosity, Violence, and the Female Body in Kristin Cashore's Graceling Trilogy'. *Bookbird: A Journal of International Children's Literature* 53 (1): 52–61. https://doi.org/10.1353/bkb.2015.0028.

Kent, Le'A. 2001. 'Fighting Abjection: Representing Fat Women'. In *Bodies out of Bounds: Fatness and Transgression*, edited by Jana Evans Braziel and Kathleen LeBesco, 130–50. Berkeley: University of California Press.

Kett, Joseph. 1977. *Rites of Passage: Adolescence in America, 1790 to the Present*. New York: Basic Books.

Kidd, Kenneth B., and Derritt Mason, eds. 2019. *Queer as Camp: Essays on Summer, Style, and Sexuality*. New York: Fordham University Press.

King, Stephen. 1974. *Carrie*. New York: Knopf Double Day.

Kokkola, Lydia. 2013. *Fictions of Adolescent Carnality: Sexy Sinners and Delinquent Deviants*. Children's Literature, Culture, and Cognition. Amsterdam: John Benjamins Publishing Company.

Kristeva, Julia. 1982. *Powers of Horror: An Essay on Abjection*. Translated by Leon Roudiez. New York, NY: Columbia University Press.

Lacan, Jacques. 2001. *Ecrits: A Selection*. Translated by Alan Sheridan. London: Routledge.

Ladson-Billings, Gloria. 1998. 'Just What Is Critical Race Theory and What's It Doing in a Nice Field Like Education?' *International Journal of Qualitative Studies in Education* 11 (1): 7–24. https://doi.org/10.1080/095183998236863.

Lassén-Seger, Maria. 2006. *Adventures into Otherness: Child Metamorphs in Late Twentieth-Century Children's Literature*. Åbo: Åbo Akademi University Press.

Lawrence-Pietroni, Anna. 1996. 'The Tricksters, The Changeover, and the Fluidity of Adolescent Literature'. *Children's Literature Association Quarterly* 21 (1): 34–9. https://doi.org/10.1353/chq.0.1082.

Len. 2007a. 'Daine, Pregnancy, and a Blayce-Less War'. *Words of Tamora Pierce* (blog), 26 August 2007. https://tpwords.wordpress.com/2007/08/26/daine-pregnancy-and-a-blayce-less-war/.

Len. 2007b. 'Pregnancy and Choices'. *Words of Tamora Pierce* (blog), 28 August 2007. https://tpwords.wordpress.com/category/daine/.
Lennard, John. 2007. *Reading Tamora Pierce 'The Immortals'*. Penrith: Humanities-Ebooks LLP.
Lerner, Gerda. 1986. *The Creation of Patriarchy*. Oxford: Oxford University Press.
Lesko, Nancy. 1996. 'Denaturalizing Adolescence: The Politics of Contemporary Representations'. *Youth and Society* 28 (2): 139–61.
Lesnik-Oberstein, Karin, ed. 2007. *The Last Taboo: Women and Body Hair*. Manchester: Manchester University Press.
Lessa, William Armand, Evon Zartman Vogt, and John Mamoru Watanabe. 1979. *Reader in Comparative Religion: An Anthropological Approach*. 3rd edition. New York: Harper & Row.
Levy, Michael, and Farah Mendlesohn. 2016. *Children's Fantasy Literature: An Introduction*. Cambridge: Cambridge University Press. https://doi.org/10.1017/CBO9781139087421.
Luske, Hamilton, Clyde Geronimi, and Wilfred Jackson. 1953. *Peter Pan*. Motion Picture.
Lykissas, Alexandra. 2018. 'Popular Culture's Enduring Influence on Childhood: Fairy Tale Collaboration in the Young Adult Series *The Lunar Chronicles*'. *Global Studies of Childhood* 8 (3): 304–15. https://doi.org/10.1177/2043610618798932.
Lykissas, Alexandra. 2020. 'Cyborg-Erella: Marissa Meyer's Cinder as a New Type of Other'. In *Woke Cinderella: Twenty-First-Century Adaptations*, edited by Suzy Woltmann, 205–16. Lanham: Lexington Books. https://www.google.co.uk/books/edition/_/62QGEAAAQBAJ?hl=en&gbpv=0.
Marshall, P. David. 2010. 'The Specular Economy'. *Society* 47 (6): 498–502. https://doi.org/10.1007/s12115-010-9368-5.
Mathison, Ymitri, ed. 2017. *Growing Up Asian American in Young Adult Fiction*. Jackson: University Press of Mississippi.
Matos, Angel Daniel. 2020. 'Adolescence'. In *The Routledge History of American Sexuality*, edited by Kevin P. Murphy, Jason Ruiz, and David Serlin, 10–20. Oxford: Routledge.
Matthews, Corinne. 2019. 'Contraception, Consent, and Community in Kristin Cashore's Graceling Trilogy'. *The Lion and the Unicorn* 43 (1): 69–89. https://doi.org/10.1353/uni.2019.0004.
Mayer, Kodi. 2016. 'The Evolution of the Disney Princess Franchise: Catching Up and Moving Forward'. *Animation Studies 2.0* (blog), 12 February 2016. https://blog.animationstudies.org/?p=1381.
Mayer, Kodi. 2019. 'The Evolution of the Disney Princess Franchise Part II: The End of an Era?' *Animation Studies 2.0* (blog), 21 October 2019. https://blog.animationstudies.org/?p=3283.
McAlister, Jodi. 2018. 'Defining and Redefining Popular Genres: The Evolution of "New Adult" Fiction'. *Australian Literary Studies* 33 (4). https://doi.org/10.20314/als.0fd566d109.

McAlister, Jodi. 2021. *New Adult Fiction*. Cambridge: Cambridge Elements.
McCallum, Robyn. 1999. *Ideologies of Identity in Adolescent Fiction: The Dialogic Construction of Subjectivity*. New York: Routledge.
McCracken, Peggy. 2003. *The Curse of Eve, the Wound of the Hero: Blood, Gender, and Medieval Literature*. The Middle Ages Series. Philadelphia: University of Pennsylvania Press.
McMahon-Coleman, Kimberl, and Roslyn Weaver. 2012. *Werewolves and Other Shapeshifters in Popular Culture: A Thematic Analysis of Recent Depictions*. Jefferson, NC: McFarland.
McRobbie, Angela. 2008. *The Aftermath of Feminism: Gender, Culture and Social Change*. London: SAGE Publications.
McSporran, Cathy. 2005. 'Daughters of Lilith: Witches and Wicked Women in the Chronicles of Narnia'. In *Revisiting Narnia: Fantasy, Myth and Religion in C. S. Lewis' Chronicles*, edited by Shanna Caughey, 191–204. Dallas, TX: BenBella Books, Inc.
Mendlesohn, Farah. 2008. *Rhetorics of Fantasy*. Middletown, CT: Wesleyan University Press.
Merrylees, Ferne. 2018. 'The Adolescent Posthuman: Reimagining Body Image and Identity in Marissa Meyer's Cinder and Julianna Baggott's Pure'. In *Posthumanism in Young Adult Fiction: Finding Humanity in a Posthuman World*, edited by Anita Tarr and Donna R. White. Mississippi: University Press of Mississippi. https://doi.org/10.2307/j.ctv5jxn92.
Meyer, Marissa. 2012. *Cinder*. The Lunar Chronicles 1. London: Puffin.
Meyer, Marissa. 2013. *Scarlet*. The Lunar Chronicles 2. London: Puffin.
Meyer, Marissa. 2014. *Cress*. The Lunar Chronicles 3. London: Puffin.
Meyer, Marissa. 2015a. *Fairest: Levana's Story*. The Lunar Chronicles, 3.5. New York: Feiwel & Friends.
Meyer, Marissa. 2015b. *Winter*. The Lunar Chronicles 4. London: Puffin.
Meyer, Marissa. 2015c. '@Le_phill Yep. But They Hardly Seem to Slow Her Down!' Microblog. *Twitter* (blog), 15 January 2015. https://twitter.com/Le_phill.
Meyer, Marissa. 2016. *Stars above: A Lunar Chronicles Collection*. The Lunar Chronicles, 4.5. New York: Feiwel & Friends.
Meyer, Marissa. 2017. *Wires and Nerve*. Wires and Nerve 1. New York: Macmillan.
Meyer, Marissa. 2018. *Wires and Nerve: Gone Rogue*. Wires and Nerve 2. New York: Macmillan.
Meyer, Stephenie. 2005. *Twilight*. Twilight Saga. New York: Little, Brown and Company.
Meyer, Stephenie. 2008. *Breaking Dawn*. Twilight Saga. New York: Little, Brown and Company.
A Mighty Girl. 2013. 'Disney: Say No to the Merida Makeover, Keep Our Hero Brave!' *Change.Org.*, May 2013. https://www.change.org/p/disney-say-no-to-the-merida-makeover-keep-our-hero-brave.

Mills, Alice. 2011. 'Spiritual, Not Sexual: The Plight of the Adolescent Human Wizard in Diane Duane's Young Wizards Series'. In *Supernatural Youth: The Rise of the Teen Hero in Literature and Popular Culture*, edited by Jes Battis, 15–27. Washington, DC: Lexington Books.

Miskec, Jennifer, and Chris McGee. 2007. 'My Scars Tell a Story: Self-Mutilation in Young Adult Literature'. *Children's Literature Association Quarterly* 32 (2): 163–78.

Mitchell, Jennifer. 2014. 'A Girl. A Machine. A Freak: A Consideration of Contemporary Queer Composites'. *Bookbird* 52 (1): 51–62.

Montz, Amy L. 2014. 'Rebels in Dresses: Distractions of Competitive Girlhood in Young Adult Dystopian Fiction'. In *Female Rebellion in Young Adult Dystopian Fiction*, edited by Sara K. Day, Miranda A. Green-Barteet, and Amy L. Montz, 107–21. Ashgate Studies on Children's Fiction. Farnham: Ashgate.

Moran, Mary Jeanette. 2018. '"Balance Is the Trick": Feminist Relationality in The Amazing Maurice and the Tiffany Aching Series'. *The Lion and the Unicorn* 42 (3): 259–80. https://doi.org/10.1353/uni.2018.0027.

Moseley, Rachel. 2002. 'Glamorous Witchcraft: Gender and Magic in Teen Film and Television'. *Screen* 43 (4): 403–22.

Muehrcke, Philip, and Juliana Muehrcke. 1974. 'Maps in Literature'. *The Geographical Review* 64 (3): 317–38.

Musgrave, Megan L. 2016. *Digital Citizenship in Twenty-First-Century Young Adult Literature: Imaginary Activism*. Critical Approaches to Children's Literature. New York: Palgrave Macmillan.

Nikolajeva, Maria. 1991. 'Where Have All the Young Girls Gone?' In *From Mythic to Linear: Time in Children's Literature*, 147–65. Lanham, MD: Scarecrow Press.

Nikolajeva, Maria. 2002. *The Rhetoric of Character in Children's Literature*. Lanham, MD: Scarecrow Press.

Nikolajeva, Maria. 2010. *Power, Voice and Subjectivity in Literature for Young Readers*. New York: Routledge.

Ohmer, Susan. 1993. '"That Rags to Riches Stuff": Disney's Cinderella and the Cultural Space of Animation'. *Film History* 5 (2): 231–49.

Orenstein, Peggy. 2011. *Cinderella Ate My Daughter*. New York: HarperCollins.

Orenstein, Peggy. 2013. 'Seriously, Disney, I'm Trying to Take a Little Break Here – MUST YOU?' *Peggy Orenstein*, 2 May 2013. https://www.peggyorenstein.com/blog/seriously-disney-im-trying-to-take-a-little-break-here-must-you.

Osman, Tarek. 2013. 'The Map That Caused a Century of Trouble'. *BBC News*, 14 December 2013, sec. Middle East. http://www.bbc.co.uk/news/world-middle-east-25299553.

Otten, Charlotte F., ed. 1986. *A Lycanthropy Reader: Werewolves in Western Culture*. Syracuse, NY: Syracuse University Press.

Owen, Gabrielle. 2020. *A Queer History of Adolescence: Developmental Pasts, Relational Futures*. Georgia: University of Georgia Press. https://doi.org/10.2307/j.ctvxhrmp2.

Page, Benedicte. 2010. 'Bullish Bologna Buyers Look to Pre-Teen Reads'. *Bookseller*, no. 5425 (March): 7.

Parsons, Linda T. 2004. 'Ella Evolving: Cinderella Stories and the Construction of Gender-Appropriate Behavior'. *Children's Literature in Education* 35 (2): 135–54.

Pattee, Amy. 2010. *Reading the Adolescent Romance: Sweet Valley High and the Popular Young Adult Romance Novel*. New York: Routledge.

Pattee, Amy. 2017. 'Between Youth and Adulthood: Young Adult and New Adult Literature'. *Children's Literature Association Quarterly* 42 (2): 218–30. https://doi.org/10.1353/chq.2017.0018.

Paul, Lissa. 1990. 'Enigma Variations: What Feminist Theory Knows about Children's Literature'. In *Children's Literature: The Development of Criticism*, edited by Peter Hunt, 148–66. London: Routledge.

Perrault, Charles. n.d. 'Cendrillon Ou La Petite Pantoufle de Verre'. In *Histoires Ou Contes Du Temps Passé*. Paris: Claude Barbin.

Perry, Evelyn M. 2010. *Robin McKinley: Girl Reader, Woman Writer*. Lanham, MD: Scarecrow Press.

Phillips, Leah. 2018. 'A Mapping Sensibility: How Mythopoeic YA (Re)Maps the Terrain of Female Adolescence'. *Modern Language Studies* 48 (1): 46–63.

Pierce, Tamora. 1983. *Alanna the First Adventure*. Song of the Lioness 1. New York: Random House.

Pierce, Tamora. 1984. *In the Hand of the Goddess*. Song of the Lioness 2. New York: Random House.

Pierce, Tamora. 1986. *The Woman Who Rides Like a Man*. Song of the Lioness 3. New York: Random House.

Pierce, Tamora. 1988. *Lioness Rampant*. Song of the Lioness 4. New York: Random House.

Pierce, Tamora. 1992. *Wild Magic*. Immortals 1. New York: Random House.

Pierce, Tamora. 1994. *Wolf-Speaker*. Immortals 2. New York: Random House.

Pierce, Tamora. 1995. *Emperor Mage*. Immortals 3. New York: Random House.

Pierce, Tamora. 1996. *The Realms of the Gods*. Immortals 4. New York: Random House.

Pierce, Tamora. 1997. *Magic in the Weaving (Sandry's Book)*. Circle of Magic 1. New York: Scholastic.

Pierce, Tamora. 1999a. *First Test*. Protector of the Small 1. New York: Random House.

Pierce, Tamora. 2000. *Page*. Protector of the Small 2. New York: Random House.

Pierce, Tamora. 2001. *Squire*. Protector of the Small 3. New York: Random House.

Pierce, Tamora. 2002. *Lady Knight*. Protector of the Small 4. New York: Random House.

Pierce, Tamora. 2003. *Trickster's Choice*. Daughter of the Lioness 1. New York: Random House.

Pierce, Tamora. 2004. *Trickster's Queen*. Daughter of the Lioness 2. New York: Random House.

Pierce, Tamora. 2011. *Mastiff*. Beka Cooper Series 3. New York: Random House.

Pierce, Tamora. 2018. *Tempests and Slaughter*. The Numair Chronicles 1. New York: Random House.

Pierce, Tamora. 2019a. 'Tamora Pierce Biography'. *Tamora Pierce*, 2019. http://www.tamora-pierce.net/about/.

Pierce, Tamora. 2019b. 'The Circle Universe Archives'. *Tamora Pierce*, 2019. http://www.tamora-pierce.net/series/the-circle-universe/.

Pierce, Tamora. 2019c. 'Tweet'. https://twitter.com/TamoraPierce/status/1202294877213450240.

Pierce, Tamora, Julie Holderman, Timothy Liebe, and Megan Messinger. 2017. *Tortall: A Spy's Guide*. New York: Random House.

Pipher, Mary. 1994. *Reviving Ophelia: Saving the Selves of Adolescent Girls*. New York: Putnam.

Powell's Books. n.d. 'Philip Pullman, Tamora Pierce, and Christopher Paolini Talk Fantasy Fiction'. *Author Interviews*, Accessed 31 July 2013. http://www.powells.com/authors/paolini.html.

Priest, Hannah. 2017. 'Sparkly Vampires and Shimmering Aliens: The Paranormal Romance of Stephenie Meyer'. In *Twenty-First Century Popular Fiction*, edited by Bernice Murphy and Stephen Matterson, 182–92. Edinburgh: Edinburgh University Press.

Prokhovnik, Raia. 1999. *Rational Woman: A Feminist Critique of Dichotomy*. Routledge Innovations in Political Theory. London and New York: Routledge.

Propp, Vladimir. 1968. *Morphology of the Folk Tale*. Translated by Laurence Scott. Bloomington: Indiana University Press.

Pullman, Philip. 2001. 'The Darkside of Narnia'. *The Cumberland River Lamp Post*, 2 September 2001. http://www.crlamppost.org/darkside.htm.

Putzi, Jennifer. 2017. '"None of This 'Trapped-in-a-Man's-Body" Bullshit': Transgender Girls and Wrong-Body Discourse in Young Adult Fiction'. *Tulsa Studies in Women's Literature* 36 (2): 423–48. https://doi.org/10.1353/tsw.2017.0029.

Raglan, Lord. 1934. 'The Hero of Tradition'. *Folklore* 45 (3): 212–31.

Raglan, Lord. 1936. *The Hero: A Study in Tradition, Myth and Drama*. Mineola, NY: Dover Publications.

Ramdarshan Bold, Melanie. 2019. *Inclusive Young Adult Fiction: Authors of Colour in the United Kingdom*. London: Palgrave Macmillan.

Rank, Otto. 1909. *Der Mythus von der Geburt des Helden*. Vienna: Franz Deuticke. http://archive.org/details/SzaS_5_Rank_1909_Mythus_von_der_Geburt_des_Helden.

Rank, Otto. 1914. *The Myth of the Birth of the Hero: A Psychological Interpretation of Mythology*. Translated by F. Robbins and Smith Ely Jelliffe. New York: The Journal of Nervous and Mental Disease Publishing Company.

Reynolds, Kimberley. 2007. *Radical Children's Literature: Future Visions and Aesthetic Transformations in Juvenile Fiction*. Basingstoke: Palgrave Macmillan. http://www.palgraveconnect.com/doifinder/10.1057/9780230206205.

Rice, Peggy S. 2000. 'Gendered Readings of a Traditional "Feminist" Folktale by Sixth-Grade Boys and Girls'. *Journal of Literacy Research* 32 (2): 211–36. https://doi.org/10.1080/10862960009548074.

Rose, Jacqueline. 1994. *Case of 'Peter Pan': Or, the Impossibility of Children's Fiction*. Basingstoke: Palgrave Macmillan Limited Macmillan Distribution Limited [distributor. https://link.springer.com/book/10.1007/978-0-333-60401-4.

Rosenberg, Alyssa. 2011. 'Tamora Pierce on "Twilight," Girl Heroes, and Fantasy Birth Control'. *The Atlantic*, 3 June 2011. https://www.theatlantic.com/entertainment/archive/2011/06/tamora-pierce-on-twilight-girl-heroes-and-fantasy-birth-control/239861/.

Ross, Val. 2009. *The Road to There: Mapmakers and Their Stories*. Toronto: Tundra Books.

Ryan, Dr Marie-Laure. 2003. *Narrative as Virtual Reality: Immersion and Interactivity in Literature and Electronic Media*. New edition. Baltimore, MD: The Johns Hopkins University Press.

Sahn, Sarah F. 2016. 'Decolonizing Childhood: Coming of Age in Tamora Pierce's Fantastic Empire'. *Children's Literature* 44 (1): 147–71. https://doi.org/10.1353/chl.2016.0012.

Sawyer, Susan M., Peter S. Azzopardi, Dakshitha Wickremarathne, and George C Patton. 2018. 'The Age of Adolescence'. *The Lancet Child & Adolescent Health* 2 (3): 223–8. https://doi.org/10.1016/S2352-4642(18)30022-1.

Sax, Boria. 1990. *The Frog King: On Legends, Fables, Fairy Tales, and Anecdotes of Animals*. New York: Pace University Press.

Saxena, Vandana. 2012. 'Growing-up Drag: Cross-Dressed Heroines in Young Adult Fiction'. 영미문학페미니즘 *[Feminist Studies in English Literature]* 20 (3): 271–309. https://doi.org/10.15796/FSEL.2012.20.3.010.

Sayantani. 2010. 'Are You There, YA Readers? It's Me, Your Period'. 3 November 2010. http://storiesaregoodmedicine.blogspot.co.uk/2010/11/are-you-there-ya-readers-its-me-your.html.

Seaman, Myra. 2007. 'Becoming More (than) Human: Affective Posthumanisms, Past and Future'. *JNT: Journal of Narrative Theory* 37 (2): 246–75.

Segal, Robert. 1990. *In Quest of the Hero*. Princeton, NJ: Princeton University Press.

Squier, Susan Merrill. 1994. *Babies in Bottles: Twentieth-Century Visions of Reproductive Technology*. New Brunswick, NJ: Rutgers University Press.

Stacks, Goddess. 2013. 'Book Review: The Song of the Lioness Quartet'. *Goddess In The Stacks* (blog), 19 November 2013. https://goddessinthestacks.com/2013/11/19/book-review-the-song-of-the-lioness-quartet/.

Stephens, John. 1999. 'Constructions of Female Selves in Adolescent Fiction: Makeovers as Metonym'. *Explorations into Children's Literature* 9 (1): 5–13.

Stetka, Bret. 2017. 'Extended Adolescence: When 25 Is the New 18'. *Scientific American*, 19 September 2017. https://www.scientificamerican.com/article/extended-adolescence-when-25-is-the-new-181/.

Stockton, Kathryn Bond. 2009. *The Queer Child, or Growing Sideways in the Twentieth Century*. Durham: Duke University Press.

Subramanian, Aishwarya. 2018. 'This Has Made the Endless Ocean Look a Bit like the Quite Large Inlet …' Direct Message. *Twitter*, https://twitter.com/messages/14340948-1096403708.

Suhr-Sytsma, Mandy. 2018. *Self-Determined Stories: The Indigenous Reinvention of Young Adult Literature*. East Lansing: Michigan State University Press.

Sullivan, Charles William. 1992. 'Fantasy'. In *Stories and Society: Children's Literature in Its Social Context*, edited by Dennis Butts, 97–109. Basingstoke: Palgrave Macmillan.

Syed, Moin, and Lauren L. Mitchell. 2015. 'How Race and Ethnicity Shape Emerging Adulthood'. In *The Oxford Handbook of Emerging Adulthood*, edited by Arnett, Jeffrey, 87. Oxford: Oxford University Press.

Thomas, Ebony Elizabeth. 2019. *The Dark Fantastic: Race and the Imagination from Harry Potter to the Hunger Games*. New York: New York UP.

Toffoletti, Kim. 2007. *Cyborgs and Barbie Dolls: Feminism, Popular Culture and the Posthuman Body*. London: I.B Tauris and Co.

Toliver, S. R. 2018a. 'Alterity and Innocence: The Hunger Games, Rue, and Black Girl Adultification'. *Journal of Children's Literature* 44 (2): 4–15.

Toliver, S. R. 2018b. 'Imagining New Hopescapes: Expanding Black Girls' Windows and Mirrors'. *Research on Diversity in Youth Literature* 1 (1): 1–24.

Toliver, S. R. 2019. 'Breaking Binaries: #BlackGirlMagic and the Black Ratchet Imagination'. *Journal of Language and Literacy Education* 15 (1): 26.

Toliver, Stephanie. 2019a. 'On the History (and Future) of YA and Speculative Fiction by Black Women'. *Literary Hub* (blog), 8 August 2019. https://lithub.com/on-the-history-and-future-of-ya-and-speculative-fiction-by-black-women/.

Toliver, Stephanie. 2019b. 'Black Girl Sci-Fi Club Makes Magic Interview by Deep Center'. http://www.deepcenter.org/2019/09/17/black-girl-sci-fi-club-makes-magic/.

Toliver, Stephanie. 2021. 'On Mirrors, Windows, and Telescopes'. *Council Chronicle*, 29–30.

Tolkien, J.R.R. 1947. 'On Fairy Stories'. In *Beowulf: The Monsters and the Critics*, edited by Christopher Tolkien, 109–61. London: HarperCollins.

Tolkien, J.R.R. 1988. *Tree and Leaf: Including the Poem Mythopoeia*. London: Unwin.

Tolmie, Jane. 2006. 'Medievalism and the Fantasy Heroine'. *Journal of Gender Studies* 15 (2): 145–58. https://doi.org/10.1080/09589230600720042.

'Tortall - Tamora Pierce - Works | Archive of Our Own'. n.d. Accessed 15 January 2019. https://archiveofourown.org/tags/Tortall%20-%20Tamora%20Pierce/works?page=1.

Trites, Roberta Seelinger. 1996. 'Theories and Possibilities of Adolescent Literature'. *Children's Literature Association Quarterly* 21 (1): 2–3. https://doi.org/10.1353/chq.0.1164.

Trites, Roberta Seelinger. 2000a. *Disturbing the Universe: Power and Repression in Adolescent Literature*. Iowa City: University of Iowa Press.

Trites, Roberta Seelinger. 2000b. '"I Don't Know the Words": Institutional Discourses in Adolescent Literature'. In *Disturbing the Universe: Power and Repression in Adolescent Literature*, 21–53. Iowa City: University of Iowa Press.

Trites, Roberta Seelinger. 2018. *Twenty-First Century Feminisms in Children's and Adolescent Literature*. Jackson: University Press of Mississippi.

Turner, Victor. 1967. 'Betwixt and between: The Liminal Period in Rites de Passage'. In *The Forest of Symbols: Aspects of Ndembu Ritual*, 93–111. New York: Cornell University Press.

Turner, Victor. 1979. 'Betwixt and Between: The Liminal Period in Rites De Passage'. In *Reader in Comparative Religion: An Anthropological Approach*, edited by William Armand Lessa, Evon Zartman Vogt, and John Mamoru Watanabe, 3rd edition, 234–43. New York: Harper & Row.

Turtschaninoff, Maria. 2016. *Maresi*. Translated by Annie Prime. London: Pushkin Children's Books.

Tylor, Edward Burnett. 1958. *The Origins of Culture*. 5th edition. New York: Harper Torchbooks.

Uther, Hans-Jörge. 2004. 'Persecuted Heroine'. In *The Types of International Folktales: A Classification and Bibliography, Based on the System of Antti Aarne and Stith Thompson*, 1: 293–4. Helsinki: Academia Scientiarum Fennica.

Vint, Sherryl. 2007. *Bodies of Tomorrow: Technology, Subjectivity, Science Fiction*. 2nd edition. Toronto: University of Toronto Press, Scholarly Publishing Division.

Viswanath, Tharini. 2019. 'Girl-Animal Metamorphoses: Voice, Choice, and (Material) Agency of the Transforming Female Body in Young Adult Literature'. *Jeunesse: Young People, Texts, Cultures* 11 (1): 112–38. https://doi.org/10.1353/jeu.2019.0005.

Walkerdine, Valerie. 1984. 'Some Day My Prince Will Come: Young Girls and the Preparation for Adolescent Sexuality'. In *Gender and Generation*, edited by Angela McRobbie, 162–84. Basingstoke: Palgrave Macmillan.

Waller, Alison. 2009. *Constructing Adolescence in Fantastic Realism*. Children's Literature and Culture. New York: Routledge.

Waller, Alison. 2020. 'The Art of Being Ordinary: Cups of Tea and Catching the Bus in Contemporary British YA'. *The International Journal of Young Adult Literature* 1 (1): 1–25. https://doi.org/10.24877/ijyal.34.

Walsh, Sue. 2013. 'The Child in Wolf's Clothing: The Meanings of the "Wolf" and Questions of Identity in Jack London's White Fang'. *European Journal of American Culture* 32 (1): 55–77. https://doi.org/10.1386/ejac.32.1.55_1.

Watson, Victor. 2004. 'Series Fiction'. In *International Companion Encyclopedia of Children's Literature*, edited by Peter Hunt, 2nd edition, 532–41. London: Routledge.

Weber, Brenda. 2005. 'Beauty, Desire, and Anxiety: The Economy of Sameness in ABC's Extreme Makeover'. *Genders*, 41. https://www.colorado.edu/gendersarchive1998-2013/2005/06/01/beauty-desire-and-anxiety-economy-sameness-abcs-extreme-makeover.

Weigle, Marta. 1989. *Creation and Procreation Feminist Reflections on Mythologies of Cosmogony and Parturition*. Philadelphia: University of Pennsylvania Press.

Weil, Kari. 2012. *Thinking Animals: Why Animal Studies Now?* New York: Columbia University Press.

Wilkins, Kim. 2019. *YA Fantasy Fiction: Conventions, Originality, Reproducibility*. Cambridge: Cambridge University Press.

Wilkins, Kim, Beth Driscoll, and Lisa Fletcher. 2018. 'What Is Australian Popular Fiction?' *Australian Literary Studies* 33 (4). https://doi.org/10.20314/als.4e3df0ec9c.

Wolf, Mark J. P. 2012. *Building Imaginary Worlds: The Theory and History of Subcreation*. Kindle. New York: Routledge.

Wolf, Mark J. P, ed. 2016. *Revisiting Imaginary Worlds: A Subcreation Studies Anthology*. New York: Routledge.

Wolf, Mark J. P, ed. 2017. *The Routledge Companion to Imaginary Worlds*. New York: Routledge.

Wolff, Josephine. 2017. 'Growing Up Female'. *Los Angeles Review of Books* (blog), 28 December 2017. https://lareviewofbooks.org/article/growing-up-female/.

Wood, Naomi. 1996. 'Domesticating Dreams in Walt Disney's Cinderella'. *The Lion and the Unicorn* 20 (1): 25–49.

World Health Organization. n.d. 'Adolescent Health'. Accessed 26 February 2022. https://www.who.int/westernpacific/health-topics/adolescent-health.

Wulandari, Siti. 2019. 'Female Masculinity of Alanna Trebond in Tamora Pierce's Alanna: The First Adventure'. *Litera-Kultura* 7 (4): 1–8.

Yarova, Aliona, and Lydia Kokkola. 2015. 'Beyond Human: Escaping the Maze of Anthropocentrism in Peter Dickinson's Eva'. *Bookbird: A Journal of International Children's Literature* 53 (1): 38–51. https://doi.org/10.1353/bkb.2015.0024.

Yep, Laurence. 1978. 'Fantasy and Reality'. *The Horn Book Magazine*, 1978.

Young, Iris Marion. 2005. *On Female Body Experience: Throwing Like a Girl and Other Essays*. Oxford: Oxford University Press.

Zähringer, Raphael. 2017. 'X Marks the Spot – Not: Pirate Treasure Maps in Treasure Island and Käpt'n Sharky Und Das Geheimnis Der Schatzinsel'. *Children's Literature in Education* 48 (1): 6–20. https://doi.org/10.1007/s10583-016-9308-0.

Index

Locators followed by "n." indicate endnotes

Aarne-Thompson-Uther (ATU) index 3
adolescence/adolescents 18, 41, 52, 60, 74, 80, 92, 112, 140, 142, 148, 151 n.2
  and adolescent identity 57
  authenticity 157 n.5
  hybridity 80, 96
  interstructural situation 151 n.2
  literature 24, 40–1
  pregnancy and 135, 137
  ritual transference 1
adolescent girlhood 1–2, 7, 12, 27, 45, 49, 66, 79, 91, 94, 96, 101, 115, 152 n.9, 152 n.13, 158 n.3
  changing perceptions 51
  colour 158 n.3
  exceptional/expectational nature 1, 3
  reframing myths 15, 19–21, 23, 31, 33, 51, 108
  shape-shifting of reframed 23
Adventures into Otherness 112
'The Age of Adolescence' (*The Lancet Child and Adolescent Health*) 41
Aisenberg, Nadya 21
Alaimo, Stacy 53
Alanna (female hero, Pierce) 6, 37–8, 42–3, 84, 92, 94, 111, 147, 149, 154 n.11, 158–9 n.6
  as beardless youth 74
  becoming Alan (hero) 55, 59–68, 72, 77, 141
  being-hero 57
  cross-dressing 37, 52, 57, 59–61, 63, 66–7, 70–1, 73–6, 88, 99, 119, 126–7, 142, 156 nn.1–2

  cultural signifier of masculinity 63
  cyclicality and ambiguity 78, 139–40
  disruptive act 78
  and George Cooper 73, 78, 124
  hegemonic masculinity 61
  King's Champion 57
  makeover 73–5
  mirror moment 64, 67
  'on the road' 61–4, 72–6
  provocative act 71
  ritual rebirths 72–3, 156 n.5
  silences her body 65–8
  Thom and 37, 55, 57–63, 141–2, 156 n.1
  twin (and child) 57–61
  un-horror-ing the blood 68–72
  warrior-woman 55, 61, 76–8
Altmann, Anna E. 1, 77
Aly (fictional character, trickster) 57, 76, 124, 136, 143
Anderson, Benedict 158 n.4
androids 46–7, 59, 82–3, 86–7, 91–5, 144–5. *See also* Iko (android female-hero, Meyer)
Angharad Crew (female-hero, McKinley) 154 n.11
Annas, Julia, knack 125
archetypal hero story 8–9, 17–19, 21, 39, 46, 75, 82, 85, 114, 116, 159 n.7
Ariel (Disney princess) 12, 151 n.1
Arnett, Jeffrey 42
Atheneum Books 38
Aurora (Disney princess) 12, 151 n.1
Averill, Lindsey 6

Index

Balsamo, Anne 97, 107–8, 145
Bardugo, Leigh 36–8, 44, 52
    Grishaverse 24, 44, 52
    Shadow and Bone 44
Bartyzel, Monika 14
Battersby, Christine 85, 137
Bayron, Kalynn, *Cinderella Is Dead* 3
Beckett, Sandra L. 154 n.17
being-cyborg 23, 83, 100, 103, 146.
    See also cyborg, Cinder
being-hero 9–10, 19–20, 23, 27, 29,
    38–9, 57, 80, 115, 117, 124
    linearity, disrupting 139–43
    modelling relation 147–9
    visuality, breaking 143–7
being-YA 25, 39–44, 51
Bella Swann (fictional character,
    Twilight) 1–3, 16, 69, 114
    absent period and pregnancy 18
    exceptional and expectational
    heroine 114
    makeover 16
    sparkle 16–17
    traditional femininity 16
Belle (Disney princess) 12, 151 n.1
Bengson, John 125
Berlant, Lauren 6
Bhaba, Homi 158 n.4
Bibbidi Bobbidi Boutiques 3
birth control 43, 72, 156 n.4
Bishop, Rudine Sims 154 n.9
Black girlhood 158 n.3
Blanchett, Cate 151 n.3
blood
    horror of xv–xvi, 55–6, 74–5, 128,
    133, 140
    from injury xv–xvi, 97
    sparkle as 9
    un-horror-ing xvi, 68–72, 84–6,
    128, 139–41, 148
Blue, Angel 14
Bologna Children's Book Fair 155 n.18
Bonham Carter, Helena 11–12
Bourdieu, Pierre, *The Field of
    Cultural Production*
    154 n.12

Broadway, Alice, Skin Books trilogy
    32
Brokefang (Long Lake Pack, Pierce)
    127, 133, 148–9
Burns, Elizabeth 152 n.15
Butler, Judith, *Gender Trouble* 63

camp, queer theories of 10, 152 n.7
Campbell, Joseph 9, 29, 47, 151 n.2,
    159 n.7
Cantavella, Anna Juan, literary maps
    32–3
Carmody, Isobelle, The Obernewtyn
    Chronicles 50
Cart, Michael 154 nn.14–15
cartography 31–2
Cashore, Kristin 38
    Graceling Realm 29, 44, 159 n.10
    Winterkeep 44
Chappell, Shelley 63
Chee, Tracie, Sea of Ink and Gold
    (*The Reader*) 52
Cher (fictional character, *Clueless*) 69
children's literature 28, 39, 41–2, 112,
    154 n.13, 158 n.3, 159 n.3
Cinderella (2015) 11, 18
Cinderella (Walt Disney) 1–2, 65, 79,
    81, 95, 101, 151 nn.1–2,
    155 n.21
    appearance 4–5, 10–11
    Bibbidi Bobbidi Boo 10, 12
    culture of princess 12
    cyborg-ness (*see* cyborg, Cinder)
    death and rebirth 3, 9–10, 13,
    95–6, 156 n.5
    dream 7
    Ella 11–12, 82
    Fairy Godmother 3, 7–8, 10–12,
    96–7, 99–100
    feminine identity 4–6, 13–14
    Gus 6, 152 n.5
    heightened fantasy femininity 4,
    6, 10, 15–16, 66, 87, 89
    hero's prize 7, 9–10, 16, 31, 45, 58,
    66, 79, 82, 91, 95–6, 119
    iconic prize 3–7

intervention 46, 81, 98
Jaq 152 n.5
Lady Tremaine 8–9, 99, 151 n.3
legacy lives 2, 15–16
pauper to princess 2, 5, 9, 12
'Sparkle On, Little Princess' 12–15
sparkly femininity 2, 9–12, 15, 58, 100
traditional versions 4–5
white femininity 2, 4, 31
YA's exceptional/expectational heroines 15–18
Cinder (female-hero, Meyer) 46, 48, 70, 79, 81–7, 111, 143–4, 157 nn.3–4
appearance 79, 99
being-hero 80
bodily awkwardness 98
cybernetic makeup/parts 68, 101–4, 106, 144–6
holographic image 107–8
human-machine self 96
as mechanic 83, 99
Pearl and Peony 82, 84, 99
as posthuman fairytale 108
as queer 157 n.2
re-attaching foot 99
sense of alterity 84
sexy body 87
too-small foot, removal 145–6
Clarke, Bruce 113
Clary Fray (fictional character) 1
Cloud (pony, Pierce) 119–21, 126, 130–3
Clover, Carol J. 153 n.16
Clute, John 28, 112
Coachman (fictional character, *Cinderella*) 151 n.3
Coats, Karen, *Looking Glasses and Neverlands* 155 n.21
colorblind ideology 99
Colthurst, Audrey, *Inkmistress* 38
common-sense feminism 1
conceptual centre xii

of opposition xv, 19, 24–5, 27–8
of possibility 42, 44, 51, 57, 81, 120, 122
contraception 159 n.10
Coram (fictional character) 59–60, 62, 67, 73, 142
Coudray, Chantal Bourgault du 153 n.17
counter-narratives 122, 158 n.4
Coward, Jo 112–13
Creed, Barbara 153 n.16
critical race theory 158 n.4
'Critical Theory and Adolescent Literature' 41
Croggon, Alison 29, 42
'Author's Note' 29
The Bone Queen 30
The Books of Pellinor 29–30, 42, 71, 148
cross-dressing 14, 23–4, 37, 52, 57, 59–61, 63–7, 72–7, 88, 99, 119, 126–7, 142, 154 n.11, 156 n.1
crossover fiction 154 n.17
Crowe, Jonathan 32
cultural materialism 159 n.2
Cummins, June 152 n.15
cyborg, Cinder 44–6, 79–87, 144, 146, 157 n.4
bodily awkwardness 96, 98
dismantling 'fixed' perfection 95–100
emancipatory potential of 85
procreation 85
reframing work 103
superficial changes 100–5
symbolic death-rebirth 98
'untouched reproductive' system 84–6

Daine (female-hero, Pierce) 38, 48, 70, 111, 143
and animals 111, 123–4, 128, 130, 158 n.5

being-hero 115, 117
being 'of the people' 119–20, 127, 131–2, 147
Broad Foot 117–18
conceptual centre 122
as demigoddess 38, 114–18
Gift and wild magic 48, 120–1, 123–8, 147, 149, 159 n.8
healing 127
heroic romance 111, 120
human-animal 111–12, 114–15, 117, 121, 128, 135, 148
knack 123–7
Miri 126, 131
'no one bird' 132, 135–8
Onau and 147
'Pack-sister' 148–9
Sarra 116–18, 123, 125, 127, 137
sense of self 119–23, 125
shape-shifting 70, 112, 115, 128–38, 143–5, 147
social and cultural situation 111
unspeakable 127–31
Weiryn 114–16, 123
in Wolf-Speaker 115
Darla (escort droid) 47, 93, 95
DC Extended Universe 26
Deleuze, Gilles, *A Thousand Plateaus* 153 n.4
Delgado, Richard 158 n.4
Dennard, Susan, Witchlands books 29
De Palma, Brian, *Carrie* 18
Didicher, Nicky 85, 93
Diehl, Amanda, *The Queen's Readers: A Collection of Essays on the Worlds and Words of Tamora Pierce* 36
Disney Princess 152 n.12. *See also specific Disney Princess*
franchise 3, 12, 15
dominant models 2, 20, 46
Douglas, Adam 153 n.17

Driscoll, Beth 153 n.2
Duane, Diane 153 n.1
Dyhouse, Carol 157 n.8

Ekman, Stefan 32
embodied self 5, 9, 18–19, 33, 38–9, 51, 53, 56, 68, 86, 113
escort-droids 47, 91, 93, 95, 100

fairy tales 4–5
Falconer, Rachel 154 n.17
FanFiction.net 154 n.6
fantasy 15–16, 25–30, 32, 36, 38, 42–5, 47, 51, 56, 58, 66, 79, 89, 91–2, 97, 99–100, 137, 142, 148, 154 n.11, 159 n.10
fat bodies 6
Fawcett, John, *Ginger Snaps* 18, 153 n.17
female-hero(es) 10, 12, 15, 18, 23, 32, 39, 46, 80, 84, 93–4, 100, 114–15, 139, 151 n.2, 154 n.9, 154 n.11. *See also specific female hero*
adolescent girlhood, reframing myths 19–21
cross-dressing 24, 37 (*see also* Alanna (female hero, Pierce), cross-dressing)
cybernetic 23, 119, 146
hybridity 80, 83, 122–3, 132
in mythopoeic YA 25, 27
femininity 3, 5, 14–16, 63, 68, 75, 80, 84–5, 88, 91–2, 95–6, 99, 101, 135, 156 n.2, 157 n.5, 157 n.7
fantasy 4, 6, 10, 15–16, 58, 66, 79, 87, 89, 99–100
heteronormative 101–2
sparkly 2, 11, 14–16, 58, 79, 100
white 2, 4, 31
Flanagan, Victoria 61, 63, 99, 156 n.2

Into the Closet: Cross-Dressing and the Gendered Body in Children's Literature and Film 60
Technology and Identity in Young Adult Fiction: The Posthuman Subject 80, 156 n.1
Fletcher, Lisa 153 n.2
Flood, Alison 36
folktales 2–3, 5, 12, 46, 151 n.3
Forman-Brunell, Miriam, *Princess Cultures: Mediating Girls' Imaginations and Identities* 152 n.8
Freud, Sigmund 2, 59

Gallo, Donald R., *From Hinton to Hamlet* 39
García, Marilisa Jiménez 158 n.3
Garner, Alexandra 57
Genette, Gérard 32
genre worlds, theory 153 n.2
Geraghty, Christine, soap operas 155 n.23
Geronimi, Clyde
   Cinderella (1950) 6–7, 13, 76, 79, 151 n.3
   Peter Pan 152 n.10
   Sleeping Beauty 6
Gilbert-Hickey, Meghan 157 n.4
   Race in Young Adult Speculative Fiction 158 n.3
Gill, Rosalind, 'Postfeminist Media Culture: Elements of a Sensibility' 13, 86–7, 91, 157 n.7
girl poisoning culture 152 n.13
girl power *vs.* saving 152 n.13
glamour 48, 87, 89, 106, 157 n.8.
   See also Lunar glamour
Gonick, Marnina, girl power and 'Reviving Ophelia' 16, 152 n.13

Grand Duke (fictional character, *Cinderella*) 151 n.3
Grant, John 28 112
Green-Barteet, Miranda A. 99, 157 n.4. *See also* colorblind ideology
   Race in Young Adult Speculative Fiction 158 n.3
Grimm, Jacob, *Aschenputtel* 4
Grimm, Wilhelm, *Aschenputtel* 4
Grosz, Elizabeth 145
   body image 145
   Volatile Bodies: Toward a Corporeal Feminism 21, 143
Guattari, Felix, *A Thousand Plateaus* 153 n.4

Hall, G Stanley 74, 151 n.2
Hand, David, *Snow White* 6, 108
Haraway, Donna 82, 85–6, 130
The Hardy Boys 155 n.23
Harris, Marvin, *Cultural Anthropology* 159 n.2
Harry Potter (fictional character) 114
Harvey, Colin B. 51
   Fantastic Transmedia – Narrative, Play and Memory across Science Fiction and Fantasy Storyworlds 153 n.3
Hayles, Katherine 93, 156 n.1
Head, Patricia 41
Heckerling, Amanda, *Clueless* 69
hegemonic fantasies/discourse 25, 39, 42, 51–2, 59, 65, 84, 98, 127, 130, 140–3
hegemonic YA 142
Hekman, Susan, material feminism 53, 64
Held, Virginia 53
Herakles (Hercules) 9
Hermione Granger (fictional character) 1

heroic romance 1–3, 5, 7–8, 20–1, 24, 37–8, 44, 46–7, 81–2, 92, 94, 99, 109, 139, 152 n.5
   Alanna (female-hero, Pierce) 55, 57–9, 61–2, 65, 67–8, 77, 139
   conceptual centre 25, 27
   Daine (female-hero, Pierce) 111, 113, 119–20, 122
   goal 58
   isolating individuality 109
   and patriarchal ideology 18
   hero's prize (Cinderella) 5, 7, 31, 37, 45, 58, 66, 73, 79, 82, 91, 95–6, 119
   ritual death rebirth 9–12
   transcendence 20
hero story 6, 17, 19, 27, 38, 62, 64–5, 74, 78, 82, 93–4, 99, 119, 123, 143, 151 n.2, 152 n.5, 154 n.10
Herz, Sarah K., *From Hinton to Hamlet* 39
HiHo Kids, 'Kids Meet an Opera Singer' 14
Hirsh, Marianne, *The Mother/Daughter Plot: Narrative, Psychoanalysis, Feminism* 2
Holdsworth, Amy 159 n.1
Holmes, Linda 17
Homer, *The Odyssey* 8
The Hunger Games 3, 16–17
   Catching Fire 18
   Katniss Everdeen (*see* Katniss Everdeen (fictional character, The Hunger Games))
hunt 115, 158 n.2
Hunt, Caroline 58, 141
   identity exchange 141
   'Theory Rises, Maginot Line Endures' 52
Hunt, Pater 23

identity exchange 141
Iko (android female-hero, Meyer) 46–7, 59, 81–2, 91–5, 100, 134
imaginary activism 30, 51
Imaginary (model) 55–6
imaginary world fiction 16, 23, 26–30, 33, 42, 44–5, 51–2, 108, 136
   assumptions 27
   imaginary world theory 153 n.3
   maps of 35
   networks of relation 24, 26–7, 48–51
imagination gap 31
imagined communities 32, 158 n.4
Insenga, Angela 80, 92–3, 108
Irigaray, Luce 56, 59, 63, 68, 141
   coining of signifiers 61–3, 67

Jackson, Wilfred
   Cinderella (1950) 6–7, 13, 76, 79, 151 n.3
   Peter Pan 152 n.10
Jameson, Frederick 81
Jarvis, Erika 4
Jasmine (Disney princess) 12, 14, 17, 151 n.1
Jenkins, Henry, intertextuality 51
Jensen, Karen 152 n.15
Johnson, Orna, *Cultural Anthropology* 159 n.2
Jonathan, Prince 68, 75–6
Joseph, Michael 103

Karl, Jean 43
Katniss Everdeen (fictional character, The Hunger Games) 1, 3, 16, 69, 114, 152 n.14
   exceptional and expectational heroine 3, 16, 114
   'hero in drag' 16
   makeover 17–18
Kearney, Mary Celeste 10

Kel (female-hero, Pierce) 38, 42, 71–2, 101, 148–9, 156 n.4
Kennedy, Melanie, *Tweenhood: Femininity and Celebrity in Tween Popular Culture* 152 n.9, 157 n.5
Kennon, Patricia 152 n.15
Kidd, Kenneth, *Queer as Camp: Essays on Summer, Style, and Sexuality* 152 n.7
Kindl, Patrice, *Owl in Love* 112
King, Stephen, *Carrie* 18
knighthood 37, 56–7, 66, 74, 124
Knight of the Realm of Tortall (Pierce) 34, 55, 57, 68, 156 n.5
Kokkola, Lydia 69, 115

Lacan, Jacques 155 n.21
   Lacanian Real 55
   system of subjectification 63
Lackey, Mercedes 153 n.1
Lady Delia 75–7
Lalasa (fictional character, Pierce) 71–2
languages 48, 55–6, 72, 112–13, 127, 130–1, 156 n.3, 157 n.1
   and signifiers 62
   speaking 157–8 n.1
Lassén-Seger, Maria 112
Lawrence-Pietroni, Anna 41
Learner, Gerda, *The Creation of Patriarchy* 152 n.6
Lesnik-Oberstein, Karin, *The Last Taboo: Women and Body Hair* 74–5
Levy, Michael, *Children's Fantasy Literature* (Introduction) 45
Lewis, C. S., The Chronicles of Narnia 27–8
linearity 21, 24, 77, 153 n.4, 154 n.10
   disrupting 27, 112, 139–43

Littler, Jo, *Against Meritocracy: Culture, Power and Myths of Mobility* 159 n.7
London, Jack, *White Fang* 124
The Lunar Chronicles (Meyer) 23, 44–5, 48, 50, 79, 83, 86, 89, 98, 101, 106, 108, 134
   Cinder 44, 46, 79, 94, 99, 150
   Cress 46, 88, 150
   Fairest 150
   Iko 46–7, 59, 81–2, 91–5, 100, 134
   Lingh Adri 82–3, 144
   mythic forms in modern shapes 27, 47
   posthumanism 80
   Princess Selene 87
   Queen Levana 48, 96, 98, 104
   Scarlet 46, 89, 94, 96, 108, 150
   Stars Above: A Lunar Chronicles Collection 150, 157 n.3
   Thorne 88
   Winter 46, 108, 150, 157 n.3
   Wires and Nerve 150
   Wires and Nerve: Gone Rogue 150
Lunar glamour 34, 81, 87–9, 101, 103
Jael 89
Levana 89–90, 100, 103–4
mirrors 105–6
secondary sex character 88, 92–3
self and appearance 89
Lury, Karen 159 n.1
Luske, Hamilton
   Cinderella (1950) 6–7, 13, 76, 79, 151 n.3
   Peter Pan 152 n.10
Lykissas, Alexandra, cyborg-erella 80, 157 n.4

Maas, Sarah J 36, 38, 44
   Throne of Glass 44
Maerad (female-hero, Croggon) 29–30, 42, 148–9, 154 n.16

makeover 2–3, 10–12, 14, 16–18, 73, 86, 90–1, 96, 104, 157 n.7
  Alanna 73–5
  Cinderella 3, 11, 13, 156 n.5
  cosmetic surgery 87, 96–7, 107
  rites of passage 1–2, 113
mammalian anatomy 126–7
mapmaking 31–4
maps 1–2, 16, 26, 30–5, 82, 153 n.5
Marchetta, Melina, Lumatere Chronicles 50
Marie, Kae 33, 154 n.7
Marvel Cinematic Universe 26
Mason, Derritt, *Queer as Camp: Essays on Summer, Style, and Sexuality* 152 n.7
Mastiff (Beka Cooper series, Pierce) 33, 150
material embodiment 93
Mathison, Ymitri, *Growing up Asian American in Young Adult Fiction* 158 n.3
Matthews, Corinne 156 n.4, 159 n.10
Maude (fictional character, Pierce) 62, 70, 140
Maud (fictional character) 73
Mayer, Kodi 15
McAlister, Jodi 153 n.2, 155 n.19
McCaffrey, Anne 153 n.1
McCallum, Robin 58, 142
McKinley, Robin 153 n.1
  The Blue Sword 154 n.11
  The Hero and the Crown 154 n.11
McMahon-Coleman, Kimberl 153 n.17
McRobbie, Angela, phallic girl 17, 67, 77
Mendlesohn, Farah 32
  Children's Fantasy Literature (Introduction) 45
menstruation 55–6, 68–9, 72–4, 77, 86, 129, 140–1, 148, 153 n.16
  absence of 129, 152 n.15
  and procreation 18, 55–6
  shameless speech (Alanna) 56, 69
Merida (Disney Pixar's *Brave*) 13–14, 151 n.1
meritocracy 126, 159 n.7
Merrylees, Ferne 80
metamorphosis 153 n.17
  Daine 112–13, 128
Meyer, Marissa 47–8, 79, 83, 86, 93, 99, 134, 157 n.4
  Lunar Chronicles (*see* The Lunar Chronicles (Meyer))
  Twilight 39
Meyers, Diana Tietjens 53
middle grades fiction (MG) 42–3
A Mighty Girl 13–14
Mistress Cooper (fictional character, Pierce) 70, 73, 140, 147–8
Mitchell, Jennifer 157 n.2
Mithros (Great God) 114
Moana (Disney princess) 151 n.1
monotheism 156 n.3
monstrosity 5–6, 18, 128
Montz, Amy 15
Mooney, Andy 12
Moran, Mary Jeanette 53, 121
Moseley, Rachel 11, 88–9, 153 n.16
Mulan (Disney princess) 12, 14, 17, 61, 151 n.1
Musgrave, Megan, *Digital Citizenship in Twenty-First-Century Young Adult Literature: Imaginary Activism* 30
mythopoeic YA 10, 21, 23, 51, 86, 101, 142, 148–9, 153 n.3, 154 n.9, 155 n.20, 155 n.23, 156 n.4
  being-YA 25, 39–44
  female-heroes in 25, 27
  founding mother 35–9
  imaginary world speculative fiction 23, 26–30, 52

intervention 24–6, 52
liminality 25, 41–2, 51
mapping sensibility 31–5
mythic forms in modern shapes 44–8
networks of relation 42, 48–51
YA and 40
myths 19–21, 31, 101, 108, 139, 143

names of things 34
Nancy Drew 155 n.23
New Adult (NA) fiction 153 n.2, 155 n.19
Nikolajeva, Maria
   hero in drag 16–17, 37, 57, 67, 77
   The Rhetoric of Character 156 n.1
   vehicle of power 127
Noddings, Nel 53
Numair (Arram) 49–50, 116–17, 121–4, 126–31, 133, 136, 158 n.5
   anti-fertility charm 136
   appearance 51

occupying position concept 5, 19–20, 29, 67, 96, 152 n.4
Ohmer, Susan 10
ontological self-sufficiency 94
Orenstein, Peggy 152 n.12
   Cinderella Ate My Daughter 14
Osman, Tarek 32
Otten, Charlotte F. 153 n.17
Owlshollow (map) 34–5, 108

Page, Benedicte, *The Bookseller* 155 n.18
Parsons, Linda 4–5, 12, 152 n.4
patriarchal ideology 3, 9, 18, 135
Pattee, Amy 155 n.19, 155 n.23
Paul, Lissa 37
Perrault, Charles, *Cendrillon, ou la Petite Pantoufle de Verre* 4

Perry, Evelyn M. 153 n.1
Pierce, Tamora 23, 27, 42, 51–2, 72, 78, 101, 111–12, 115, 137, 148–9, 153 n.1, 156 n.4, 159 nn.10–11
   Circle Universe 33, 35, 149
   The Magic in the Weaving 149
   as mythopoeic YA's founding mother 35–9
   pseudo-medieval universe 48, 52
   'Tamora Pierce's Unofficial Fan Community' 36
   Tortall Universe (*see* Tortall Universe (Pierce))
   The Woman Who Rides Like a Man 57
   YALSA Edwards Award 43
Pipher, Mary, *Reviving Ophelia: Saving the Selves of Adolescent Girls* 152 n.13
plague research 144
Plato 8
   Love and Beauty 8
   The Symposium 8
Pocahontas (Disney princess) 12, 14, 17, 151 n.1
poignant (UK) 159 n.9
postfeminist media sensibility (Gill) 13, 86–7, 91, 157 n.7
posthumanism 80, 156 n.1, 157 n.2
Posthumanism in Young Adult Fiction: Finding Humanity in a Posthuman World 80
Prince Charming (fictional character, *Cinderella*) 7, 16, 76, 151 n.3
Prince Kai (fictional character, Pierce) 82, 84, 92, 98, 101–2, 157 n.3
procreation 9, 18, 84, 129
   menstruation 56
   as monstrous 5, 18
   as other to creation 85
   pregnancy 6, 72, 129, 134, 136–7

Prokhovnik, Raia, *Rational Woman: A Feminist Critique of Dichotomy* 19–20
pseudo-children 5
Pullman, Philip 28

Queenclaw (goddess of house cats) 114, 116
quest myth 1, 21, 24, 44, 112

Rabelais, François 8
racism 99, 157 n.4
　colour-blindness 115
Raglan, Lord, 'The Hero of Tradition' 82
Ramdarshan Bold, Melanie 115, 158 n.4
The Rampion (spaceship, *Scarlet*) 47, 93–4
Rank, Otto 151 n.2
　Der Mythus von der Geburt des Helden 151 n.1
Rapunzel (Disney princess) 12, 46, 151 n.1
raw talent (real-world concept) 126
relational 6, 19, 38–41, 53, 70, 94, 111, 119, 122, 131, 139–41, 147–9
rhizome 153 n.4
Rhodes, Cristina 158 n.3
Roses, Jacqueline 59–60

Sahn, Sarah, 'Decolonizing Childhood: Coming of Age in Tamora Pierce's Fantastic Empire' 56
Sax, Boria 115, 158 n.2
Sayantani 152 n.15
Scarlet (Little Red Riding Hood) 46, 89, 108
selfhood model 2–3, 9, 18, 20–1, 23, 35, 39, 41, 58, 94, 118–19, 122, 132, 138–40

Smith, Claire 43
Snow White (Disney princess) 12, 46, 108, 151 n.1
sparkle 2–3, 9–12, 15–18, 64, 96
sparklemation 12, 18, 73
sparkly femininity 2, 11, 14–16, 58, 79, 100
Squier, Susan, *Babies in Bottles: Twentieth-Century Visions of Reproductive Technology* 157 n.6
Star Wars 26, 47
Subramanian, Aishwarya 33
Suhr-Systma, Mandy 158 n.3
Sweeney, Kathleen 105
　Maiden USA: Girl Icons Come of Age 100–1
Sweet Valley High 155 n.23
symbolic/ritual death and rebirth 2, 9, 13, 16, 18, 64, 72, 95–6, 98, 113, 117, 156 n.5

Tale Type index 3, 151 n.2
Tarr, Anita 156 n.1
Thayet, Queen 76, 129
Thomas, Ebony Elizabeth 158 n.3
　The Dark Fantastic: Race and the Imagination from Harry Potter to the Hunger Games 17, 31
Tiana (Disney princess) 12, 14, 17, 151 n.1
Tinkerbell (fictional character, *Peter Pan*) 152 n.9
Toffoletti, Kim 156 n.1
Toliver, Stephanie 158 n.3
　'Imagining New Hopescapes: Expanding Black Girls'' 154 n.9
　'On Mirrors, Windows, and Telescopes' 154 n.9
Tolkien, J.R.R. 23
　Eowyn 27
　'Mythopoeia' 28

The Return of the King 27
Secondary World 27–8, 48
Tolmie, Jane 15
topography 31, 34–5, 108
Tortall Universe (Pierce) 24, 29, 33, 35, 44, 48–50, 101, 114, 123
    Beka Cooper trilogy 33, 50, 156 n.4
        Bloodhound 150
        Mastiff 33, 150
        Terrier 150
    Carthakis 50, 124
    Daughter of the Lioness
        Trickster's Choice 76, 150
        Trickster's Queen 76, 150
    Immortals 38, 51, 76, 111, 116, 148, 150, 154 n.10
        Emperor Mage 150
        The Realms of the Gods 114, 150
        Wild Magic 48, 121, 124, 126, 147, 150
        Wolf-Speaker 115, 150
    mythopoeic YA 154 n.10
    north-south divide mapping 111
    The Numair Chronicles 50
        Tempests and Slaughter 36, 49–50, 150
        Tortall: A Spy's Guide 35–6, 50, 150
        Tortall and Other Lands 150
    Protector of the Small 38, 51
        First Test 150
        Lady Knight 34, 136, 150
        Page 150
        Squire 34–5, 150, 156 n.4
    The Song of the Lioness 42, 49–51, 57, 68, 142, 150, 154 n.6, 154 n.10
        Alanna: The First Adventure 35, 37, 66, 150
        In the Hand of the Goddess 150, 156 n.5
        Lioness Rampant 43, 57, 76, 150, 156 n.5
        The Woman Who Rides Like a Man 150
touch 143–5, 147
transgender YA 95
Tris Prior (fictional character) 1
Trites, Roberta Seelinger 40–1, 120
    Disturbing the Universe: Power and Repression in Adolescent Literature 154 n.13, 159 n.8
Turtschaninoff, Maria, Red Abbey Chronicles 30
tweenhood 157 n.5

'Unpacking World Folk-Literature' (Tale Type Index) 151 n.2
Urban, Shawn 151 n.2

Vaughn, Holly, *The Queen's Readers: A Collection of Essays on the Worlds and Words of Tamora Pierce* 36
Vint, Sherryl 156 n.1
visuality 11–12, 81, 105, 139, 143–7

Walkerdine, Valerie 152 n.4
Waller, Alison 71, 118, 140
Walsh, Sue 124
Weber, Brenda, *Extreme Makeover* 13
Weigle, Marta, birthing speech 56
Weil, Kari 130
West, Lindy 36
Western culture 2, 12, 17–18, 121
    contemporary 12–13, 17–20, 24–6, 49, 52, 65, 69, 80–1, 86, 91, 95–6, 98, 103, 107, 113, 119, 148
    makeover paradigm 13
    myth of original unity 85
    oppositional pairs 19–20

selfhood 2 (*see also* selfhood model)
White, Donna R. 156 n.1
Wildmage (demigoddess) 111
Wilkins, Kim 3, 38, 153 n.2
Wisewing ('Song Hollow Colony of bats') 133
Wolf, Mark 26, 50
   Building Imaginary Worlds 153 n.3
   Revisiting Imaginary Worlds: A Subcreation Studies Anthology 153 n.3
Wolff, Josephine 43
Wood, Naomi 5
   'Domesticating Dreams in Walt Disney's Cinderella' 7
world-building 24, 26, 28–32, 50
World Health Organization 41

Wrede, Patricia 153 n.1

Yep, Laurence 47
Young, Iris Marion 92
Young Adult Library Services Association (YALSA) 43
Young Adult (YA) fiction 1, 13, 153 n.2, 154 n.13, 154 n.15, 155 n.23, 156 n.1, 158 n.3, 159 n.3, 159 n.10. *See also* mythopoeic YA
books and beings 25
dystopia 45
exceptional/expectational heroines 3, 15–18, 57, 114
hegemonic 142
and mythopoeic YA 40
opposing pairs 42
position-taking 40, 51

www.ingramcontent.com/pod-product-compliance
Lightning Source LLC
Chambersburg PA
CBHW061828300426
44115CB00013B/2291